First People:
A Revised Chronology for San Diego County

First People:
A Revised Chronology for San Diego County

Dennis R. Gallegos

StorySeekers
San Diego, California

Cover graphic:
Potential First People routes into San Diego County. Windsong Shores SDI-10965 Silver Lake point, crescent and scraper.

Copyright © 2017 by Dennis R. Gallegos
ISBN 978-0-9822671-7-2
Library of Congress Control Number: 2017934284

StorySeekers
PO Box 27343
San Diego, CA 92198-1343
www.story-seekers.com

*To the ancient ones
who continue to fascinate us
with their elegant simplicity and
overall complexity, innovation and perserverence*

Contents

Illustrations	ix
Acronyms	x
Acknowledgements	xi
Prologue	xiii
Abstract	xv

CHAPTER 1

Early Holocene Setting and First People Sites	1
Late Pleistocene-Holocene Setting	4
Early Holocene Sites	6
La Jolla: Spindrift Site SDI-39/W-1	6
La Jolla: Chancellor's House SDI-4669/W-12	6
Tijuana Lagoon: Remington Hills SDI-11079	11
Agua Hedionda: UCLJ-M-15	11
San Dieguito Lagoon: Del Mar Man Site SDI-10940/W34	13
Agua Hedionda: Windsong Shores SDI-10965/W-131	14
San Dieguito River Valley: C.W. Harris Site SDI-149/W-198	16
Summary	21

CHAPTER 2

Pleistocene-Holocene La Jolla Occupation	25
La Jolla Environmental Setting and Archaeological Sites	25
La Jolla Bay to UCSD Cultural Resources (La Jolla Archaeological Area)	26
La Jolla Shores W-2	33
Sites on Pleistocene Marine Sandstone Terrace North of Spindrift	34
SIO Upper Cliff site SDI-11075/UCLJ-M-7/W-3683/W-151 and Lower Cliff Site W-2240	34
Scripps Estates Site (W-9) SDI-525, SDI-11019	35
Middle Midden SDI-4670/W-5	38
Chancellor's House SDI-4669/W-12 A, B	38
Summary	42

CHAPTER 3

Rogers' San Dieguito Plateau:	
Dating San Dieguito and Warren vs. Rogers' Chronology	45
Rogers: San Dieguito Plateau Sites	45
San Dieguito Plateau, Locus I	48
San Dieguito Plateau Locus IV-Scraper Hill Site SDI-8330/W-240	54
Rogers: Shell-Midden People, Materials, Occupation Areas, and North County Lagoons	56
Rogers vs. Warren: San Dieguito Cultural Pattern	62
Summary	65

Chapter 4
Late Holocene and Late Period Occupation — 69
- Climate and Setting — 69
- Northern Uto-Aztecan-Takic Movement into Southern California — 70
- NUA Expansion, Obsidian Trade, Bow and Arrow, and Takic/Luiseño Movement into SDC — 70
- Languages and Boundaries — 71
- Late Period: Site Type, Density and Distribution — 71
- Late Period Villages, Cultural Materials and Traditions — 77
- Summary — 82

Chapter 5
Chronology and Discussion — 83
- Environmental Setting, Subsistence and Radiocarbon Dating — 83
- Early Archaic (12,000–9000 B.P.) — 83
- Middle Archaic (9000–3500 B.P.) — 87
- Late Archaic (3500–1300 B.P.) — 89
- Late Period (1300 B.P. to Historic Contact) — 89
- Summary — 92

Epilogue — 97
References — 99
Index — 115
About the Author — 118

Illustrations

Figures

1.	Late Pleistocene Shoreline and Great Basin Lakes	2
2.	Generalized Representation of Pleistocene to Holocene La Jolla Shorelines	5
3.	Early Holocene Sites	7
4.	Remington Hills SDI-11079, Bifaces and *Olivella* sp. Beads	12
5.	Windsong Shores SDI-10965 Bifaces, Scrapers and Crescents	15
6.	Harris Site Loci I and II Geologic Cross-Section	17
7.	Radiocarbon Dates and Land-use Patterning for the Otay Management Plan Area	22
8.	La Jolla Archaeological Area with Sites Adjacent to the Bay and Submarine Canyons	28
9a.	1930s USGS Map with Rogers W-1 Spindrift and W-2 La Jolla Shores	30
9b.	Present Day La Jolla Shores Developed, Showing Rogers SDI-39/W-1 Spindrift and W-2 La Jolla Shores	30
10.	Linguistic Western Groups, Obsidian Sources and Lake Cahuilla	41
11.	Generalized Distribution of Crescents in California; and, the San Dieguito Plateau Loci I, II, III and IV Showing Sites with Crescents.	46
12.	Selected Crescents from the San Dieguito Plateau; and North San Diego County Sites	47
13.	Agua Hedionda, Batiquitos Lagoon, and San Dieguito Plateau Locus I Sites Recorded by Rogers with Radiocarbon Dates	50
14.	Harris Site Artifacts: Locus I E-Stratum and Locus II	59
15.	Bifaces from Cactus Street SDI-11424 and La Costa Site SDI-4405	61
16.	Kumeyaay and Luiseño Boundary Map	72
17.	Late Holocene Radiocarbon Dated Sites in San Diego County	73
18.	Site Type and Artifacts	74
19.	Climate Zones for San Diego County with Record Search and Inventory Corridors	75
20.	Late Period Village Locations	78
21.	Features, Artifacts and Ecofacts from Dated ca 7500-3500 B.P. (Middle Archaic) Sites	90

Tables

1.	Early Holocene Radiocarbon Dated Sites in San Diego County	8
2.	Early Holocene Calibrated Radiocarbon Dates	9
3.	Early Holocene Site Summaries	10
4.	La Jolla Archaeological Area Cultural Site Summaries	29
5.	La Jolla Sites by Radiocarbon Dates and Shell Species Dated	31
6.	Radiocarbon Dates for Rogers' Sites near Agua Hedionda and Batiquitos Lagoons, and San Dieguito Plateau Locus I	49
7.	San Dieguito Plateau Site Summaries	51
8.	Site Summaries for Warren's San Dieguito Sites	64
9.	A Chronology and Culture History for San Diego County	84

Acronyms

AMS	Accelerator Mass Spectrometry
BLM	Bureau of Land Management
B.P.	Before Present. Present is defined as A.D. 1950
CRM	Cultural Resource Management
CSUN	California State University Northridge
DSN	Desert Side-Notched
IGPP	Institute of Geophysics and Planetary Physics
IV	Imperial Valley
Lit I, II, III	Littoral/Shell-Midden/La Jolla
LJ	La Jolla/La Jolla Cultural Pattern/La Jollan/Shell-Midden/Lit I,II,III
LJCP	La Jolla Cultural Pattern/La Jolla
LJAA	La Jolla Archaeological Area
LGM	Last Glacial Maximum
MLD	Most Likely Descendent
NUA	Northern Uto-Aztecan
NRHP	National Register of Historic Places
OMPA	Otay Management Plan Area
PCT	Paleo-Coastal Tradition
PDL	Piedra de Lumbre
SD	San Dieguito/Scraper-Maker/San Dieguito Cultural Pattern
SDC	San Diego County
SDCP	San Diego Cultural Pattern
SDP	San Dieguito Plateau
SDSU	San Diego State University
SEUT	Steep Edge Unifacial Tool
SIO	Scripps Institution of Oceanography
SM	Scraper-Maker/San Dieguito/San Dieguito Cultural Pattern
UCSD	University of California San Diego
WPLT	Western Pluvial Lakes Tradition
WSPT	Western Stemmed Point Tradition

Acknowledgements

I thank Malcolm Rogers for his leadership and for providing us with the wealth of records we have from his site forms, notes, publications, and collections from 1919 to 1960; as well as inspiring those who followed. Beginning around 1959, Claude Warren was probably the first to provide controlled professional methods in San Diego County, as well as publishing his work for Scripps Estates and Batiquitos Lagoon; and, for compiling Rogers' 1938 work at the Harris site, and subsequent Harris site/San Dieguito publications. Dr. James Moriarty III (Doc) was associated with the Scripps Institution of Oceanography in the 1950s, recording sites on or near the UCSD campus. He later taught at the University of San Diego and stayed involved in contract archaeology into the 1990s. Doc was always available to talk to you, give you his viewpoint, as well as a good story. But it was Dr. Paul Ezell who trained the first wave of archaeologists/historians/cultural resource managers (CRM) at San Diego State University, as well as inspiring those he came into contact with, including myself. Many of us trained in anthropology/archaeology in the late 1960s and 1970s and were given the opportunities of a lifetime to have careers in archaeology.

A thank you to all those I learned from in college as we taught each other and trained on the job at State Parks early salvage projects: reservoir projects Castaic, Hardluck and Pyramid; and road and parks projects in the 1960s and 70s for Fritz Riddell and Bill Olsen, in what was later called CRM. And, working with Roberta Greenwood at the Ventura Mission and her deft hand at CRM, before it was called CRM. Also a thank you to fellow classmates, mentors and compadres such as Rick Hanks, Chris White and Richard Carrico who were ahead of the game early on and provided sage advice over my career. Learning on the job with Dr. Emma Lou Davis, a hard-driving, fun lady, who was more comfortable in the field than any place in the world. She was a researcher, lithic analyst, and artist who was amazing and inspiring to work with. She was instrumental on my early desert studies for the BLM Class II Central Mojave and Colorado Desert Regions, 2.5 million acre inventory, and the East and West Mesa Regions Imperial Valley inventory.

A thank you to Jeff Flenniken for sharing his in-depth knowledge of lithic technology and therein insight into the simplicity and efficiency of stone tools, by area, material, and resource needs that made this manuscript possible. And to the illustrators I have worked with (Jay Thesken and Mike Caldwell) who were able to capture the beauty, skills and craftsmanship. A thank you to Rick Hanks, Jeff Flenniken Richard Carrico, Rod McLean, Diane Douglas, Winston Zack and Chris White for your comments.

I also thank my Kumeyaay and Luiseño friends who kept a spiritual and watchful eye over me, especially Carmen Lucas (Kwaaymii).

The production team of Brian Spelts, Barry Age, and Shelley Chung provided the graphics and initial manuscript. Peggy and Vincent Rossi of StorySeekers took the manuscript to a finished publication. Gary Breschini and Trudy Haversat are thanked for their support of publishing CRM work. And a shout out to Mike Waters, Dennis Jenkins and others whose work at the Paleoamerican Odyssey Conference was inspirational.

This publication is dedicated to all those I have worked with at State Parks, BLM, Wirth, Westec, SRI, and Gallegos & Associates who did the heavy lifting; shared a beer; told a good story; and made me think as well as laugh, and work harder to prove or disprove statements in conversation and in print. I trust that this publication provides you with a good read, provokes thought, challenges the norm, and challenges you to create a better chronology/history. That is my overall goal.

The errors and omissions I take full credit for. The good stuff, I stole from you—you know who you are and do not need to be personally thanked.

Prologue

This journey began by following Malcolm Rogers' trail via his site record forms, notes, and publications, which documented what he saw beginning in 1919 and his understanding of San Diego County's archaeology. San Diego's first archaeologist, born in 1890, was not a trained archaeologist. He was a geologist with a passion for archaeology. Rogers provides the records for most of the early work in San Diego County, the eastern California desert, and Baja from ca. 1919 to his death in a car accident in 1960. His publications began in 1929 with his: *The Stone Art of the San Dieguito Plateau*, and ends with posthumous publications in 1966 of *The San Dieguito Type Site: M. J. Rogers' 1938 Excavation on the San Dieguito River Valley* edited by C. Warren; and, *Ancient Hunters of the Far West*, edited by R. Pourade with contributions by H. M. Wormington, E. L. Davis, and C. W. Brott.

The first site Rogers recorded was W-1 (SDI-39), the Spindrift site, one of the oldest sites, dated 9585–9025 cal B.P., in SDC and perhaps the founding location for the First People of San Diego County. His second recorded site, W-2, he describes as the most important prehistoric station in Southern California, which he watched being destroyed by a steam shovel in 1926 for the development of La Jolla Shores. He also recorded a number of sites on Pleistocene sandstone bluffs north of La Jolla Shores including Scripps Estates (W-9/SDI-525), Middle Midden (W-5/SDI-4670), and the Chancellor's House (W-12/SDI-4669) dated to 9740–9545 cal B.P. These sites, from Spindrift to the Chancellor's House, Rogers identified to a people he called Shell-Midden and later referred to as La Jolla.

Rogers recorded Scraper Hill (W-240/SDI-8330), a Scraper-Maker site, which he also referred to as the discovery site, and upon which he identified as a key site in his chronology. He referred to both the people and the artifacts as Scraper-Maker, which he later termed San Dieguito. Rogers recorded a number of sites in north SDC (east of lagoons, and east and west of the foothills and the Harris site (W-198/SDI-149), an area he identified as the San Dieguito Plateau. The Harris site, the San Dieguito Plateau sites, and the Scraper-Maker site were instrumental in Rogers' description and understanding of San Dieguito. Rogers initially identified the La Jolla as First People and later revised his chronology with San Dieguito as First People.

Following Rogers via his site forms, notes, and publications; reading Warren's work; plus the author's 40+ years of archaeological experience; and his review of CRM's gray literature provided the basis for this publication. But it was Rogers that was the most insightful and helpful in providing a trail to follow his twists and turns in preparing this publication.

Abstract

The chronology for San Diego County (SDC) has been addressed a number of times resulting in numerous terms with overlapping time periods for the peopling of SDC over the past 12,000 years. Questions to be answered include: Who were the First People? Where did they arrive from? What tools/tool kit identify these early settlers? Where did they initially settle? Is there a relationship between the First People and the Kumeyaay living here today? Also, how did the tool kit change over time; what were the changes in site patterning and use of resources through time; and what adaptations can be noted to environmental change during the Holocene, as well as technology change and resource intensification through time. Addressing these questions necessitated a review of early researchers' notes, site forms, and publications, as well as recent Cultural Resource Management (CRM) archaeological work and the author's work in CRM over the past 40+ years in SDC.

This publication includes a discussion on First People arriving by sea via the "Kelp Highway" into SDC at the end of the Pleistocene; and a discussion on Early Holocene people leaving the drying Great Basin and entering north SDC at the beginning of the Holocene, settling adjacent to the mouths of river valleys that were forming into lagoons with the rise in sea level ca. 9000 B.P. Chapter 1, Early Holocene Setting and First People Sites, provides an overview of the earliest sites dating from the end of the Pleistocene and beginning of the Holocene. These sites include Remington Hills SDI-11079, Del Mar Man SDI-10940, C.W. Harris Site SDI-149, Agua Hedionda site UCLJ-M-15, La Jolla Spindrift SDI-39, Chancellor's House SDI-4669, and Windsong Shores SDI-10965. A number of these Early Holocene sites (SDI-11079, SDI-10940, SDI-39, SDI-4669) are similar in content (artifacts and ecofacts) and focus on coastal resources of shellfish and fish. Tools from these coastal sites are primarily non-formal and made from local beach cobbles that were adequate for the task at hand while other sites (SDI-149 Locus I E-Stratum, UCLJ-M-15 basal level, and SDI-10965) contain a high number of formal tools (i.e., bifaces, crescents and scrapers) of fine-grained metavolcanic material from local quarries. Two areas of occupation for these kinds of sites are discussed in Chapter 2 (Pleistocene-Holocene La Jolla Occupation) and Chapter 3 (Rogers' San Dieguito Plateau, Dating San Dieguito, and Warren Vs. Rogers Chronology). Along with the Chapter 3 discussion of San Dieguito sites on the San Dieguito Plateau is a discussion on the chronology, individually and collectively built by Malcolm Rogers (1919 to 1960) and Claude Warren (1959 to present), used for most of the past 80 years. Both individuals have strong credentials and personalities and their chronologies appear similar, but there are substantial differences given typing of sites as San Dieguito, and therein the time period for San Dieguito. Warren had the benefit of radiocarbon dating and initially limited his San Dieguito definition to primarily the Harris Site as the "Type Site" with specific types of tools, workmanship, and radiocarbon dates older that 8000 B.P. It should be noted that radiocarbon dating was only available towards the end of Rogers' career, therefore Rogers identified his San Dieguito sites on the basis of types of artifacts (bifaces, scrapers, and crescents), material and craftsmanship.

Chapter 4, Late Holocene and Late Period Occupation, provides a discussion on climate, environmental change, adaptation, cultural material, language, intrusion of Uto-Aztecan/Takic (Luiseño/Cahuilla), and resource intensification. Chapter 5, Chronology and Discussion, builds from the four previous chapters to provide a chronology for SDC occupation from ca. 12,000 B.P. to present. This 12,000 year chronology is divided into Early, Middle and Late Holocene; as well as Early Archaic (12,000 to 9000 B.P.), Middle Archaic (Phase I 9000-

7500 B.P., and Phase II 7500–3500 B.P.), Late Archaic (3500–1300 B.P.) and Late Period (1300 B.P. to historic contact). These divisions are identified to focus research on poorly known but significant periods of initial occupation (Early Archaic); stability with change (Middle Archaic); resource depletion/change with associated depopulation and population movement (Late Archaic); and, Late Period with increased population, innovation and resource intensification.

The locations for First People, Early Holocene sites, tool kits, Harris type site, site patterning, differing views of Malcolm Rogers' and Claude Warren's SDC chronology, time periods, terminology, and environmental setting and change, are all part of the story of the past 12,000 years. This work provides new information on the initial and continuous occupation of SDC and addresses potential First People sites and cultural material across the landscape and through time. Chronologies are by their very nature "a work in progress," as is this one, to be changed and updated as new information is added. It is the author's goal to make you question, think, and to challenge this chronology and previous ones, and to therein improve, clarify, and build a better overall understanding of the past 12,000 year history of SDC.

First People:
A Revised Chronology for San Diego County

Chapter 1
Early Holocene Setting and First People Sites

New World exploration and settlement began after 20,000 years B.P. (Last Glacial Maximum), wherein a warming period melted glaciers that raised sea levels worldwide and created inland lakes and coastal lagoons. Melted glaciers also enhanced inland and coastal regions with plentiful fish, shellfish, game, and plant foods for the initial settlers. In 1929, Malcolm Rogers believed that the initial peopling was by those who left behind the shell middens. He used the term "Shell-Midden" to describe both the people and the artifacts and stated: "The first and probably the older is chiefly characterized by numerous shell middens. These middens are to be found not only on the coast, but as far as four miles inland. The surface finds from these shell middens include metates, manos, hammerstones, teshoa flakes, and a great amount of split stone, but no chipped stone artifacts which may be recognized as finished implements" (Rogers 1929:456–457). He believed at this time that the Scraper-Makers followed the Shell-Midden people. Malcolm Rogers' Shell-Midden people were later referred to as La Jolla, La Jolla Complex, Pauma Complex, Millingstone Horizon, Encinitas Tradition, Archaic, and La Jolla Cultural Pattern. However, in 1945, he reversed his chronology stating: "Immediately after the disappearance of the San Dieguito [Scraper-Maker] people with their excellent stone-flaking technique, a new stock [La Jolla] with a seafood-seed-gathering complex and no ability to work stone moved in..." (Rogers 1945:171).

Rogers renamed the Scraper-Makers as San Dieguito. This cultural pattern has also been referred and/or related to Western Pluvial Lakes Tradition (WPLT), Western Stemmed Point Tradition (WSPT), Paleo-Coastal Tradition (PCT), and San Dieguito Cultural Pattern (SDCP). Claude Warren, following Rogers, also hypothesized the initial occupation (SDCP) reflected an inland orientation and use of more formal tools such as bifaces, scraping tools, and crescents; followed by the La Jolla Cultural Pattern (LJCP) reflecting a coastal orientation with shell, cobble-based tools, milling tools, and burials; followed by the Late Period Kumeyaay (Ipai, Tipai)/Yuman and Luiseño occupation (Rogers 1945; Warren 1966, 1967, 1968; Warren and True 1961; Warren et al. 1961).

By the 1960s, publications by Rogers, Warren, and others identified the initial occupation of SDC by a people following game from northeastern Asia, crossing the land bridge in Beringia after the Last Glacial Maximum and moving into the Great Basin where changes in climate during the Late Pleistocene ca. 15,000 years ago, created large pluvial lakes from Oregon and Utah to California (Figure 1). One of the earliest well-dated occupations is at Paisley Caves, Oregon, wherein six human coprolites were radiocarbon dated from 12,140–12,400 B.P. (average date of eight additional samples = 12,240 B.P. calibrated to 14,340 ±60 cal B.P.) (Jenkins et al. 2013; Waters and Stafford 2013:548). Jenkins (2013) considers Paisley Caves lithic assemblage as Western Stemmed Point Tradition (WSPT). The WSPT is defined by Willig and Aikens (1988:3) as "characterized by large stemmed, shouldered and lanceolate points, often associated with crescents and heavy core tools ... from southern British Columbia to northern Mexico and from the Rockies to the Pacific Coast—there is a certain diversity of regional styles, but all complexes share similarities in technology, typology, and implied settlement-subsistence patterns." The WSPT includes the San Dieguito, Lake Mohave, and Hascomat complexes; Western Lithic Co-Tradition; Western Pluvial Lakes Tradition; and regional styles for Lake Mojave, Silver Lake, and Lind Coulee (Willig and Aikens 1988:4). Warren et al. (1998:II–46) states: "The Lake Mojave culture ... is a regional expression of the Western Pluvial Lakes Tradition, and is included in the San Dieguito ... and is associated with fresh water stand of Lake Mojave that dates to between ca. 8,500 and 10,500 years ago" (Warren and Ore 1978; Wells et al. 1989).

2 *First People: A Revised Chronology for San Diego County*

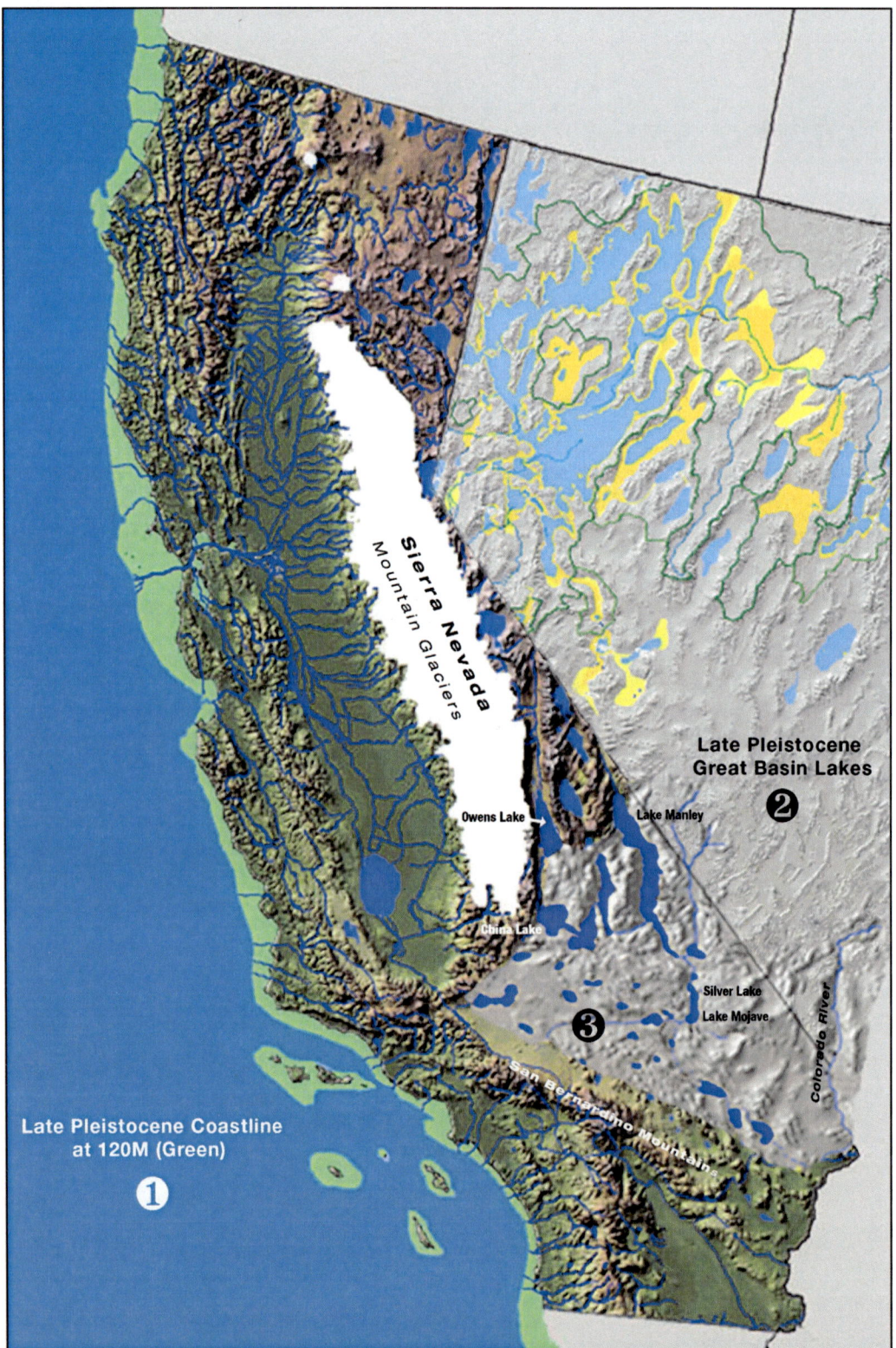

Figure 1. Late Pleistocene Shoreline and Great Basin Lakes.
Sources Taken/Adapted From: 1. geologycafe.com 2012; 2. USGS and Reheis 1999; 3. USGS.gov 2004.

The radiocarbon date for the Awl site SBR-4562 on an olivella sp. bead from the lowermost stratum is 9450 B.P. (11,110–9830 cal B.P.) (Erlandson et al. 2007a:59). With the drying of these pluvial lakes ca. 8,000 to 11,000 years ago, some of these early people likely found their way southwest from the southern edge of the Great Basin to SDC's coastal lagoons. The rise in sea level at the end of the Pleistocene and during the Early to Middle Holocene flooded canyons and mouths of river valleys to create submarine canyons and lagoons, resulting in rich environmental settings of shellfish and fish, as well as associated marine and land resources for the Early Holocene settlers.

Erlandson et al. (2007b) proposed the "Kelp Highway" hypothesis, wherein it was proposed that during the end of the Late Pleistocene, kelp forests from northeastern Asia to South America provided the route by boat into the Americas, and the Kelp Highway facilitated the voyage by providing highly productive, nutrient-rich kelp forests with associated fish, birds, sea mammals, and shellfish as a food source. Late Pleistocene-Early Holocene island occupation sites associated with the Kelp Highway include: Arlington Springs site CA-SRI-173, dated to 10,960 B.P. (12,900 cal B.P.); and Daisy Cave CA-SMI-261, dated to 10,390 B.P. (1-sigma calibrated age 12,060–12,460 cal B.P.) (Agenbroad et al. 2005; Erlandson et al. 1996; Rosenthal and Fitzgerald 2012). It is highly possible that the First People arrived in SDC by sea in the vicinity of La Jolla Bay, submarine canyons, caves, and sandstone terraces. A second location (Remington Hills SDI-11079) for an Early Holocene arrival by sea is also near a submarine canyon, which would have been accessible 10,000 to 12,000 years ago. It should be noted that these Early Holocene sites are oriented to coastal/ocean resources.

What was initially described by Rogers as Scraper-Makers (San Dieguito/SDCP) and Shell-Midden (La Jolla/LJCP) have both been dated to the Early Holocene (11,000–9000 B.P.). In order to explain the presence of both the Shell-Midden/La Jolla/LJCP and the Scraper-Makers/San Dieguito/SDCP in San Diego County during the Early Holocene, Warren proposed five models: Abandonment, Displacement, Acculturation, Transformation, and Non-transition (Warren et al. 1998). All five models assume San Dieguito as first occupants arriving by an inland route. However, with the work by Erlandson and others (Erlandson et al. 1996; Erlandson et al. 2007a,b; Erlandson 2013), an initial coastal SDC occupation via the Kelp Highway cannot be ruled out. Therefore, two additional models (models 6 and 7) identifying LJCP as the initial occupation are proposed. Model 6 identifies the LJCP as initially occupying San Diego County (SDC), with the LJCP adding SDCP tools for the purpose of better exploiting inland resources. Model 7 also identifies LJCP as First People, however, sites with more of a SDCP (e.g., bifaces, stemmed points, and crescents) such as the Windsong Shores site SDI-10965, UCLJ-M-15, and the Harris site may represent a people who entered SDC from the drying inland lakes of the Great Basin and present-day dry lake beds of Silver Lake and Lake Mojave—into an area (north SDC) already occupied by a coastal oriented people, the LJCP.

On the basis of Early Holocene radiocarbon dates and site location, the two potential First People site locations include: (1) the La Jolla Archaeological Area, extending from La Jolla Bay to the UCSD Chancellor's House, and (2) Remington Hills site SDI-11079, situated just east of the Tijuana Lagoon.

It should also be noted that the LJCP appears to have had contact with the Great Basin/desert since initial occupation, given early dates on coastal olivella sp. spire-removed beads found in the interior of California, and obsidian from the interior of California found at Early Holocene coastal SDC sites (see Chapters 1 and 5 for model discussions). The First People had their choice of coastal and inland locations ("sweet spots") and for the occupation of SDC, this founding settlement and settlers could have been by land or by sea. This does not negate that the SDCP and LJCP may simply represent coastal and inland tools for the purpose of hunting, fishing, collecting, and processing both coastal and inland resources.

Late Pleistocene-Holocene Setting

For coastal north San Diego County, the setting at the end of the Pleistocene and beginning of the Holocene may have been similar to that described by Erlandson et al. (1996:369–370) for Daisy Cave (San Miguel Island) wherein he states: "...prior to ca. 12,000 cal B.P. a pine forest grew outside the cave, probably covering a more extensive coastal plain exposed by lower sea levels. The pollen spectra take on a more modern character after ca. 12,000 yrs ago, when the percentage of pine pollen declines dramatically and Compositae, Rosaceae, and Quercus (oak) pollen all increase significantly. . . . These vegetation changes are closely linked to postglacial warming, which also led to dramatic sea level rise. . . . By the Late Holocene, it appears that the environment . . . had taken on an essentially modern character."

The environmental setting of sea level rise, sand transport, and climate change (e.g., rainfall and droughts) greatly affected native populations over the past 12,000+ years. At the transition from the Pleistocene to the Holocene for the South Coast Range, West et al. (2007:25) describes the changing climate: "There is a rapid increase in oak, herbs, and chaparral taxa and a corresponding decrease in conifers, signaling the initial development of Holocene-type plant communities (e.g., oak woodland, chaparral, and coastal sage scrub)." For San Elijo, the Holocene setting is described as: "Early Holocene period (from cal 9600 B.C. to cal 5600 B.C. [11,550–7550 cal B.P.] was one of abundant ferns, which declined dramatically between cal 6000–5000 B.C. [7950–6950 cal B.P.])" (Byrd et al. 2004:345). The abundance of ferns reflects an initial wetter Early Holocene climate and coastal fog. For northeastern California, a period of more effective moisture ca. 4000–3000 B.P. and 1500 B.P. is identified (West and McGuire 2004). The Early Neoglacial from ca. 4000–2500 B.P. is described as a period of cooler temperatures and higher precipitation (West et al. 2007). This is followed by a Late Holocene dry period from 2800–1850 cal B.P. (Mensing et al. 2013); and, then unusual warmth and aridity identified as the Medieval Climatic Anomaly from 1200–750 cal B.P. (Mensing et al. 2013); followed by the Little Ice Age, a period of relative cool climate from ca. 750–150 B.P. (West et al. 2007).

Sea level from the end of the Pleistocene (ca. 20,000 B.P.) through most of the Holocene rose 120 m to present-day sea level: -120 m at 20,000 B.P.; -55 m at 12,000 B.P.; -35 m at 10,000 B.P.; -18 m at 8000 B.P.; and -5 m at 6000 B.P. to roughly present-day sea level ca. 4000–3000 B.P. (Inman 1983; Masters and Aiello 2007) (Figure 2). With sea level rise, San Diego County's coastal setting over the past 12,000 years changed from a rocky shore to a sandy, soft-bottom habitat for shellfish and fish, thereby affecting the type, quantity, and availability of coastal foods. Late Pleistocene/Early Holocene rise in sea level flooded coastal canyons and created submarine canyons and lagoons with highly productive habitats for shellfish and fish. Around 6000 B.P., sea level rise and sand transport created San Diego Bay; and, by ca. 3500 B.P. with sea level somewhat stable, and with sand and cobble bars across north SDC lagoon mouths, the lagoons filled with silt and sediment, depleting the lagoon shellfish and fish habitat. The closing of a number of lagoons is documented by coring studies along with radiocarbon dating the presence/absence of archaeological sites at Batiquitos Lagoon (Miller 1966; Gallegos 1985); and, by Byrd's study at San Elijo Lagoon, which identified "the initial formation of a brackish to marine open lagoon at San Elijo between cal 7500–6700 B.C. [9450–8650 cal B.P.] . . . with deep, open lagoon conditions exist[ing] until at least cal 3300–3000 B.C. [5250–4950 cal B.P.] . . . No evidence of open lagoon conditions were documented at the start of the Late Holocene between cal 1500 B.C. and cal A.D. 900 [3450–1050 cal B.P.]. . . . Open lagoon conditions . . . reappeared at cal A.D. 1000 . . . and existed at least until cal A.D. 1300 [950–650 cal B.P.]" (Byrd et al. 2004:346).

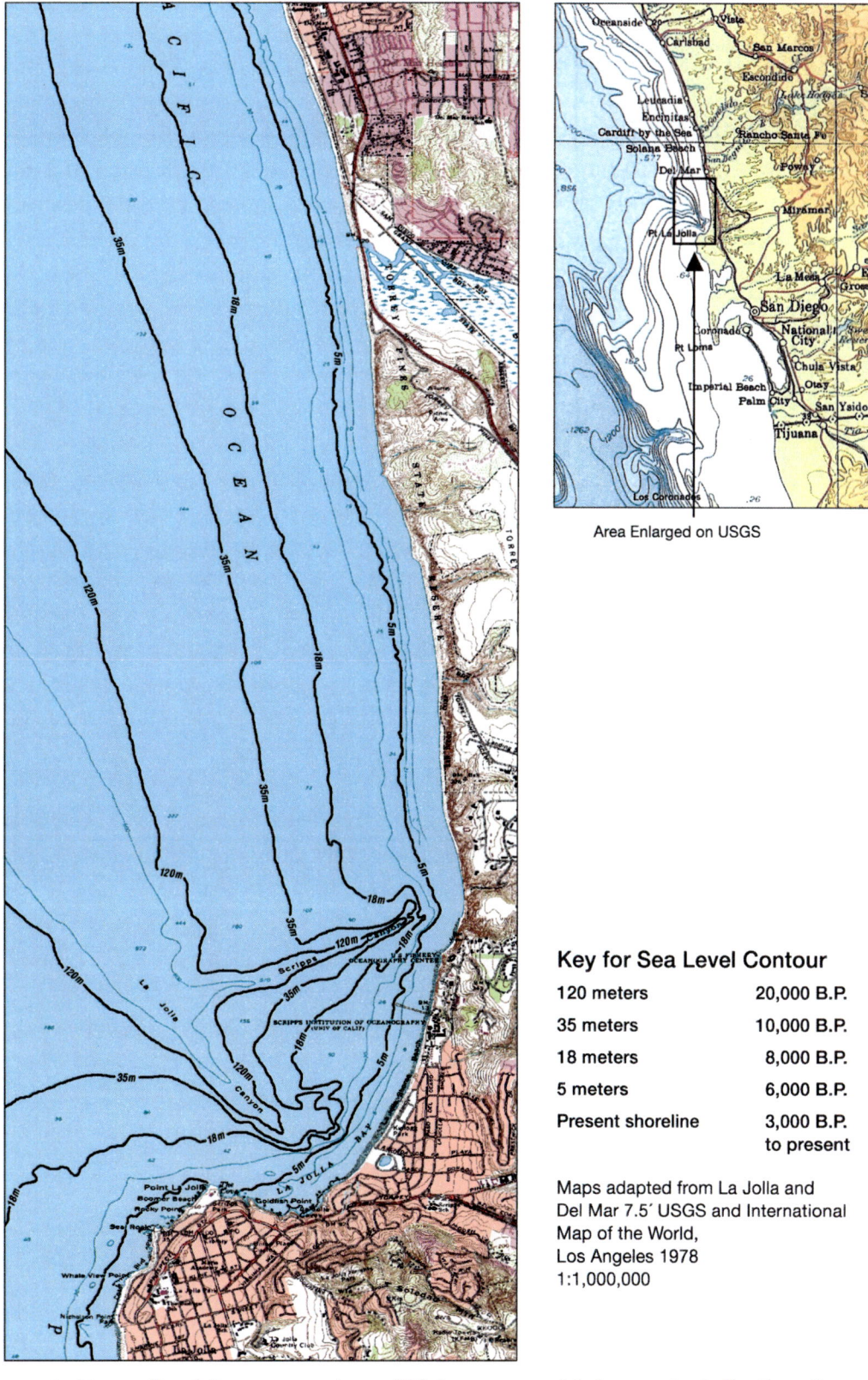

Figure 2. Generalized Representation of Pleistocene to Holocene La Jolla Shorelines.

Early Holocene Sites

The earliest sites (over 9000 years B.P.) in SDC are primarily along the coast either situated adjacent to a lagoon, submarine canyon, or coastal valley (Figure 3). These sites include: Remington Hills SDI-11079; Del Mar Man SDI-10940/W-34; Agua Hedionda UCLJ-M-15; La Jolla Spindrift SDI-39; Windsong Shores SDI-10965; and UCSD Chancellor's House SDI-4669; as well as over 60 additional Early Holocene sites (dated ca. 9000–7000 B.P.) located adjacent to lagoons and coastal valleys (Table 1). The Harris site SDI-149 is situated approximately 10 miles from the mouth of the San Dieguito Lagoon. The material dated for these early coastal sites is primarily shell, with the exception of soil/charcoal (black organic layer) from the Harris site SDI-149. It should be noted that: *Olivella* sp. spire-removed beads provided AMS dates for the Remington Hills site SDI-11079; a single *Argopecten* sp. shell provided an AMS date for the Windsong Shores SDI-10965 earliest date; and bone from the Chancellor's House SDI-4669 was dated, thereby providing direct association of radiocarbon dates to occupation as opposed to the Harris site, wherein black organic material from a geologic stratum within a river channel that was not in direct association with cultural material was used to date this site.

Erlandson and others' work (Erlandson et al. 2007a,b) on a Late Pleistocene-Early Holocene coastal route into the new world via the Kelp Highway provides support for hypothesizing that early explorers from northeastern Asia may have entered SDC via a coastal route. Presently, we have pieces of this remarkable story of New World occupation in SDC beginning ca. 10,000– 11,000 years ago. Future work may provide earlier radiocarbon dates to assist in completing the story of the earliest SDC settlers. Radiocarbon dates calibrated for 2 sigma using IntCal13 show the range for 95 percent confidence (Table 2). It should be noted that this range is as small as 195 years (Chancellor's House) or as large as 1,865 years (Harris Site) or 2,415 years (Agua Hedionda site UCLJ-M-15), and simply means that there is a 95 percent confidence that the actual date is within this range and does not identify a specific point. Table 3 provides cultural summaries for each Early Holocene site. The Early Holocene sites listed on Table 1 and shown on Figure 3 are discussed below.

La Jolla: Spindrift Site SDI-39/W-1

The Spindrift site, located adjacent to La Jolla Bay, the La Jolla and Scripps submarine canyons, the La Jolla Caves, and an estuary was initially reported by Nelson ca. early 1900s and later recorded by Rogers ca. 1919 as SDM-W-1. Rogers recorded W-1 as a 20-acre shell midden with three acres of intense occupation, including cobble hearths, burials, and both La Jolla and Yuman occupation (Rogers 1920s, W-1). Nelson recorded the Spindrift site as No. 39 refuse heap with a midden depth of one to eight feet (0.3 to 2.44 m) from south to north, dipping under the marsh level and beach sands at the north end (Gifford 1916). Site occupation appears continuous throughout the Holocene, given the Early Holocene radiocarbon dates beginning ca. 9,000 years ago and continuing to historic contact. See Chapter 2 for a discussion on Spindrift, and Early to Middle Holocene occupation from La Jolla Bay to the adjacent Pleistocene marine terraces to the north.

La Jolla: Chancellor's House SDI-4669/W-12

Rogers may have recorded this site earlier, but cites working on W-12 in 1929 (Rogers field notes 1929). He identifies this eight-acre site as a highland midden with a trace of Yuman III overlying Littoral II (La Jollan) burials, and a buried San Dieguito III midden. He states: "The first occupation here was on a ridge of marine coarse grey sand, which . . . has all been destroyed by recession of the sea cliff margin except for a landward pitching margin" (Rogers field notes 1929). He reports crude scrapers, manos, metates, hearths, midden of three feet with shellfish (mostly mussel and pecten), with some fish and mammal bone (Rogers field notes 1929).

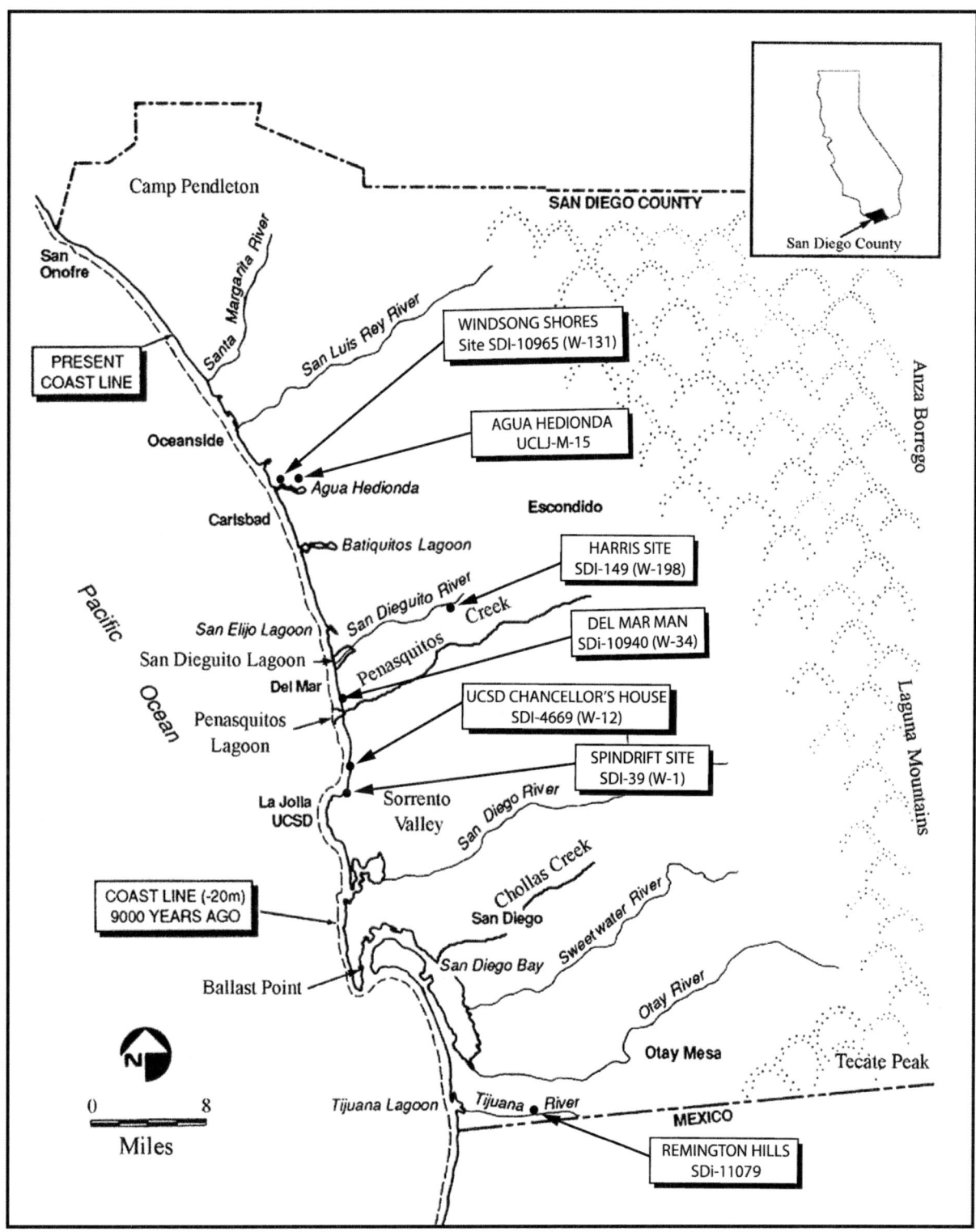

Figure 3. Early Holocene Sites.

Measured Age-Range B.P.	Conventional Date B.P.	Calibrated 2 Sigma cal B.P. Date *	Location	SDI-No.	Other No.	Lab No.	Material	Reference
9400±60	9810±60	10625 -10250	Remington Hills, Tijuana Lagoon	11079		BETA-118072	Shell, *Olivella* sp. bead	Kyle, Schroth & Gallegos 1998
9280±60	9700±60	10505 -10180	Remington Hills, Tijuana Lagoon	11079		BETA-118073	Shell, *Olivella* sp. bead	Kyle, Schroth & Gallegos 1998
9070±100		9740 -9295	Del Mar Man San Dieguito Lagoon	10940	W-34	LJ-3177	Shell, *Chione* sp	Linnick 1977:33
9050±60	9460±60	10205 -9840	Remington Hills, Tijuana Lagoon	11079		BETA-118071	Shell, *Olivella* sp. bead	Kyle, Schroth & Gallegos 1998
9030±350		11190 -9400 9345 -9325	Harris Site San Dieguito River Valley	149	W-198	A-722A	Soil/Charcoal	Haynes et al. 1967
9020±500		10695 -8280	Agua Hedionda		UCLJ-M-15	LJ-967	Shell, *Mytilus c*	Hubbs et al. 1965
9000±70	9410±70	10185 -9690	Remington Hills, Tijuana Lagoon	11079		BETA-118074	Shell, *Olivella* sp. bead	Kyle, Schroth & Gallegos 1998
8940±100		9585 -9025	La Jolla Spindrift	39	W-1	Beta 263877	Shell, *Mytilus c*.	Pigniolo and Brodie 2009
8890±40	9290±40	9930 -9580	Windsong Shores, Agua Hedionda	10965	W-131	BETA-199587	Shell, *Argopecten* sp.	Gallegos (this publication)
8690±40		9740 -9545	UCSD Chancellor's House	4669	W-12	UCR-3714	Bone	Hector 2007

*All 2 Sigma Calibrations completed by Dardon Hood, Beta Analytic using IntCal13

Table 1. Early Holocene Radiocarbon Dated Sites in San Diego County.

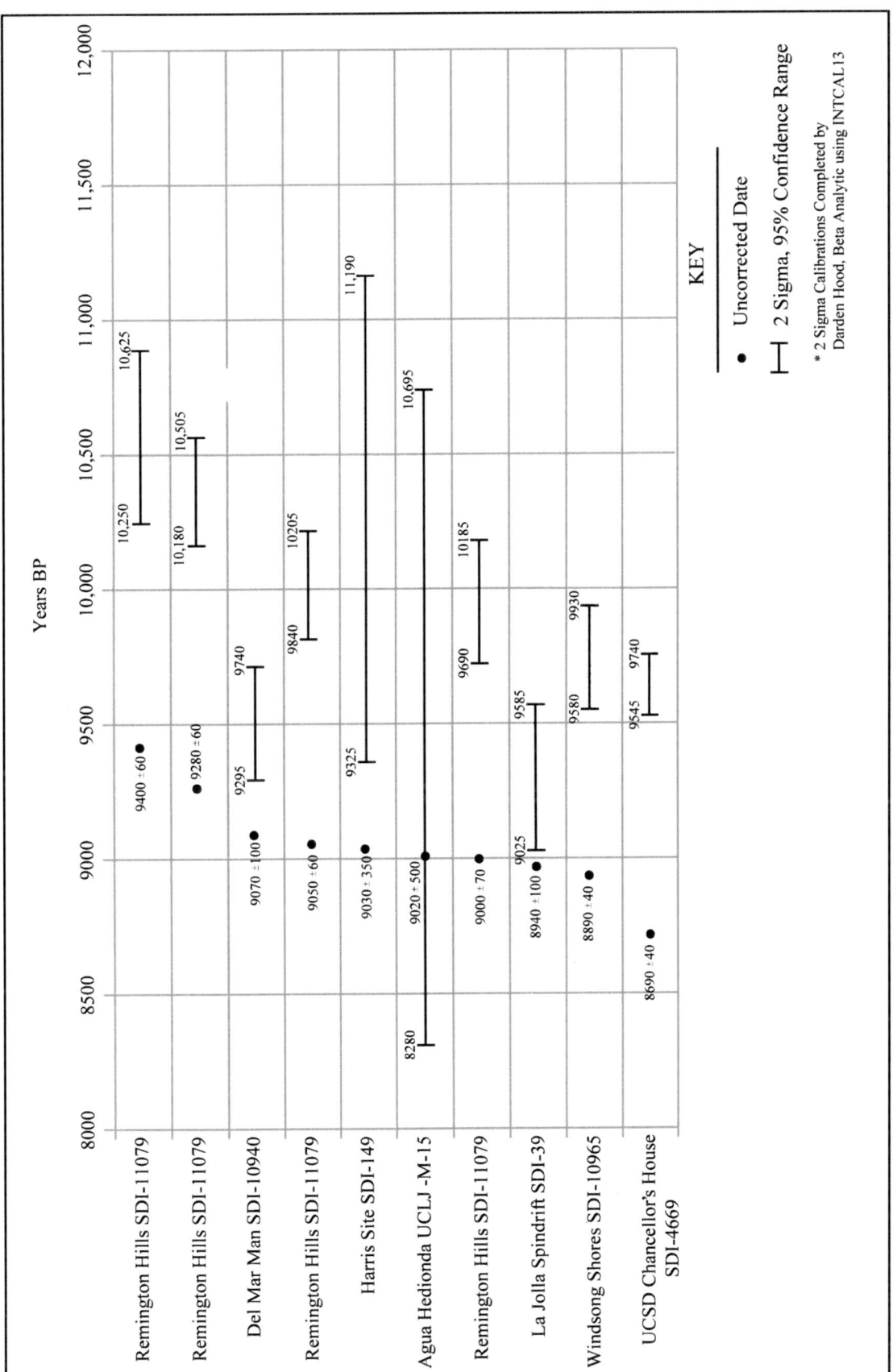

Table 2. Early Holocene Calibrated Radiocarbon Dates.

Cultural Material	Remmington Hills SDI-11079		Agua Hedionda UCLJ-M-15	Del Mar Man SDI-10940, W-34	Windsong Shores SDI-10965, W-131		Chancellor's House** SDI-4669, W-12A/B		C.W. Harris Site SDI-149 Locus I E-Stratum	
	Count	Percent	Count	Count	Count	Percent	Count	Percent	Count	Percent
Biface/Knife/Point	4	1.1%	1	2	10	6.9%	3	1.0%	90	44.8%
Crescent	0	0.0%	0	0	5	3.4%	0	0.0%	2	1.0%
Scraper	50	13.9%	X	0	61	42.1%	70	22.5%	97	48.3%
Chopper	5	1.4%	X	0	9	6.2%	0	0.0%	0	0.0%
Cobble Tools	0	0.0%	0	0	0	0.0%	28	9.0%	0	0.0%
Hammerstone	22	6.1%	X	0	14	9.7%	34	10.9%	9	4.5%
Core	19	5.3%	0	0	7	4.8%	56	18.0%	3	1.5%
Utilized/modified Flake	91	25.3%	0	0	12	8.3%	26	8.4%	0	0.0%
Debitage/Flake*	27090	0.0%	X	X	7735	0.0%	4403	0.0%	0	0.0%
Mano	120	33.3%	0	0	5	3.4%	63	20.3%	0	0.0%
Metate	8	2.2%	X	X	1	0.7%	10	3.2%	0	0.0%
Stone Bowl	0	0.0%	0	0	0	0.0%	2	0.6%		
Groundstone	10	2.8%	X	0	4	2.8%	0	0.0%	0	0.0%
Pestle	5	1.4%	0	0	0	0.0%	0	0.0%	0	0.0%
Stone ball	0	0.0%	0	0	7	4.8%	8	2.6%		
Donut Stone	0	0.0%	0	0	0	0.0%	2	0.6%		
Shell Bead	25	6.9%	0	0	0	0.0%	1	0.3%	0	0.0%
Shell Worked	0	0.0%	0	0	0	0.0%	1	0.3%		
Bone Tool	0	0.0%	0	0	10	6.9%	7	2.3%		
Bone Bead	1	0.3%	0	0	0	0.0%	0	0.0%	0	0.0%
Total	27450	100.0%			7880	100.0%	4714	100.0%	201	100.0%
Total*	360				145		311			
Total Shell (gms)	487			X	2539		2508			
Total Bone (gms)	166.36			X	X		X			
Burial	None		None	2	None		42		None	

*Excludes Flakes/angular waste/debitage

Number of 1x1m Units	42.5				37		48	Trench
C-14 Dates	6750 to 9400 B.P.		7420, 7450 9020 B.P.	4500 to 9070 B.P.	7040 to 8890		7680-8690 B.P.	8490, 8490, 9030 B.P.
					8 Trenches		38 Trenches	
Number of Dates:	7		3	10	6		7	3
Notes:	8 ochre grinders 25 Olivella beads 2 otoliths			2 SD felsite knives	Coso and Casa Diablo Obsidian		Olivella bead Stone & shell beads	
Source	Kyle et al. 1998		Moriarty 1967	Rogers site form Linick 1977	Gallegos & Carrico 1984		Rogers site form Roth & Berryman 1996 Hector 2007 J. Smith 1976	Warren et al. 1998

See Table 4 for La Jolla Spindrift SDI-39, W-1

**Includes Chancellor's House and Eberlin

Table 3. Early Holocene Site Summaries.

Dates for this site range from ca. 8690–7500 B.P. The 8690 B.P. date using 2-sigma calibration provides a date of 9740–9545 cal B.P. (see Table 1). Cultural material recovered from this site is shown on Table 3.

Tijuana Lagoon: Remington Hills SDI-11079

Remington Hills SDI-11079, situated just east of the Tijuana Lagoon and just north of the US-Mexico border, is the oldest (uncorrected) radiocarbon dated site in SDC. In all, 25 *Olivella* sp. spire-removed beads were recovered from SDI-11079 (Figure 4). Seven radiocarbon dates (six on *Olivella* sp. spire-removed beads and one on Haliotis sp.) produced the following uncorrected AMS dates: 9400, 9280, 9050, 9000, 8640, 8250, 6750 B.P. (Kyle et al. 1998). Using 2-sigma calibration, the 9400 B.P. date is corrected to 10,625–10,250 cal. B.P. Circa 10,000 B.P., the -35 m shoreline would have been near a submarine canyon, "a sweet spot" for Early People traveling the Kelp Highway. As sea level rose ca. 10,000–3500 B.P., the submarine canyon and shoreline would separate by eight km (five miles), given the shallow ocean floor. However, the loss of direct access to the submarine canyon with rising sea level would have been offset by the creation of the Tijuana Lagoon ca. 9000 B.P., wherein the Tijuana River mouth would fill with ocean water to create a large and attractive lagoon. Occupation at Remington Hills SDI-11079 and other Otay Mesa sites throughout the Holocene would have focused on both coastal resources as well as inland river valley and Otay Mesa plant and animal resources. Artifacts for this site and region include bifaces, scraping tools, milling and cobble tools, but crescents are absent.

The Remington Hills site is an Early to Middle Holocene habitation site occupied for ca. 3000+ years, but as with most SDC sites, mixing of soil and artifacts is likely due to agricultural use and bioturbation; therefore, caution should be used to identify the relationship of artifacts directly associated with the Early Holocene. Cultural material recovered from the 42.5 1x1 m excavation units includes scraping tools, milling tools, flake tools, bifaces, and beads (Table 3). Debitage material was identified as primarily fine-grained metavolcanic (76%) and metasedimentary (15.3%). Nonlocal materials include crypto-crystalline quartz (n = 97, 0.3%), obsidian (n = 25, 0.1%), and Piedra de Lumbre chert (n = 1, 0.1%). One obsidian sample was sourced to the West Sugarloaf Coso Volcanic Field. The San Dieguito hallmarks of bifaces and scrapers made of fine-grained metavolcanic material are present, but are a minor part of the collection (see Figure 4).

Faunal remains include 2,285 primarily small bone fragments with one medium size and 60 large mammal bone fragments. The identified bones include rabbit (jack, desert cottontail, brush), California ground squirrel, pocket gopher, rays/skates/shark, and snake. The large mammal likely represents deer. Shell, 487.2 g representing 18 species, was divided between bay/estuary (47.9%), rocky (42.6%), and sandy (9.6%) habitats. Pollen analysis identified pine, oak, buckwheat, cattail, blackberry, and sunflower. Protein residue analysis identified chia, Chenopodiaceae, Gramineae, deer, rabbit, and dog. The Remington Hills site is situated at the head of the Tijuana Lagoon, and the occupants had access to both coastal and inland resources, as reflected by the range of faunal remains and milling tools, as well as both cobble and finely worked metavolcanic tools.

Agua Hedionda: UCLJ-M-15

In 1962, Moriarty directed the excavation of site UCLJ-M-15, and published a short synthesis providing results in 1967. However, no complete report identifying methods and results was provided. This site, located at the northeast edge of the Agua Hedionda Lagoon, was excavated using controlled 2x2 m units and excavated in 10 cm levels to a depth of 170 cm. Moriarty (1967) identified the site as La Jollan from surface to 130–140 cm, "when milling stones no longer appeared." From 130 to 170 cm, he noted a distinct change with an increase of small felsite flakes and the recovery of the base of a large biface similar in technique, pattern, and material to San Dieguito. Moriarty (1967:555) further states: "Intermingled with these artifacts were choppers, scrapers, and

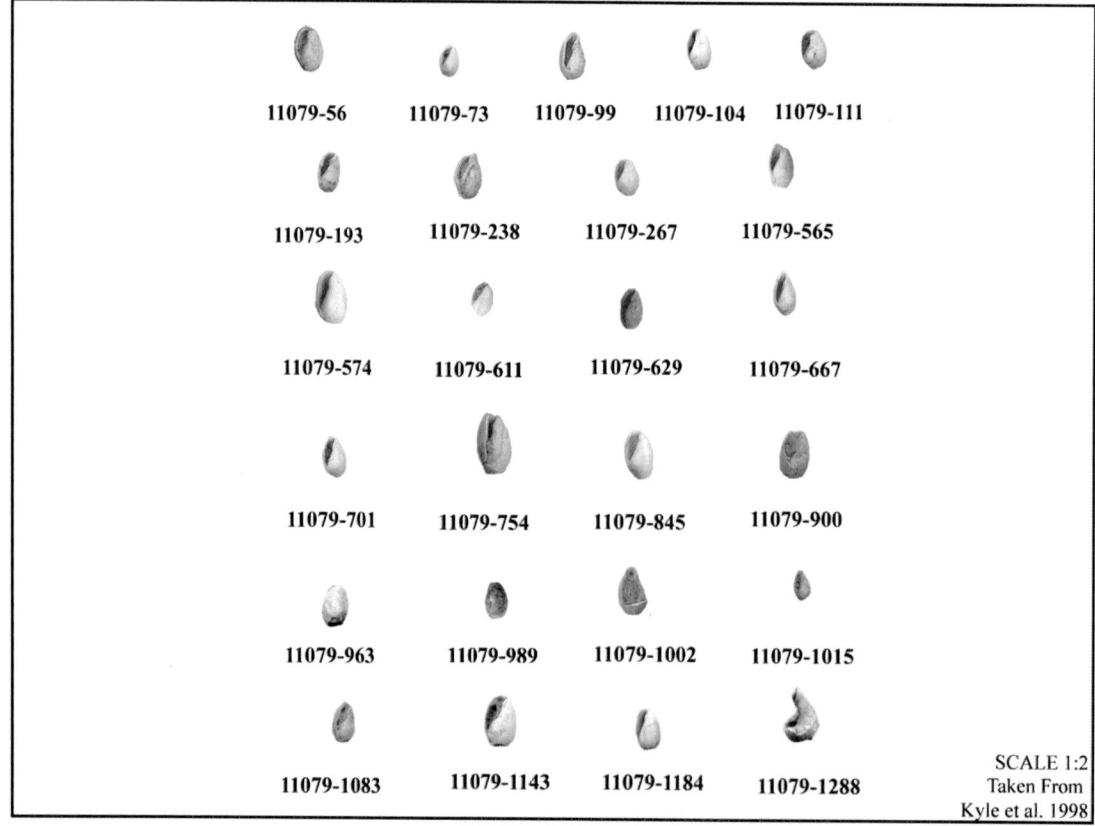

Figure 4. Remington Hills SDI 11079, Bifaces and *Olivella* sp. Beads.

hammerstones typical of La Jolla Phase I. No variation in the profile occurred and there appeared to be an unbroken continuity of occupation from this lowest level up through the overlying midden to the surface." Uncorrected radiocarbon dates on shell by level are 7420 B.P. and 7450 B.P. (130–140 cm), with the basal level (160 to 170 cm) dated 9020 ±500 B.P. (corrected to 10,695–8280 cal B.P. using 2-sigma calibration). Hubbs et al. (1965) states: "A breakthrough date for the inception of shellfish gathering along mainland coast of California . . . Because green felsite implements of the San Dieguito type increased as base level was approached Moriarty concluded that he had finally encountered a transition between San Dieguito and La Jollan cultures . . . Transitional complex may be related to "Pauma complex" of True (1958)" (Hubbs et al. 1965:109).

Moriarty (1967:555) uses the term "Transitional" [Transformation Model] and states: "Radiocarbon evidence from the Agua Hedionda site tends to indicate that the first occupants had already entered a transitional phase between a hunting and a milling culture. The necessity for the creation of large projectile points (that is, continuance of the hunter tradition) on the coast is abrogated to a large extent by the abundance of faunal material in the marine shoreline ecologies which produced more than sufficient protein. . . . Environmental variation, therefore, may well have been the major factor which led to the transition of the hunting culture into the Milling Complex."

San Dieguito Lagoon: Del Mar Man Site SDI-10940/W-34

The Del Mar Man site SDI-10940/W-34, recorded by Rogers in the 1920s, is situated at the northwest edge of the San Dieguito Lagoon. The upper terrace was identified as W-34, and the lower terrace with burials as W-34A. As reported by Rogers, the site had been reduced in size due to the recession of the sea cliff with "one burial in the erosion notch between the lower and upper midden . . . The second burial was exposed in the lower midden and most of it has fallen into the sea" (Rogers 1920s, W-34). He identified this site as La Jollan and reported a metate, stone flaking, shell, and two San Dieguito knives of local felsite material. Using the 1977 results from the UCSD Radiocarbon Laboratory (Linick 1977:33), the uncorrected radiocarbon dates on *Chione* sp. shell for the upper midden (W-34) are: 4500, 5290, 7390, and 9070 B.P. Six dates were produced on *Chione* sp. shell from the lower midden (W-34A) and range from 5930 to 8860 B.P. (Linick 1977:33). Using 2-sigma calibration, the 9070 ±100 B.P. date is corrected to 9740–9295 cal B.P. (see Table 1). The Del Mar Man site is probably best known for amino acid racemization dating by Bada, which produced a date of 48,000 years B.P. (Bada et al. 1974) that was later corrected to 5400 B.P. (Stafford and Tyson 1989; Taylor et al. 1985). Tyson was reported saying: "If the Del Mar Man gets any younger, we'll have to call the coroner and make him a forensics case." This site was also used to test accelerator mass spectrometry (AMS) dating on charcoal, shell, and bone (Stafford and Tyson 1989). The Del Mar Man site is situated adjacent to the ocean and the San Dieguito Lagoon and appears to represent a coastal-oriented people (LJCP) with a hint of SDCP tools. However, due to rising sea level and accompanying bluff failure, as well as the absence of an adequate controlled sample excavation, this site is poorly understood.

Additional Early Holocene sites adjacent to the San Dieguito Lagoon with uncorrected radiocarbon dates include SDI-194 (1 date, 8600 B.P.), SDI-293 (2 dates, 8420–7400 B.P.), SDI-322 (2 dates, 8290–7720 B.P.), SDI-685 (2 dates, 8450–8030 B.P.), and SDI-5369 (2 dates, 8650–3930 B.P.). With respect to artifacts recovered from these Early Holocene sites, Norwood and Walker state: "Obsidian recovered . . . is a very high quality possibly . . . Coso . . . In considering the content of the sites, there is no criteria for suggesting occupations representing culture patterns other than La Jolla. . . . However, four bifaces as well as scrapers were reported" (Norwood and Walker 1980, 156, 251-260).

Agua Hedionda: Windsong Shores SDI-10965/W-131

For SDI-10965/W-131, Rogers in the 1920s reported: "SD-II [San Dieguito] people first camped here on hard packed estuary sands of Quaternary age ... On the south slope a max. depth of 18" was found in the Lit. II [La Jolla] midden ....Metates (granite and schist) here are all relatively thin and light" (Rogers 1920s, W-131). This site, situated adjacent to the mouth of the Agua Hedionda Lagoon, was disturbed by a house, driveway, and septic tank. Due to proposed development, site testing/evaluation and data recovery work were conducted (Gallegos 1991).

The test and data recovery program included the excavation of 37 1x1 m units and eight backhoe trenches to a depth of 90 cm (Gallegos and Carrico 1984). This work resulted in the recovery of a range of tools to include bifaces (points and knives, 6%); scrapers (43%); choppers (6%); hammerstones (9.7%); cores (5%); milling tools (7%); stone balls (5%); bone awls (rabbit and deer bone, 7%); crescents (3.5%); ochre, seeds (pine nuts); and faunal remains (see Table 3). Faunal remains consisted of shell (2,539 g, 26 taxa, primarily lagoon, 89% *Chione*, 4% *Argopecten*); fish (counts as high as 382 vertebrae in one unit and included kelp and sand bass, surfperch, halibut, barracuda, shark, herring or sardine, sheephead, and ray); bird remains, including Chendytes lawi (extinct flightless sea duck/scoter), loon, and mallard; and mammal bone (n = 1025, including n = 887 rabbit and n = 21 deer) (see Table 3).

Windsong's lithic materials, compared to most Early Holocene coastal sites, is more diverse and includes fine-grained metavolcanic, basalt, quartz, chert, Piedra de Lumbre chert, obsidian, quartzite, rhyolite, and chalcedony, with numerous micro-flakes recovered. Obsidian was sourced to both Coso and Casa Diablo in the Sierra Nevada mountain range. Bifaces included two finished points (one Silver Lake) and eight bifaces (broken knives/point bases and midsections) all in finished condition and showing damage (Figure 5). Crescents are made of basalt, fine-grained metavolcanic, and chert, and three of five are complete (see Figure 5). This site is likely the best SDC representative of the San Dieguito Complex as defined by Warren (1967:177). Lake Mohave (also referred to as Lake Mojave) and Silver Lake points, along with a number of Early Holocene point forms, as well as crescents, end and side scrapers, gravers, notches, and burins are included in the Western Stemmed Point Tradition (WSPT), which includes a broad region of the West (Beck and Jones 2013:281–283). The WSPT includes the San Dieguito and Lake Mohave complexes; Western Lithic Co-Tradition; Western Pluvial Lakes Tradition; and the regional styles of Lake Mohave, Silver Lake, and Lind Coulee (Willig and Aikens 1988:4).

Radiocarbon dates for Windsong Shores are 8390 B.P., 8280 B.P., 8060 B.P., and 7040 B.P. (Gallegos 1991). All of these dates were taken on bulk shell, are not AMS dates, and are uncorrected. Bulk shell samples usually included three or more *Chione* sp. shells submitted together to achieve a minimal weight of 30+ g. The problem with this type of dating is that it produces an aggregate date, younger than using a single shell for AMS dating. In order to achieve a more accurate date for Windsong Shores, two additional *Argopecten* sp. shell samples (one shell for each date) were submitted for AMS dating in 2004, and produced the uncorrected dates of 8890 B.P. and 8780 BP. Using IntCal13 and 2-sigma calibration, the 8890 B.P. date is corrected to 9930–9580 cal B.P., thereby identifying Windsong Shores with 95 percent confidence as occupied ca. 9930–9580 years ago.

Given the bifaces, radiocarbon dates, Silver Lake point, crescents, and scrapers, the Windsong Shores site appears to represent a people who moved from the drying inland lakes (e.g., Silver Lake) to Agua Hedionda Lagoon 9930–9580 cal B.P. The cultural and faunal assemblage represents a diet of shellfish, fish, birds, and small to large mammals; and, given milling tools the processing of plant foods.

Early Holocene Setting and First People Sites 15

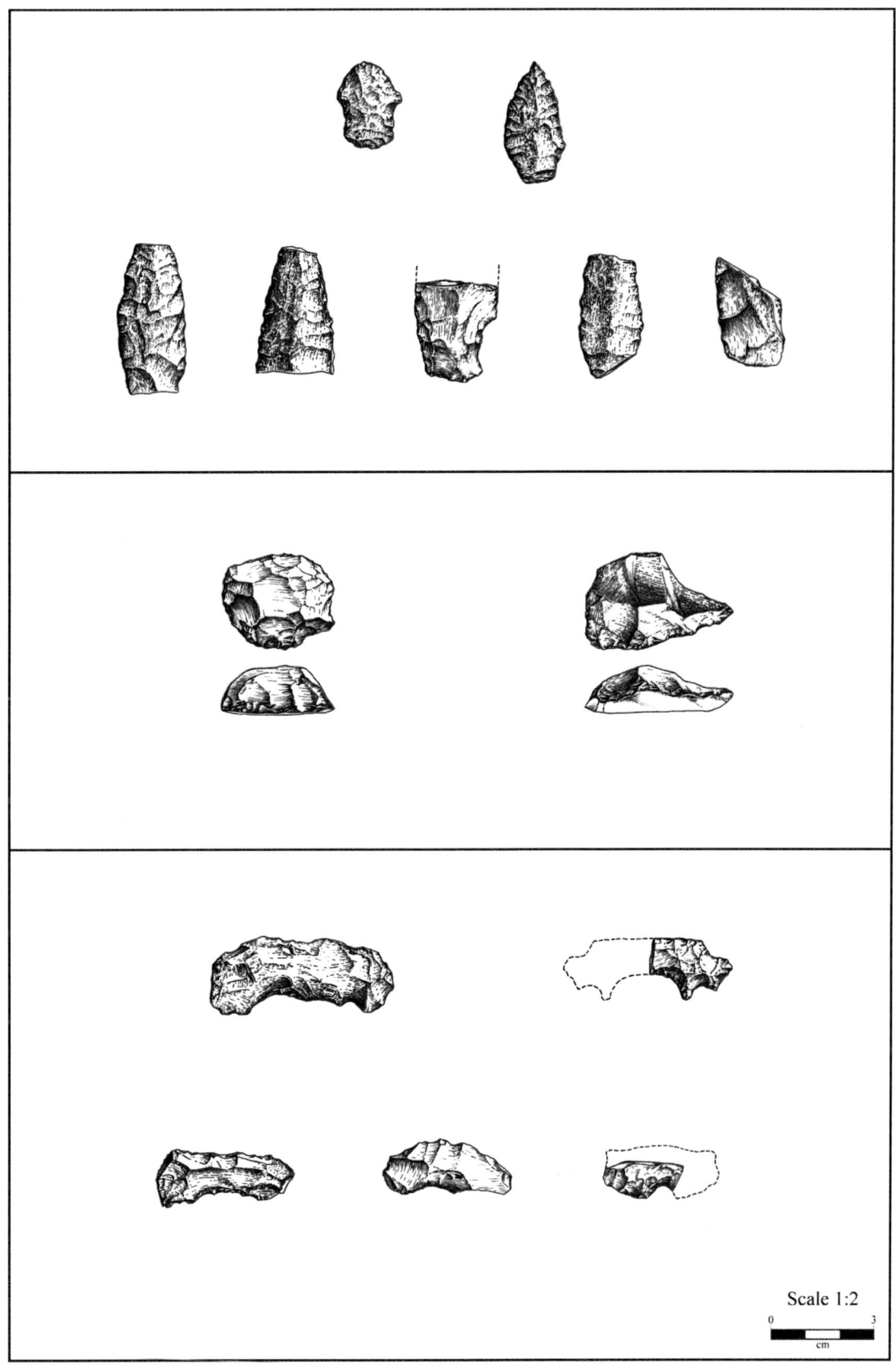

Figure 5. Windsong Shores SDI-10965 Bifaces, Scrapers and Crescents.

San Dieguito River Valley: C. W. Harris Site SDI-149/W-198

The C.W. Harris site (Harris site) (SDMM-W-198/SDI-149/316), located in north San Diego County within the San Dieguito River Valley channel, was discovered in 1928 by Rogers after the 1926 flood, which "exposed a culture-bearing stratum in the southeast bank of the channel." (Figure 6). Rogers describes the Harris site after the 1926 flood as: "[T]he margin of the fossil channel fill was scoured sufficiently to disclose something of the nature and approximate depth of the deposits. It was observed that the thick basal stratum was composed of large boulders, gravel, and sand lenses. Further inspection disclosed San Dieguito III factory floors at different elevations throughout the structure, and the fact that the sand lenses had actually been camped on, as they contained finished artifacts. All had been altered by subsequent river flow, but the combined evidence indicated that during the time this entire structure was being laid down by intermittent flash floods, the San Dieguito III people continued to camp here during the dry seasons" (Warren 1966:5).

Reports usually cited to discuss and define the Harris site and the San Dieguito Complex are M. J. Rogers' 1938 excavation (edited by Warren 1966); Warren and True's 1958 excavation (Warren and True 1961). Additional studies include Carrico and Ezell 1978; Carrico et al. 1991; Ezell's 1964 excavation/no report; Warren 1965 and 1967 excavations/no report; and Cooley and Carrico 2001 excavation/no report.

Primarily on the basis of work by Rogers and Warren (Warren 1966; Warren and True 1961) and artifacts recovered at Locus I E-Stratum (San Dieguito component), Warren defined the San Dieguito Complex as comprised of knives of several varieties; small leaf-shaped points; stemmed and shouldered points, generally termed "Lake Mohave" and "Silver Lake" points; ovoid, domed scrapers; engraving tools; and crescents (Warren 1967:177). Warren et al. (1998) states: "Milling tools are not found in the San Dieguito assemblage of the Harris site ... However, millingstones are found with similar early man materials as far north as the states of Washington and Oregon" (Daugherty 1956; Cressman 1960).

The Harris site has been identified by Warren et al. (1998) and others as one of the earliest sites in San Diego County and the type site for San Dieguito (Warren 1966). This site is related to the WPLT (Warren 1966, 1967; Warren et al. 1998), which has been subsumed under the WSPT.

Radiocarbon Dates

The earliest date of 9030 B.P. (A-722A) was taken on carbonaceous residue within a river channel. The two younger dates of 8490 B.P. (A-724) and 8490 B.P. (A-725) were reported as follows: "Sample A-724 charcoal (?) ... was disseminated throughout alluvial sand and gravel ... [and sample] A-725 Charcoal (?) ... charcoal lumps from alluvial sand and gravel unit ... was confined to single sand lens" (Haynes et al. 1967). These samples were collected from a stream channel that demonstrates a high amount of disturbance and collected on materials that may or may not be directly associated with cultural material. With respect to the radiocarbon dates and location for SDI-149/W-198, Hubbs stated, "[T]he problem needs further elucidation, especially because stratigraphic relations in reworked flood-plain deposits like those at SDMM-W-198 are suspect" (Shumway et al. 1961).

Site Disturbance

Rogers, discussing the Harris site disturbance, stated: "The factories often produce one or more broken blades.... The sand lenses produced a high percentage of intact implements and a much smaller number of spalls, suggesting that these areas served as temporary campsites when they were bars and beaches during arid periods.... None were found which did not show an evidence of having been degraded by subsequent stream flow. This evidence is well-exemplified in the large lens in E3 where the long axes of blades were oriented up and down stream ... None of the artifacts from the sand lenses displayed battering or stream-wear, an indication

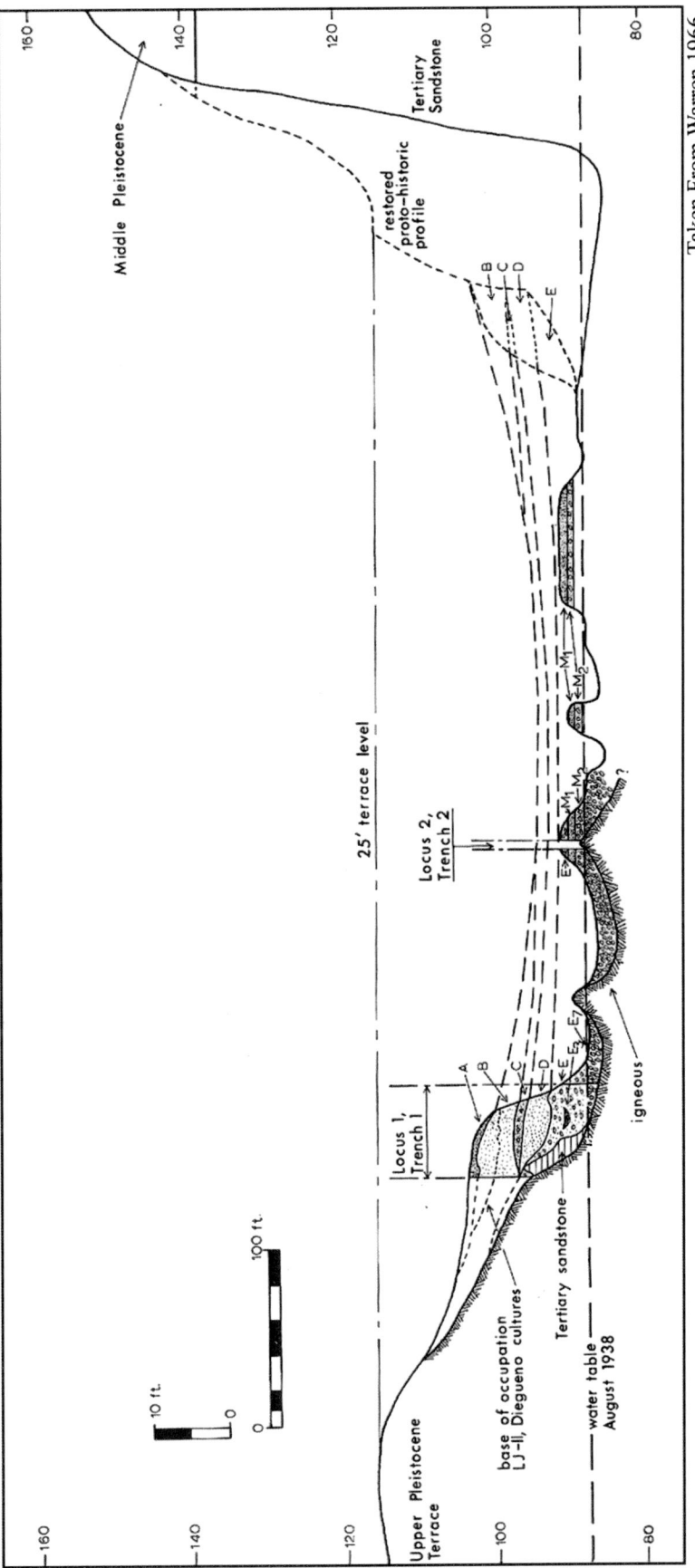

Figure 6. Harris Site Loci I and II Geologic Cross-Section.

that they had not been moved any distance. All flakes from E-Stratum were unpatinated except for a few in the lower third, which displayed some stream wear" (Warren 1966:8).

Site Type: Factory Description

The Harris site is identified as the "type site" for the San Dieguito (Warren 1966). The question asked here is what type of site does the Harris site Locus I E-Stratum represent and how does this site fit into the SDC chronology? Researchers including Rogers, Ezell, Cook, Flenniken, and Knell have identified the Harris site as a factory or workshop, with short-term camping, and Warren and Vaughan identified the Harris site as a habitation site. Ezell, who worked with Rogers at the Harris site, states: "The C.W. Harris Site should not be regarded as a 'Type Site' or as in any way a standard against which any site should be measured; the artifacts from the C.W. Harris Site should not be regarded as a standard against which to measure similar, but not identical, artifacts from other sites; [and] ...The C.W. Harris Site should be seen as a special-purpose site, a factory site primarily devoted to the exploitation of a localized natural resource" (Ezell 1987:18-20).

Rogers

Rogers, describing the San Dieguito component Locus I E-Stratum after the 1938 excavation states: "Stratum E: rests disconformably on Tertiary sandstone [Torrey Formation] ... and older igneous intrusive ... E-Stratum exhibits not only cross-bedding throughout, but also resorted factory material and some factories in situ ... The factories often produce one or more broken blades surrounded by many trimming flakes, all located around a large boulder, as if the individual making the artifacts used a boulder for a seat or an anvil" (Warren 1966:8).

Vaughan

Vaughan, with Warren as her committee chairman, completed her master's thesis using a sample of Harris site artifacts from Warren's 1965 and 1967 excavations (Vaughan 1982). Vaughan, in addressing Rogers' use of the term "factory" to describe activities conducted at the Harris site, determined that the term factory "can be equated with the activity of quarrying lithic material for the manufacture of stone tools" (Vaughan 1982:13). Vaughan cited Bucy (1971:92), who stated: "A quarry site represents an area where high quality material was sought and reduced to transportable form, the greatest percentage of waste being left at the source." Vaughan determined that the Harris site was not a quarry or initial workshop and that "primary debitage was not found in the detritus collections from the C.W. Harris Site, indicating that all tool blanks were produced at another locale and subsequently brought to the site." Vaughan used the definition of quarry to identify the Harris site as not being a factory/workshop.

Cook

Rancho Cielo is the most likely quarry for the Harris site, located just north of Del Dios Highway across the road from the Harris site. Cook states: "It is apparent that almost all of the major tool types known to the San Dieguito were being produced in some form ... All of the predominant uniface and biface forms could conceivably have been produced at Rancho Cielo, at least in their early and intermediate stages of reduction (Cook 1985:228). Examination of the tool blank and preform morphologies allows us to strongly infer that the deposits are San Dieguito in origin ... This combined site type designation [quarry-workshop for Rancho Cielo] is appropriate because the stone was quarried and then subjected to some form of reduction at the same locale ... what we have found is that the stone was worked to an intermediate stage of reduction [Flenniken's Stages 1 and 2] where the flintknapper could be assured the piece was amenable and acceptable for further refinement, and then transported off-site. What results [at the Rancho Cielo Quarry] is large quantities of lithic debitage ranging from decortication flakes and shatter, to abandoned near completed blanks and preforms aborted for some material or workmanship flaw" (Cook 1985:219).

Cook (1985:67) states: "The definition of the San Dieguito tool complex can ... be better defined as a chain of mechanical processes that begin with procurement of lithic resources and end with final implements ... Sufficient data now exists to define ... the processes of lithic procurement, reduction, modification, use and discard ... At present three site types can be defined at which portions of the lithic ... behavior took place: the quarry, the workshop, and the habitation site."

Cook (1985:75) states: "Vaughan [1982:134] comes to a very significant conclusion for establishing relationships between habitation sites, workshops, and quarries: that blank procurement or quarry operations and initial primary flaking are not activities enacted by the San Dieguito inhabitants at the C.W. Harris site. Rather, these early stages of manufacturing are performed elsewhere and trimmed blanks are then brought to the Harris site where they undergo subsequent reduction operations ... The apparent spatial separation of activity sets representing different stages of the lithic behavioral model requires some explanation ... The least effort principle would encourage the stone knapper to produce blanks at the quarry to reduce the weight they had to carry away. The principle of choice may also apply: if the material at Rancho Cielo was of a better quality than surrounding geological sources for stone tool production, then special trips to this hilltop location were purposefully planned. Because the quarries in this case occur in inhospitable locations [on unshaded mountain slopes], they would also want to limit the time at the quarry, so tool finishing would take place in the more welcome surroundings of the [adjacent San Dieguito] river valley."

Flenniken

Flenniken et al. (1998:IV–21) provides the following analysis and description of Rogers' 1938 artifacts from the San Dieguito component (Locus I E-Stratum): "Stratum E was described as a San Dieguito factory level ... all the artifacts from this unit were from Stratum E, and as such, represent the San Dieguito factory materials described by Rogers ... lithic technology represented by the sample (n = 920) ... is considerably different than other inland site lithic assemblages. While cobble core reduction is present in the assemblage, the major focus of knapping activities that occurred prehistorically at the site was oriented toward biface production, most likely for transport as biface blanks ... Biface reduction dominated the sample at CA-SDI-149 with 71% ... of the technologically diagnostic debitage sample. The majority of the biface reduction debitage consists of early percussion bifacial thinning flakes ... edge preparation activities are represented by only one bulb removal flake and three edge preparation flakes. Items with detachment scars indicate that bifaces at the Harris Site were produced by direct freehand percussion from flake blanks, presumably manufactured at the nearby Rancho Cielo quarry (Cook 1985), other similar sites in the area, or cobbles found in the vicinity of the Harris site."

Flenniken et al. (1998:II–22) with respect to use-wear states: "It is interesting to note that most of the felsites [fine-grained metavolcanic] bifacial thinning flakes have extremely abraded and rounded platform margins. This damage appears to be the result of edge preparation for flake removal during biface thinning rather than the result of use-wear. The sharp edges of the margins were abraded at an angle perpendicular to the plane of the biface and abrasions on the margin are also perpendicular. We expect that use as a cutting tool, similar to use as a knife, would have produced rounded margins with abrasions parallel to the plane of the biface. Some experimentation verified that this configuration is consistent with platform preparation but does not exclude other types of use-wear. This metavolcanic material is easily eroded by abrasion, even given the durable knapping attribute of the material." Of the analyzed diagnostic debitage 99.6 percent is metavolcanic materials, with 0.4 percent chert or chalcedony.

The use of stages of reduction is a mental construct used to break a continuum into coherent analysis subsets. Flenniken's stages for biface reduction include: Stage 1) acquisition of raw material and initial reduction debitage; Stage 2) biface with cortex removed and bifacial percussion reduction debitage; Stage 3) biface blank completely thinned producing percussion bifacial thinning debitage; Stage 4) outline of perform has been determined with some pressure bifacial reduction debitage; and Stage 5) finished biface, knife, point with hafting element, or discard (Flenniken et al. 1998:IV–11; Schroth 1998). Flenniken identifies the majority of biface reduction debitage at the Harris site as Stage 3, percussion bifacial thinning debitage. "In summary, based on the analyzed sample and a critical technological appraisal of the remainder of Malcolm Rogers' recovered lithic assemblage from CA-SDI-149, the Harris site appears to be a biface production workshop whose inhabitants produced large bifaces for transport" (Flenniken et al. 1998:IV–23).

Knell

Knell (2010:1–5) completed an analysis of Warren and True's (1961) Harris site work and identifies his work as "an assemblage-level analysis of Claude Warren's 1958 and 1959 excavations at the Harris site to assess how the site occupants—specifically the San Dieguito complex occupants—organized their chipped stone technology." The collection included 391 chipped stone artifacts: 119 tools, four cores, and 268 debitage. Materials selected were local: 98 percent Santiago Peak Volcanics (also referred to as fine-grained metavolcanic or felsite), with three chert, one quartz crystal, and one quartz debitage. Knell (2010:3-5) stated: "The 328 tool manufacture-related artifacts comprise 83.9% of the assemblage, clear evidence that tool production was a major on-site trajectory at the Harris site . . . The 49 bifacial tool[s] . . . support the manufacture trajectory . . . [and] indicates that all but two of the bifaces from the Harris site are unfinished . . . Given that most [47 of 49] of the bifaces broke or were discarded during manufacture [18 perverse fractures, 16 breakage along flaw in stone, 7 bend brakes/end shock, 6 step and hinge fractures], they cannot be labeled as "knives" which form a distinct functional tool class. The bifaces may have been intended as knives, but as manufacture rejects this function cannot be supported."

Harris Site Discussion

Flenniken et al. (1998), Knell (2010), and Vaughan (1982) all identified the absence of both Stage 1 (obtaining the blank) and Stage 2 (primary flaking) as evidence of a distant quarry operation for the purpose of obtaining flake blanks. Vaughan used this evidence to state that the Harris site was not a factory, however, she equated the term factory with quarry. Quarry is where raw material was acquired and initially worked, and, factory/workshop is an acceptable term for processing the flake blank/preform to a more finished tool. Rogers was correct to use the term factory since the Harris site is not a quarry, but a factory or workshop where tools were manufactured, and to a limited extent used for short-term camping.

As a result of the Harris site and Rancho Cielo Quarry, lithic studies by Vaughan, Knell, Cook, and Flenniken, a more complete picture of Early Holocene lithic reduction and tool production activities with specific reference to the Harris site can be reconstructed. First, materials were quarried and initially processed (Stages 1 and 2) at the Rancho Cielo Quarry or a site similar to Rancho Cielo. Then flake blanks were brought back to a river valley location (e.g., the Harris site), close to water, shade, and food to be further reduced through percussion bifacial thinning (Stage 3). In some cases, probably for short-term camping, the tools (scrapers and knives/points) were finished and used at the Harris Site. In other cases, they were transported to the habitation site to be finished as scrapers or knives/points.

The Harris site is neither a quarry nor habitation site, but should be identified as a factory or workshop with temporary campsites where Stage 3 tool production activities were conducted as part of the production cycle of stone tools from quarry (Rancho Cielo) to workshop (Harris site) to habitation site(s) (e.g., San Dieguito Plateau). Other San Diego County sites, especially those near lagoons to the west such as Windsong Shores SDI-10965, UCLJ-M-15 at Agua Hedionda Lagoon, and sites on the San Dieguito Plateau, such as the Great Western site SDI-4392/W-49, may represent more complete views of Early Holocene occupation exploiting both coastal shellfish and fish, and inland small to large mammals and plant resources using bifaces, scrapers and crescents, along with milling and cobble tools. The Harris site is an important site that may date initially from Early Holocene 8,000 to 10,000 years ago and certainly connects San Diego County to the Great Basin WPLT/WSPT.

Summary

Given the radiocarbon dates ca. 11,000–9000 B.P., there are a number of candidates for First People site locations and these include: Remington Hills SDI-11079, Agua Hedionda UCLJ-M-15, Del Mar Man SDI-10940, Windsong Shores SDI-10965, Spindrift SDI-39, Chancellor's House SDI-4669, and the Harris site SDI-149 (see Figure 3 and Tables 1–3). However, there is no report for the excavation of site UCLJ-M-15 and the Del Mar Man site SDI-10940 lacks an excavation and report to fully characterize this site. Coastal orientation is apparent for all of these Early Holocene sites except for the Harris site. Specialized analyses for the Harris site SDI-149 by Cook, Flenniken, and Knell identified the Harris site Locus I E-Stratum as a workshop with temporary camping where Stage 3 tool production activities were conducted. It should be noted that Harris site tools are primarily bifaces (45 percent) and scrapers (48 percent), with nine hammerstones, three cores, and two crescents, which is in stark contrast to the other Early Holocene sites listed on Table 3.

It should be noted that most SDC sites have some problem with soil mixing and stratigraphy, but all of these Early Holocene sites, except for the Harris site, have some milling tools with Remington Hills (138/38 percent) and the Chancellor's House (75/24 percent) having the highest percentages. The Harris site has the highest number of bifaces (90/45 percent), followed by Windsong Shores (10/7 percent), followed by counts of less than four each for the remaining sites. And all of these Early Holocene sites except for the Harris site have a range of tools suggesting multiple activities and a wide range of resources sought and processed. In contrast, the Harris site SDI-149 Locus I E-Stratum with primarily bifaces and scrapers identifies limited Early Holocene workshop activities.

The Remington Hills site SDI-11079 has four of the earliest SDC radiocarbon dates beginning with 10,625–10,250 cal B.P., and this site has cobble tools, milling tools, bifaces, scrapers, beads, shell, and bone identifying habitation and activities conducted. There is a submarine canyon just east of the Tijuana Lagoon that would have been accessible 10,000 years ago. But by 3,500 years ago, given the rise in sea level and the shallow sea floor, the distance from shoreline to the submarine canyon increased eight km (five miles). However, with the rise in sea level, the Tijuana Lagoon was formed, providing lagoon shell and fish resources throughout the Holocene. Also, the continuous radiocarbon dates for sites within the Otay Management Plan Area (OMPA) (Figure 7) documents continuous occupation of this portion of SDC (Gallegos 1998). Early and Middle Holocene OMPA sites are found around the lagoon, river valley, on the mesa, and at the foothills of the San Ysidro Mountains (see Figure 7). High quality, fine-grained metavolcanic cobbles and boulders are present as float across Otay Mesa and vein quarries are present in the San Ysidro Mountains. These quarries represent both Early to Middle Holocene large biface reduction, as well as Late Holocene arrow point production. The Tijuana Lagoon was open throughout the Holocene producing both shellfish and fish as demonstrated by the archaeological sites adjacent to the lagoon dating from over 9000 B.P. to historic contact. However, by the Late Holocene-Late Period, habitation focused at three village locations: La Punta, Otay, and Milejo, all situated adjacent to reliable water sources. Remington

22 *First People: A Revised Chronology for San Diego County*

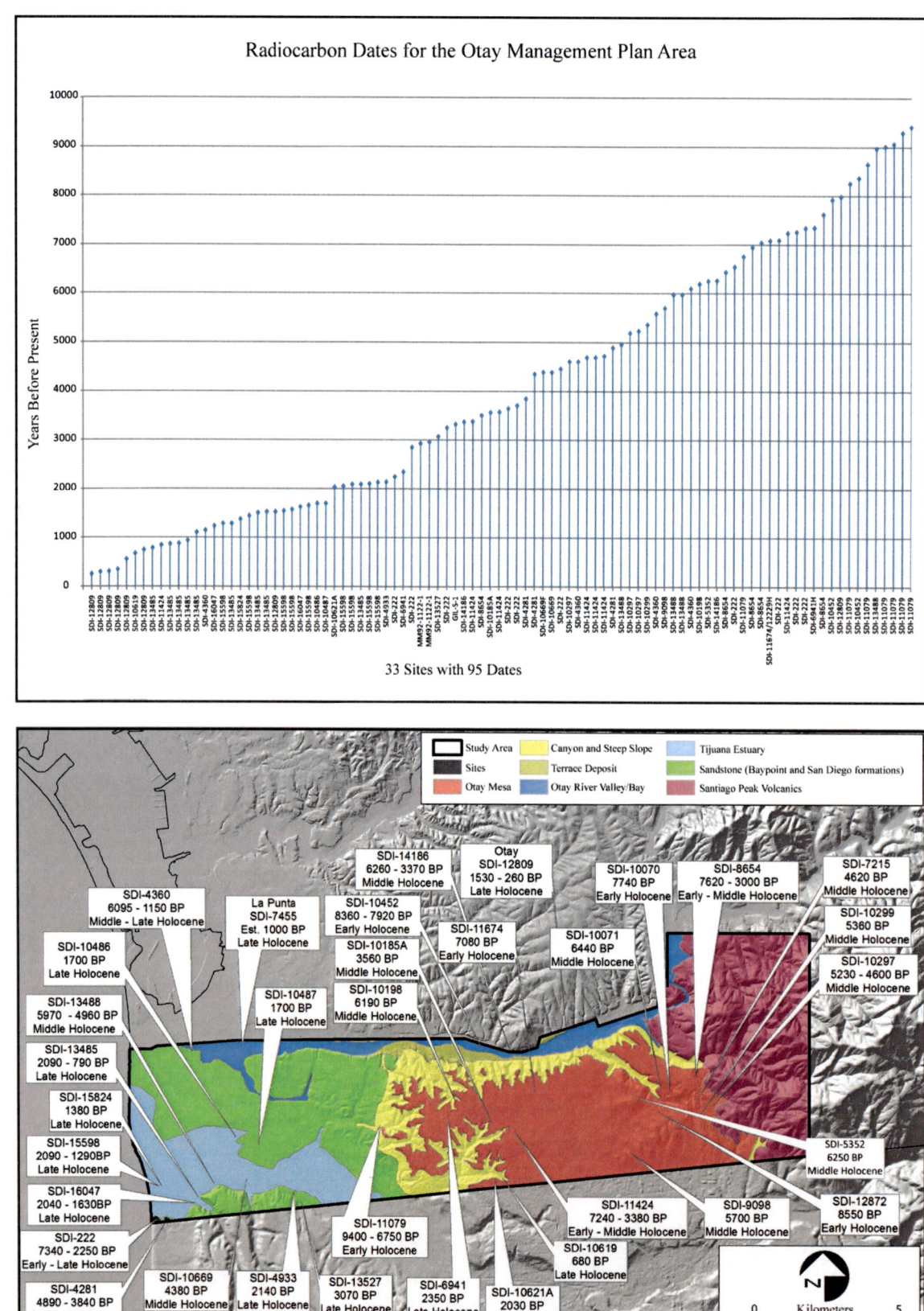

Figure 7. Radiocarbon Dates and Land-use Patterning for the Otay Management Plan Area.

Hills/OMPA is a good candidate for First People occupation, given the early radiocarbon dates and the submarine canyon that would have been accessible ca. 10,000 years B.P. People could have arrived by land or sea, but it is apparent that coastal resources were a major part of the occupants diet and there is no gap in the archaeological dates or major change in the cultural material recovered during the Early to Middle Holocene for the OMPA, suggesting that the early settlers likely stayed in this area throughout the Holocene (see Figure 7).

The Del Mar Man site has very early dates beginning 9740–9295 cal B.P., but lacks a sufficiently large excavation sample to compare this site to other Early Holocene sites. In contrast, the Agua Hedionda site UCLJ-M-15 had a sufficiently large excavation, but no report. The Windsong Shores site SDI-10965 is unique in that it best represents a tool kit (e.g., bifaces, Silver Lake point, and crescents) reflective of a people who left the drying lakes of the Great Basin and settled in north SDC 9930–9580 cal B.P.

However, on the basis of environmental setting (e.g., submarine canyons and lagoons) as well as Early Holocene dates, both Remington Hills SDI-11079/OMPA and the La Jolla Archaeological Area (LJAA) appear to be the best candidates for First People. The LJAA includes the Spindrift site SDI-39, Chancellor's House SDI-4669, and over two miles of nearly continuous coastal occupation, dating from over 10,000 years ago to historic contact. Between Remington Hills and LJAA, the LJAA may well be the best candidate for First People given the setting (e.g., protected on the east by hills; and situated adjacent to submarine canyons, La Jolla Bay, and ocean and lagoon resources of shellfish and fish). The LJAA's density of sites and continuous occupation for over two miles long, situated directly on the coast, demonstrates the pull of the ocean/coastal resources and thereby may point to the occupants' origin. The dense occupation in the La Jolla region especially from Spindrift, Scripps Estates, and the Chancellor's House is also demonstrated by the estimated 100–200 burials reported by Rogers (1920s), Moriarty (Hanna 1980) and Shumway et al. (1961). La Jolla sites within the LJAA including Spindrift, Scripps Estates, and the Chancellor's House are discussed in Chapter 2.

CHAPTER 2
Pleistocene–Holocene La Jolla Occupation

La Jolla Environmental Setting and Archaeological Sites

World climatic events at the end of the Pleistocene and throughout the Holocene affected ocean temperature and currents, sea level rise, change in rocky coast to sandy beaches, flooding of coastal valleys and creation of lagoons, loss of coastal lowlands, and shrinking and reforming of islands. Climate change included cool-wet or warm-dry periods that affected Pleistocene-Holocene plants' and animals' survival or extinction and also affected humans with adaptation and change throughout the Holocene.

Beginning at the LGM (20,000 B.P.), sea level along the Southern California coast was 120 meters lower than present and the rise in sea level during the Early Holocene (ca. 12,000 to 10,000 years ago) would have filled both La Jolla and Scripps submarine canyons, providing a coastal avenue into La Jolla Beach-Spindrift (W-1), La Jolla Shores (W-2), and the adjacent coastal sandstone caves and terraces (see Figure 3). During the Early Holocene, the climate would have been cooler and wetter with Torrey pines and other Late Pleistocene-Early Holocene vegetation along the SDC coastline, and rainfall may have been close to 50 cm (20 inches) per year. By 12,000 years ago during the Younger Dryas (12,800–11,400 years ago), sea level had risen to the -55 m level (see Figure 2) and had created a wave-cut platform during the stillstand, where kelp beds later flourished (Masters and Aiello 2007). "The rocky kelp-forest . . . would have provided a resource-rich environment that may have outranked terrestrial resources for early people" (Masters and Aiello 2007:40). By 10,000 years ago, sea level had risen to the -35 m level (see Figure 2). As the La Jolla and Scripps canyons filled during sea level rise ca. 20,000–8,000 years ago, the adjacent canyon rim shoreline would have been somewhat stable, given the canyon depth and steep slope. Circa 6,000 years ago sea level was -5 m and the stillstand at this time cut another platform on which sand would deposit. By 5,000 years ago, sandy beaches were noticeable; and by ca. 4,000 years ago the shoreline had moved a considerable distance from both La Jolla and Scripps submarine canyons, to roughly our present-day shoreline (Masters and Aiello 2007; Inman 1983).

The La Jolla and Scripps submarine canyons are the result of Pleistocene river cutting and the Rose Canyon and Mount Soledad faults. And, these faults may explain the presence of fresh water springs reported for this area. The resource-rich La Jolla and Scripps submarine canyons allowed deepwater fish to move closer to the shoreline, thereby enriching and enhancing coastal resources of fish from deep water, rocky kelp beds, and sandy bottom habitats during the Holocene. The deep submarine canyons attracted a wide range of fish and provided an excellent habitat for squid runs and anchovy swarms. Hastings et al. (2014:227) reports: "The heads of these canyons come within a few hundred meters of the shore, and the canyons descend to depths of over 500 meters within 7 km of the coastline. These canyons include steep rock walls, as well as sand and mud substrates that support a variety of fishes. Species recorded there number 123, with 68 common, 40 uncommon and 15 rare species . . . Notable among the canyon species are a surprisingly large number of rockfishes . . . The present study compiles records of 265 species collected within the immediate vicinity of the marine protected areas [MPA] of La Jolla. Thus, these MPAs have the potential to provide some measure of protection for half of the 519 marine fish species recorded from state waters."

Shellfish were also plentiful as demonstrated by the spindrift shell midden containing rocky, sandy bottom and lagoon species reflecting multiple habitats and habitat change through time. Carter (1980:145–146) stated:

"At La Jolla there are added attractions. When the sea level was lower, the heads of the great submarine canyons were exposed . . . and their rocky walls increased the amount of shore suitable for abalones and mussels. Furthermore, this lowering [lower sea level] exposed springs that are known to be present at shallow depths off the beach at La Jolla."

Limitations to a more complete understanding of early occupation for the La Jolla area include: (a) the loss of archaeological sites due to sea level rise; (b) coastal cliff erosion; (c) historical development; (d) excavations with no reports; and (e) few archaeological reports with controlled unit excavation with associated radiocarbon dates. It should be noted that archaeological work on private, City or State lands in the early 1900s was not required by law and only through the good graces of the land owner, developer, and heavy equipment operators working with the San Diego Museum of Man (e.g., Malcolm Rogers) staff and/or UCSD personnel (e.g., Moriarty III) were allowed to record what was being steam shoveled and/or bulldozed from the 1920s to the 1970s. Rogers did extensive work during this time and kept site notes and letter reports, but few if any technical reports came out of these early La Jolla site visits. Rogers would conduct surveys, especially along cliff bluffs and excavate small trenches, usually near the cliff edge; and Moriarty would conduct excavations or follow the bulldozers when he found out about construction activity. In addition to the loss of archaeological sites due to early development, there were also excavations with no reports, such as those directed by Jason Smith and students from California State University Northridge (CSUN) in 1976, involving 100 excavation units at SDI-4670/W-5 and 48 units at SDI-4669/W-12. The first reports of any substance documenting the archaeological work at Scripps Estates SDI-525/W-9 was by a number of UCSD professors, who had bought house lots within a large Early to Middle Holocene archaeological site (SDI-525/W-9) containing burials (Moriarty et al. 1959; Shumway et al. 1961).

Improvements in archaeological studies over the past 40 years are the result of City, County and State requirements for surveys, excavation, analysis, and reporting. Professional publications on coastal environmental setting and change throughout the Holocene; and sea level and sand transport studies by Inman and Masters for SDC have greatly helped to fill in the environmental record on this important archaeological area.

Since the 1950s, radiocarbon dates for environmental and archaeological purposes worldwide including the La Jolla and UCSD area were completed by the La Jolla Radiocarbon Laboratory and published in La Jolla Natural Radiocarbon Measurements by local researchers. However, these early dates simply provide the uncorrected measured date with a plus/minus variable. Dating problems since the 1950s include the use of multiple shells (bulk samples) for a radiocarbon date vs. AMS single-shell dating. Even with AMS availability, bulk shell samples were and still are a common practice due to cost. AMS provides a more precise date for the single item submitted, and bulk sampling provides the researcher with an average date for the number of items processed (usually 30 g from multiple shells). Radiocarbon dating improvements include better dating equipment that allows for the use of smaller single item samples (AMS) for more precise dating, and calibration correction methods. For this manuscript, uncalibrated dates are provided as uncorrected B.P. (measured age range) unless otherwise stated. Calibrated dates are provided as cal B.P.

La Jolla Bay to UCSD Cultural Resources (La Jolla Archaeological Area)

Erlandson used the term "sweet spot" to identify locations of rich coastal resources such as underwater canyons adjacent to land and estuaries/lagoons as possible landings for the earliest explorers (Erlandson 2013). One such sweet spot is La Jolla Bay with La Jolla Submarine Canyon, Scripps Submarine Canyon, La Jolla Caves, La Jolla Beach, La Jolla Shores, and the adjacent Pleistocene marine sandstone terraces north to UCSD (Figure 8). Within this area, Early to Middle Holocene occupation is demonstrated by shell middens with burials.

Sites situated near La Jolla Bay and submarine canyons, identified here as the La Jolla Archaeological Area (LJAA), include: Spindrift SDI-39/W-1; La Jolla Shores W-2; Middle Midden SDI-4670/W-5; SIO Upper Cliff site SDI-11075/W-3683/UCLJ-M-7; Scripps Estates SDI-525/W-9; and Chancellor's House SDI-4669/W-12 (see Figure 8). These sites are discussed below by site number with cultural material shown on Table 4.

Spindrift SDI-39/W-1

Rogers reported the entire embayment stretching from the cliffs at La Jolla Caves to the Scripps Institution of Oceanography (SIO) as an archaeological site with two places (W-1 and W-2) of intense occupation (Rogers 1926). Rogers described the Spindrift site as: "The greatest Lit. I [La Jolla] ... concentration on the entire coast exists here ... Much of its former extent has been destroyed by a change of sea-level (at least half). As this cultural phase is confined to the immediate present coast line and all other sites have suffered through recession of the coast line, it is quite probable that many of their middens have been destroyed, perhaps even larger ones" (Rogers 1926a).

Sea level rise at this unique location is shown on Figure 2 and discussed below. La Jolla Bay, from ca. 13,000 to 8,000 years ago, is described as having a cobble beach bar between La Jolla Submarine Canyon and a large estuary adjacent to the Spindrift site (Pigniolo and Brodie 2009). From 8,000 years ago to historic times, with the continued rise in sea level, the estuary was reduced in size and depth, and the distance from the shoreline to the submarine canyon increased (Inman 1983; Pigniolo and Brodie 2009).

The lagoon (since destroyed by sea level rise and modern development) was described in Shumway et al. (1961:50) as: "La Jolla Shores ... At the southern end of this lowland area there existed, until a few decades ago, a salt-water lagoon ... Near the former entrance, the intertidal beach is underlain with peat, indicative of an older lagoon that existed ... borings in the beach ... indicate a buried lagoon salt-flat deposit at a depth of about 8 m below the present surface." The location and depth of the peat sample dated 4230 +/-200 (LJ-208) is identified as "off center of La Jolla Beach and Tennis Club ... ca. 137 m seaward from Club ... 2.0 m below mean sea level" (Hubbs et al. 1962:212). The Spindrift site SDI-39/W-1 with present-day development is shown on Figures 9a,b.

Spindrift Habitat and Shellfish

The submarine canyon provided the rocky habitat for Mytilus and was accessible to divers (free diving) as sea level rose. The lagoon, which changed as sea level rose, may have been present throughout the Holocene providing lagoon shellfish species; and, by 5430 B.P., a sandy beach provided the habitat for Pismo clams (Tivela stultorum). Given the presence of Mytilus dated from ca. 9000–1300 B.P., Tivela stultorum (Pismo) dated from 5200–2300 B.P., Pseudochama dated from ca. 1600–1000 B.P., and *Argopecten* dated ca. 2600 B.P. suggests that these habitats (rocky shore, bay/estuary, and sandy beach) changed through time and may have overlapped in time at Spindrift (Table 5).

Pigniolo and Brodie (2009) report 50 species of shellfish from rocky shore, sandy beach, and bay/estuary habitats, with Unit 3 producing 13,061 g of shellfish predominately taken from a rocky shore habitat. The dominant species were Mytilus 10,138 g; Balanus 466 g; Chiton 432 g; and Haliotis 414 g. Radiocarbon dates taken on Mytilus shell from Unit 3, 60–70 cm and 110 to 120 cm are 6600 B.P. and 8940 B.P., respectively, providing evidence for Early to Middle Holocene occupation focusing on rocky shore shellfish. Using 2-sigma calibration, this 8940 B.P. date is corrected to 9585–9025 cal B.P. (see Table 1). Roth and Berryman (1993), for a portion of the Spindrift site dated ca. 1100–1500 B.P., reported: "[O]ccupants had immediate access to fresh water, marshland, sandy beach, bay, rocky foreshore, tide pool, kelp bed and deep water habitats. Thus, a wide array of marine invertebrate resources

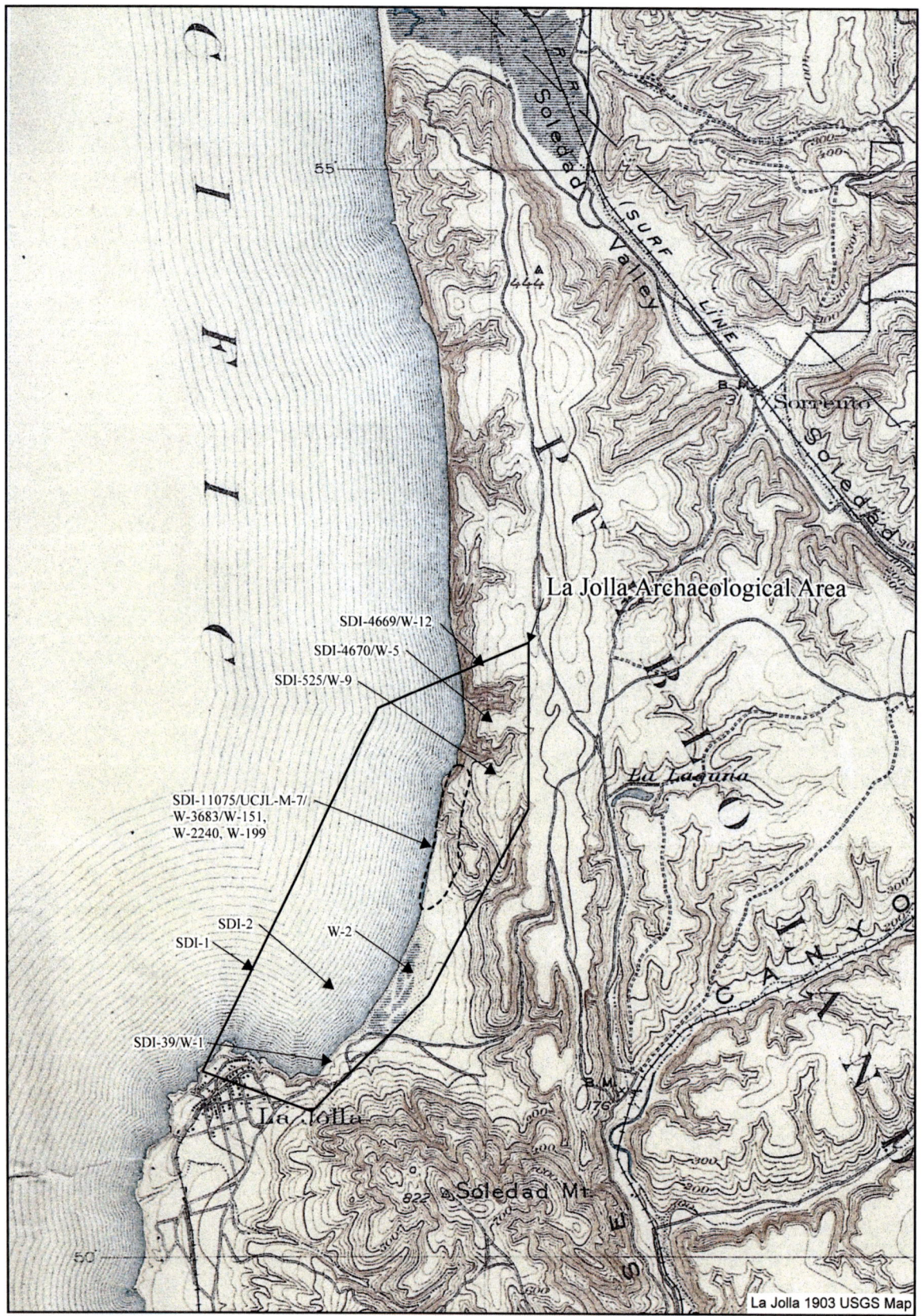

Figure 8. La Jolla Archaeological Area with Sites Adjacent to the Bay and Submarine Canyons.

Table 4. La Jolla Archaeological Area Cultural Site Summaries.

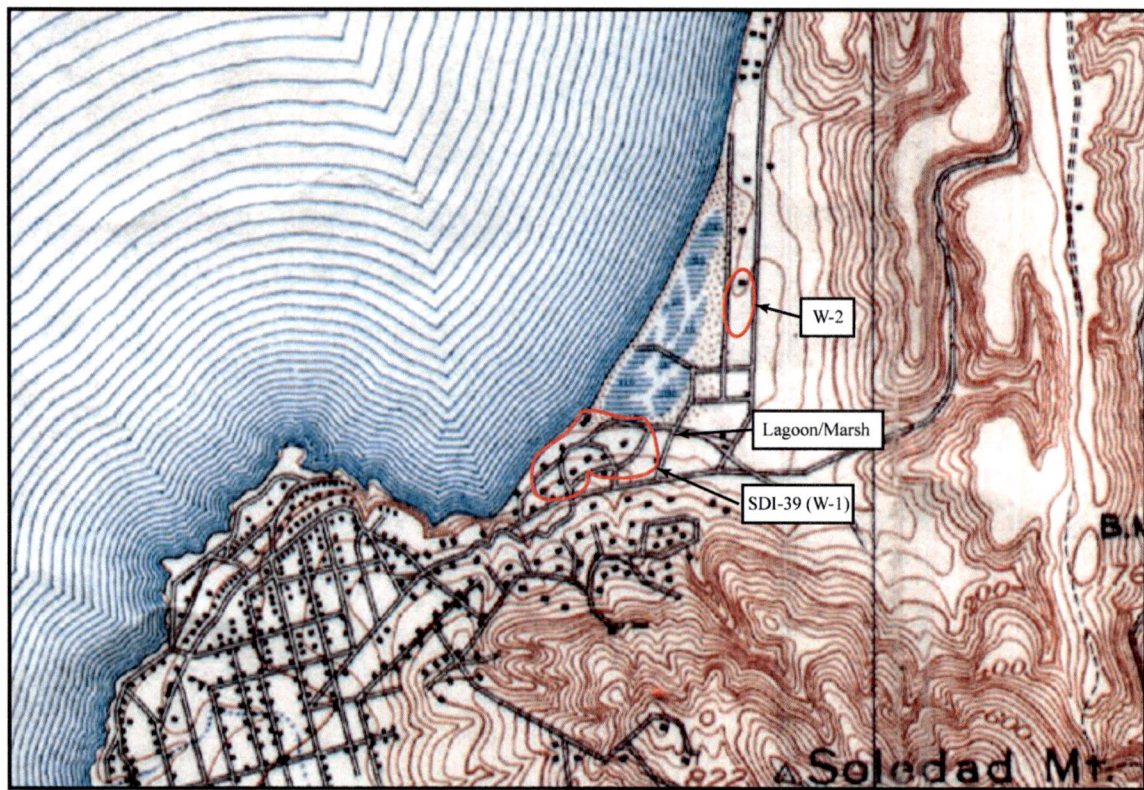

Figure 9a. 1930s USGS Map with Rogers W-1 Spindrift and W-2 La Jolla Shores.

Figure 9b. Present Day La Jolla Shores Developed, Showing Rogers SDI-39/W-1 Spindrift and W-2 La Jolla Shores.

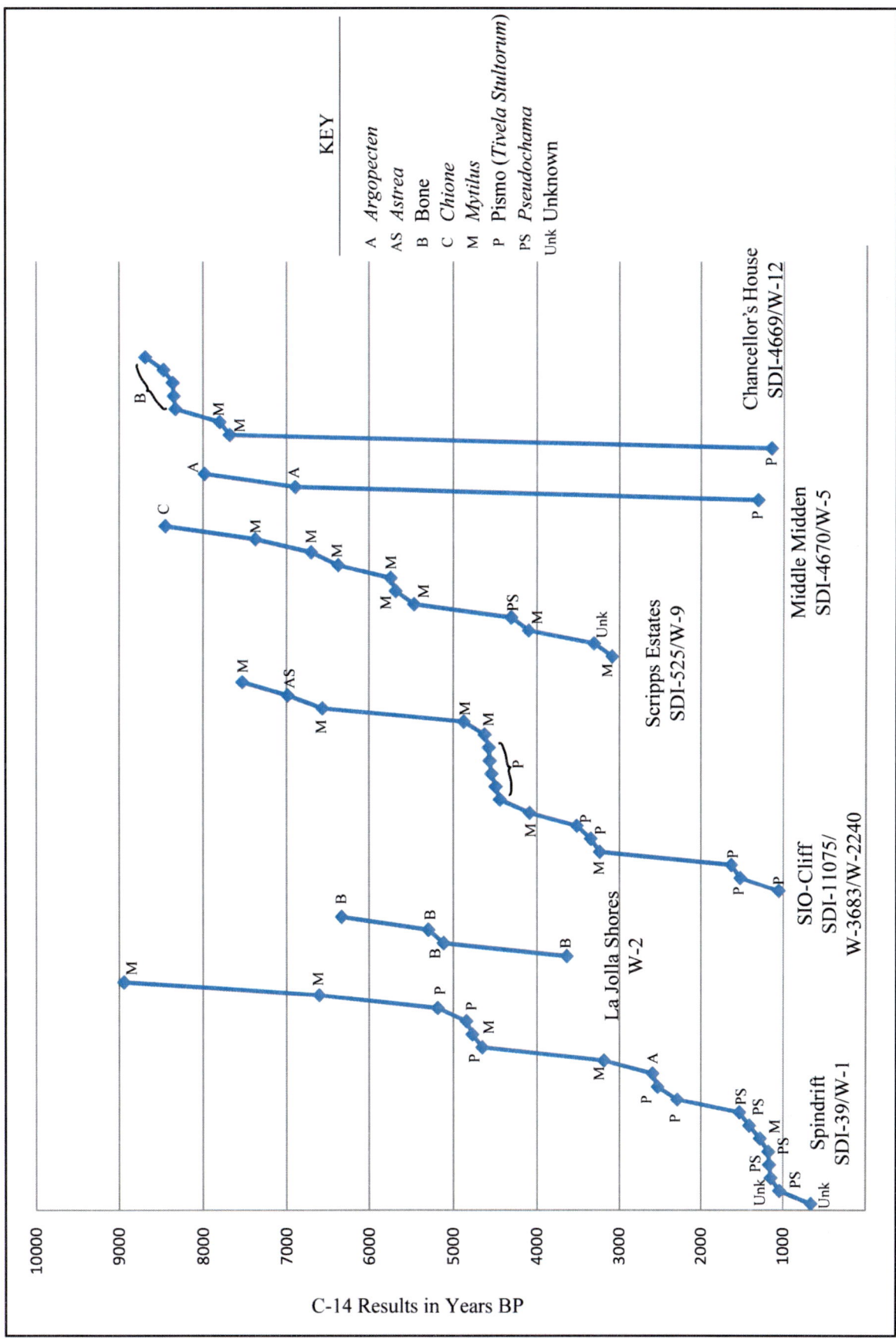

Table 5. La Jolla Sites by Radiocarbon Dates and Shell Species Dated.

would have been readily available…all of these environments were exploited" (Roth and Berryman 1993). Using Rogers' site boundary (est. 300 x 400 m), over 20 archaeological monitoring and excavation reports have been conducted within streets and residential lots of the Spindrift site (Pigniolo and Brodie 2009).

This site could possibly date much older than 9585–9025 cal B.P., as it is situated near the La Jolla Submarine Canyon and an Early Holocene lagoon; and given the rise in sea level of over 35 m during the Holocene's past 10,000 years, a good portion of this site may be underwater. Therefore, the portion of the site on the mainland may only represent less than 50 percent (as suggested by Rogers), and much of the remaining mainland site has been disturbed and/or destroyed by development (see Figure 9).

Offshore Findings

Underwater sites SDI-1, SDI-2, and W-556 are located between the head of La Jolla Submarine Canyon and La Jolla Beach and Tennis Club. SDI-1 and SDI-2, recorded by Baumhoff (1955) from a publication titled Ocean-Bottom Artifacts (Tuthill and Allanson 1954), wherein SDI-1 was reported: "On the edge of La Jolla Canyon in water about 100 feet deep [30.5 m], and nearly a half mile from shore…Area of artifacts on ocean bottom." The second site (SDI-2) is reported: "…800' [246 m] off the La Jolla Beach and Tennis Club in 20' [6.15 m] of water …Area of artifacts on ocean bottom." Morin (1974) reported a third underwater site (W-556) as under 6 ft (1.8 m) of water, and reported a collection of 11 small mortars and 12 grooved stones.

In discussing the history of SIO (1976:134) it was stated that in the early 1950s divers found hundreds of small mortars underwater south of Scripps and stated that "there must have been a grinding complex almost amounting to a compulsion…" For the most part, only one to three artifacts were recovered from these localities and these were primarily small portable sandstone mortars or bowls approximately 20 cm in diameter and 7.5 cm thick (Laylander 2012). Other artifacts reported include manos, metates, pestles, net weights, scrapers and projectile points. This diverse artifact set could be the result of cliff failure or sea level rise (Laylander 2012, Masters and Gallegos 1997).

A study by Masters and Schneider (2000:574–577) reports: "…200 mortars were retrieved from exposed cobble patches off CA-SDI-39 at depths of one to six meters…These mortar/bowls are remarkably uniform in size, ranging between 13 and 22 cm maximum diameter…[The first] clustering of finds [is] in the intertidal zone and near shore rocky reefs to a depth of 5 m…The second cluster of sites…occurs between depths of 10–20 m. These localities are predominantly kelp beds with a rocky, exposed substrate and a few occur at the heads of the submarine canyons at La Jolla. The sites recorded at 25 m depth and greater are all on ledges within the submarine canyons." The coastal orientation of small stone mortars may have extended up to 1.6 km (one mile) and to a depth of 30.5 m (100 ft.), given the finding of 42 underwater prehistoric sites, 36 with small mortars (Masters and Schneider 2000:577). Sites with small mortars have been reported from the Channel Islands, and from Santa Barbara to San Diego. For the small mortars, Masters and Schneider (2000:573) propose " … were part of prehistoric fishing strategies…in conjunction with the use of watercraft."

Spindrift: Moriarty's Work

Moriarty's work at the Spindrift site is notable for an anomalous burial, the La Jolla-Diegueño amalgamation hypothesis, and his dating of the introduction of pottery. Moriarty reports an anomalous burial dated to 3190 B.P. as placed in supine, lying on back extended position (Moriarty and Moriarty 1982). The burial was surrounded by Astraea undosa covered by metates, which is associated with food offerings; a small cache of quartz crystals; and a steatite charmstone. The individual was a male between 50–55 years old and given biting scars on long bones and missing skeletal material may have been killed by a large mammal, such as a bear (Moriarty and

Moriarty 1982). With respect to the La Jolla and Diegueño amalgamation, Moriarty stated: "There is a layer of Diegueño [Late Period/Yuman/Kumeyaay] material overlying the La Jolla [material] . . . there is no stratigraphic break between the La Jolla and the Diegueño . . . when excavated, demonstrated in its vertical profile the entire sequence from La Jolla II, at the base, through Diegueño 1 . . . It appears that the process of amalgamation between the two cultures covered a relatively long period, beginning about 3000 B.P. and extending to about 2000 B.P. . . . The amalgamation is marked by an increase in the diversification of pressure-flaked artifacts. The variations and importation of mineral types expands with quartzites, obsidian, felsites, and crypto-crystalline materials now beginning to appear in quantity (Moriarty 1966:23). The mixing of the two cultures brought about changes distinguishable in the artifact assemblage, and possibly resulted in the modification of burial practices" (Moriarty 1966:23-24). The stratigraphic level with pottery was dated to 1270 B.P. (Moriarty 1966:27).

Spindrift: Village of Mut La Joy

Rogers (1920s, W-2) reports that W-1 was a great Y-III (Yuman/Late Period) center, and that "Diegueño continued to come down from the interior to fish and gather shellfish seasonally until 1890" (Rogers 1920s, W-1). The Late Period village of Mut La Joy (Shipek 1976) was also referred to as "Mut lah hoy ya" (Leftwich 1984) or "Mat kwlahuy" or "Mat kulaahuuy," and identified as place of caves (Couro and Langdon 1975:135). This village may also be the setting for the book titled Salt Water Boy (Lee 1949). Yuman/Kumeyaay/Late Period cultural materials reported from the Spindrift site includes: arrow points; arrow shaft straighteners; manos, metates, pestles, scrapers, cores, debitage with obsidian from Obsidian Butte, Imperial Valley; ceramics (Colorado Buff, Salton Brown, and Tizon Brown Ware); ceramic pipe fragments; shell beads (*Olivella* biplicata and *Olivella* dama), bone, and stone beads; Spanish glass trade beads; and cremations (Pigniolo and Brodie 2009). Junipero Serra reported, "The natives . . . live well on various seeds and on fish which they catch from rafts made of tules and formed like canoes, with which they venture far out on the sea" (Engelhardt 1920:21).

Spindrift demonstrates continuous occupation from over 9,000 years ago to historic contact. Historic development since the late 1800s includes houses, roads, utility lines, parking lots, and parks. However, since the 1970s, with the passage of CEQA and City of San Diego guidelines requiring archaeological work to be conducted for any subsurface disturbance in sensitive archaeological areas, the Spindrift site is being rediscovered and redefined on a street-by-street and lot-by-lot basis. A summation of both burials and cremations, including Rogers' early work, Moriarty's work, and over 20 CRM studies identified 27 burials and 15 cremations (Pigniolo and Brodie 2009). Given the loss of site due to sea level rise and historical disturbance, the reported burials and cremations may simply represent a less than 10 percent sample of this large and important site.

La Jolla Shores W-2

W-2, situated just north of W-1 on the north side of the relic pond/lagoon and adjacent to La Jolla Shores and La Jolla Submarine Canyon, was identified by Rogers (1920s, W-2) as a large seven-acre "shell midden capping an estuary sand with human remains scattered through it." In 1926, Rogers reported the destruction of this site by the development of the La Jolla Shores subdivision project and stated: "[T]he steam shovel . . . unearthed an unknown number of burials . . . The bottom stratum which produced . . . human remains, did indirectly produce one whole *Olivella* shell bead which was cemented to a rib of one of the mineralized burials. Metates were both deep oval basined and trough type . . . Ball manos present . . . La Jolla collectors have removed hundreds of manos and at least 100 metates from this site . . . It is impossible to say how many skeletons and fragments were encountered in the excavations . . . During the ensuing three months, the site was completely demolished, and with it probably the most important prehistoric station in southern California" (Rogers 1926a). A minimum of nine burials were reported by Rogers (1920s, 1926a, W-2), and radiocarbon dating of four bone samples from the white dune sand (also referred to as yellow) stratum, 2 m below ground level, produced dates from 6330–3640 B.P. (Stafford et al. 1987). The site was described by Rogers (1920s, W-2) as a sand dune, and he reported the upper one-foot of dune consisted of a shell midden with no skeletal material, followed by red sand with human bone in good condition. The basal deposit is a yellow or white sand with burials and mineralized human bone.

Rogers (1920s, W-2) describing the midden at W-2, noted "at least two different horizons . . . My interpretation . . . is that the thin Lit. I stratum [La Jolla I, basal stratum] . . . scattered mineralized human bones were from burials washed out . . . by tidal action during its destruction. This period was followed by a recession of the mean sea-level and alluviation of sandy outwash from . . . back of site . . . After an elapse of time during this aggrading Lit. II [La Jolla II] people moved on to the site and built up an extensive thin bedded midden." The tidal action and wash out of burials could have been caused by unusually high tides, or the result of a tsunami ca. 6330 to 3640 years ago.

Sites on Pleistocene Marine Sandstone Terrace North of Spindrift

The deep Early to Middle Holocene middens, characterized by cobble tools, milling tools, fire-affected rock, burials, and shellfish are nearly continuous from the Spindrift site north to the Chancellor's House. These sites include: Scripps Institution of Oceanography (W-199, SDI-11075, UCLJ-M-7, W-3683, W-151, W-2240), Scripps Estates Subdivision (SDI-525/W-9), Middle Midden (SDI-4670/W-5), and UCSD's Chancellor House site (SDI-4669/SDI-201/W-12). Sites situated on the Pleistocene sandstone terraces north of Spindrift SDI-39/W-1 and W-2 primarily reflect occupation ca. 10,000 to 3000 years ago with a trace of Late Period occupation.

The setting for these coastal sites includes mesas and exposed sea cliffs with conglomerate lenses that provided volcanic and crystalline rock material for flake and cobble tools, as well as slabs of Eocene sandstone, found along the beach and the canyon rim, for metates (Shumway et al. 1961). The midden, as described by Shumway for W-9/SDI-525 (Scripps Estates) is a good general description of upper terrace sites SDI-4670/W-5 and SDI-4669/W-12, wherein he reports: "Horizon A—Soft Dark Soil, caliche cementation increasing downward; followed by Horizons B1, B2 and B3 with caliche cemented and yellow sand; resting on Horizon D— Sandstone, Eocene Rose Canyon Formation" (Shumway et al. 1961:53). Rogers (1920s, W-9) describes W-9 specifically and coastal sites in general as "a slight amount of SD-III [San Dieguito] . . . to indicate that the site was visited . . . After this the Lit. I people [La Jolla I] built a thin bedded midden on the highest part, which rests on marine sandstone . . . It is cemented as usual, and runs to mussels almost exclusively, like most Lit I middens. The Lit II [La Jolla II] and capping midden is deeper and of greater extent, reflecting a longer or more intensive occupation . . . [and] has the usual profusion of mano stones and metates . . . [with] a trace of Y-III [e.g., arrow points or ceramics]." Vegetation for these coastal bluffs includes Torrey pines and shrubs and herbs (Shumway et al. 1961:51). La Jolla/UCSD coastal terrace sites are discussed below.

SIO Upper Cliff Site SDI-11075/UCLJ-M-7/W-3683/W-151 and Lower Cliff Site W-2240

Rogers (1920s, W-151; 1929a) recorded W-151 (SDI-11075/UCLJ-M-7/W-3683/W-151) and reported: "[W]e had missed a large site on the grounds of the Scripps Biological Institute." He reported a site size of one-half acre and midden depth of six feet (1.84 m) on a flat bench overlooking the ocean (Rogers 1920s, W-151; 1929a). For the upper stratum, shellfish (Donax, Mytilus, Tivela, Astraea) from rocky and sandy shellfish habitats were reported; and, for the basal stratum, only mussel shell from a rocky habitat was reported (Rogers 1920s, W-151; 1929a).

In 1962, due to the proposed construction of the Institute of Geophysics and Planetary Physics (IGPP) building, a salvage excavation by San Diego State University (SDSU) Anthropology Club, under the direction of Ezell and Moriarty was conducted (Hanna 1980:58). Cox, a student of Ezell's, documented the 1962 excavation in a student paper (Cox 1963). In all, two trenches and 14 1.52 x 1.52 m (5x5 foot) units were excavated across the site (Cox 1963). The excavation produced scraping tools (scraper plane, domed, side scraper, flake scraper, and concave scraper/spokeshave), chopping tools, hammerstones, and manos (see Table 4). Cobble and flake tools were identified as from local material. Shell was from sandy beach and rocky shore habitats. Cox's report did not identify artifact counts by artifact type, burials, metates, or ceramics. One 1x1 m unit, located at the west edge of the site adjacent to the cliff edge, was used to provide controlled shell samples for radiocarbon dating. Shell from Levels 1 and 4 (Tivela) produced dates of 1620 B.P. and 1510 B.P., respectively; and Mytilus from Levels 8, 12, and 16 produced dates of 4090, 4870, and 7530 B.P., respectively (Hubbs et al. 1963, 1965) (see Table 4). The site apparently truncated at the cliff edge at a depth of 1.83 m, thereby identifying that a good amount of the Early to Middle Holocene portion of the site had fallen into the ocean due to cliff failure. Masters (2006) discusses the "Tivela Proxy" as identifying the change from rocky coast to sandy beach habitats in the La Jolla region stating: "[O]nce sea level had moved inshore of the La Jolla submarine canyon heads ... The transition to sand beaches for the southernmost part of the cell [Torrey Pines subcell] is particularly well documented at SDI-11075 ... Rocky exposed coast mollusks were most abundant in the earliest occupation levels, but after ~5 ka sand beach taxa became the dominant remains in the midden" (Masters 2006:87).

Sussman and Masters (1990) conducted a survey and test for SDI-11075 (W-3683) in 1987. This work included the excavation of 11 (1x1 m) units in the eastern area (20 m east of cliff edge) near the Martin Johnson House (T-29) and two units near the cliff edge (see Table 4). Depth of midden in the eastern area was approximately 20 cm, however an activity floor with a possible hearth dating ca. 4500–3500 B.P., along with stone tools and marine shell (Pismo clam, abalone, rock oyster, and turban) was reported (Sussman and Masters 1990). The eastern area (11 units) produced one groundstone, six tools, 530 debitage, and 1,967 g of shell (Masters 1990; Sussman 1990). In addition to the 11 units, a 1x2 m unit was excavated near the cliff edge to a depth of 220 cm. Artifacts recovered from these two units included three groundstone, 23 tools, and 183 debitage (Sussman 1990). In all, 26,820 g of shellfish were recovered with Mytilus (46 percent) the dominant species (Masters 1990). Radiocarbon dates for this study ranged from 6980–3350 B.P. (see Table 4).

Lower Cliff Site W-2240 is located adjacent and south across a small canyon from SDI-11075, along the edge of the bluff. One unit was excavated under the direction of Jacquelin Miller in 1960 and three shell samples produced radiocarbon dates of 1050, 3240, and 4620 B.P. (see Table 4). Moriarty, in an interview with Hanna stated the finding of "shell and typical La Jolla artifacts, no pottery ... and no human remains" (Hanna 1980:63). The Lower Cliff site is mostly destroyed due to development and cliff failure.

Scripps Estates Site (W-9) SDI-525, SDI-11019

Rogers initially recorded W-9 in 1929 as a six-acre shell midden disturbed by disking, with hearth features found below the plow zone (30-40 cm) (Rogers 1920s). He identified the site as SD-III (San Dieguito), Lit I and II (La Jollan) and a trace of Y-III (Yuman/Late Period), with high shell content, manos, metates, and one mortar. The site (approximately 140,000 sq m) extends from the coastal bluffs on the west and includes the Scripps Estates development, a large protected open space area; Coast Apartments; and SDI-11019 on the east. Portions of this site exist under Scripps Estates houses, yards, streets, Coast Apartments, and within a large vacant lot. In the winter of 1943, Rogers, with the assistance of a U.S. Army Camp Callan work detail and volunteers, reviewed the bulldozer damage to this site and recorded burials. As taken from Rogers' notes: "The burial area is 250' long and 35' wide [however, this area may simply identify the bulldozed area] ... [near] edge of a deep canyon. The site had been completely gone over with a grader to the average depth of two feet [0.61 m] before my arrival and the resultant muck trucked off to Camp Callan for landscaping. The cemetery was almost completely laid bare, metate markers pulled off many of the burials and an unknown number ... of burials smashed and parts trucked off in the dirt loads. Ten [burials] had parts still in situ so that their horizontal position could be marked" (Rogers 1920s, W-9; 1943). Rogers provided mapped locations for 33 burials for Shumway as part of the Scripps Estates project (Shumway et al. 1961). With reference to the number of burials, Moriarty stated that "it was incredibly rich with burial, after burial, after burial ... He [Rogers] always said about 200 burials along the edges there ... I found about 40, and recorded them, and measured them, and left them in place ... he worked on the canyon edge [west and north edges of the site], and I worked in from it" (Hanna 1980:32). Moriarty (Hanna 1980:36) also relayed a story about how the gardener had said: "We want that soil [from SDI-525/W-9], Jim, because it is great, because we're going to need it for the lawns around Revelle Hall."

As a result of SIO staff having purchased lots and constructing houses on archaeological site SDI-525/W-9, a number of SIO staff (e.g., Shumway, Hubbs, Inman, and Isaacs) along with Moriarty were involved in the excavation of the Scripps Estates Subdivision and reported the findings (Moriarty et al. 1959; Shumway et al. 1961). Students from UCLA, under the direction of Clement Meighan and Claude Warren, participated in the excavation. The impetus for initiating the archaeological work was the finding of a burial in Shumway's front yard: "Although shell middens are numerous along the California coasts, middens with burials are not abundant. Scripps Estates Site, described in this report, is of special significance because of its antiquity and because of the concentration of burials ... It is estimated that the site originally held more than 100 burials; some of these have been destroyed in the hurried advance of civilization and, undoubtedly, many others remain to be found" (Shumway et al. 1961:41).

The Scripps Estates Subdivision excavation area was primarily house lots 16 and 17, owned by Shumway and Isaacs. The results from the excavation of three trenches are reported in Moriarty et al. (1959), with additional work and an overview and discussion in Shumway et al. (1961) (see Table 4). The midden is described as: Stratum A1-Dark Midden; Stratum B2-Lime Pan. It was suggested that the lime pan developed after burials were placed, and that A1 and B2 may not represent different strata, but represent the formation of lime from the upper shells breaking down (Shumway et al. 1961). In 1953, Moriarty reported two burials discovered as a result of grading for Ellentown Road for the Scripps Estates Subdivision (Shumway et al. 1961:56). And, 17 burials were encountered and reported as part of the Scripps Estates project (Shumway et al. 1961:60). "Most of the burials are devoid of ornaments or offerings. Burial 7 was an exception ... with a ... necklace" (Shumway et al. 1961:64). As the burial was not removed, the necklace was estimated to be around 90 *Olivella* sp. spire-removed beads and a central pendant of Tivela stultorum (Pismo clam) about three cm in diameter and one cm thick (Shumway et al. 1961:90–91). Mytilus associated with Burial 7 was dated to 6700 B.P. (Shumway et al. 1961:212); and, additional radiocarbon dates for the site, also taken on Mytilus, ranged from 5460–7370 B.P. (Hubbs et al. 1960, 1962, 1965; Shumway et al. 1961) (see Table 5). Shumway et al. (1961:97) states: "Because shell and artifacts of rather consistent type occur throughout the soil horizons ... and because the dates were obtained from composite shell samples presumably not representing the extreme times of the establishment and abandonment of the site, we may assume that the site was occupied continuously or nearly so for a period of more than 2 millenia, from roughly 7500 to about 5000 years ago."

Artifacts included scrapers (e.g., scraper planes, small domed, rectangular side, and thumbnail), chopper, a possible crescent, hammerstones, cores (multiface and platform), manos (unifacial and bifacial, and some with pounding on end), metates (unshaped and shaped, thin flat to deep basins), pitted stones, flake tools, obsidian and chert flakes, debitage, pestle, stone balls, *Olivella* spire-removed beads, mortar, donut stones, bone tools (bone gorge), one arrow point, shell (56 species but mostly rocky shore) with some fish bone, crab, and bird bone (Moriarty et al. 1959; Shumway et al. 1961) (see Table 4). "An outstanding feature of the large artifact assemblage from the Scripps Estates Site is the abundance of utilitarian objects and the extreme paucity of specimens interpretable as of ceremonial or recreational significance" (Shumway et al. 1961:69). No San Dieguito artifacts were reported (Shumway et al. 1961:58–59). With respect to Rogers' two development phases for the La Jolla (Lit 1 and Lit 2), Shumway et al. (1961:126) states: "The artifactual complex does not conform with the tantalizingly brief and indefinite distinction between 'La Jolla I' and 'La Jolla II' and lends no support to such a division." And Warren states: "[T]hese phases may represent seasonal economic differences or differences in artifact sample rather than differences in time" (Moriarty et al. 1959:212).

Burial 3 is on the right side, body oriented to the north with head to west (Shumway et al. 1961:63): "All skeletons ... were in flexed position ... In most cases ... a line from the pelvis to the skull points toward the ... north ... the La Jolla people were of moderate stature and apparently were reasonably free of vitamin deficiency or food-deficiency diseases. There is little, if any, sign of poor nutrition ... apparently the abundance of seafood, supplemented by land vegetation, insured relatively straight and sturdy bones" (Shumway et al. 1961:61–67).

Shumway et al. (1961:102) reports: "Among the molluscs [e.g., Mytilus, Pseudochama, Haliotis, and Astraea], those from the rocky foreshore constituted about eight tenths [80%] of the total shell ... the California mussel vastly predominated at all levels." The remaining shellfish was around 16 percent bay/estuary (e.g., *Argopecten*, *Chione*, and Ostrea) with around 4 percent from the sandy beach habitat (e.g., Tivela, Donax, and *Olivella*). With respect to diet, Shumway et al. (1961:98) states: "The type of molluscs eaten, the abundance of tools for grinding plant food, and the great scarcity of vertebrate remains all indicate a simple food-gathering culture, with little or no hunting for larger animals, either on land or on the high sea."

Shumway et al. (1961:104) further reports: "Conspicuously lacking are remains of pinnipeds, sea otters ... Nor have any traces been found of large pelagic fishes, such as swordfish ... and tunas ... The fish remains ... indicate that fishing was done primarily from the shore, probably in several habitats. For the most part, the fish could have been caught in rocky or sandy habitats near shore, except for the rockfish (Sebastodes) ... would have required the use of a raft or boat. Either hooks or gill nets might have been used." With respect to the setting, Moriarty and Shumway hypothesize "that with the rapid rise of sea level a number of small deep bays developed where presently there are sloughs and valley floors full of sediment. Such narrow deep bays would abound in sea food and provide for a considerable population of sea food eating people" (Moriarty et al. 1959:200). These narrow deep canyons, presently filled with sediment and situated adjacent to and north of Scripps Estates, provided rocky shellfish until sand transport post 5000 B.P. blocked the canyon mouths, therein destroying the habitat for rocky shellfish and the need for habitation in this location, sealing Scripps Estates site occupation primarily to the Early and Middle Holocene.

Coast Apartments

For the UCSD Coast Apartments portion of the site, Moriarty reported 13 burials during his salvage excavation for the development of Coast Apartments (Shumway et al. 1961:42). A radiocarbon date, taken on Mytilus shell at 1.25 m, near bottom of midden in association with the burials, produced a date of 6370 B.P. (Hubbs et al. 1962). Results of the Pigniolo and Wahoff (1998) excavation are provided on Table 4. One additional burial was encountered in 1998 during Coast Apartments renovations (Hector 2007).

Middle Midden SDI-4670/W-5

Rogers recorded W-5 in 1929 as a SD-III, Lit I and II (San Dieguito and La Jolla) site containing the "'usual number' of burials . . . cobble hearths, shell midden, one fish hook reamer of the San Clemente gray lava, three digging weights, one . . . blade . . . origin SD-III? . . . The recession of the high sea-cliff has destroyed the major portion [of the site]" (Rogers 1920s). Site size was estimated at eight acres with disturbance due to agricultural use (Rogers 1920s, W-5). Previous work included the site recording with some excavation by Rogers; and, the excavation of 25 2x2 m units under the direction of Jason Smith and Darcy Ike as a 1976 CSUN field class (see Table 4). CSUN did not complete a report for this work (Hanna 1980; Roth and Berryman 1996). Ike (1978) identified the depth of midden as 60 to 120 cm; and, the "neutral soil pH was reported to preserve bones, seeds, and charcoal in abundance" (Hanna 1980:30). Radiocarbon dates for this site are 7980, 6880, and 1300 B.P. (Roth and Berryman 1996:22) (see Table 5). This site is presently identified as an ecologically sensitive area and protected within the University of California Natural Reserve System.

Chancellor's House SDI-4669/W-12 A, B

Rogers referred to this coastal ridge top site as Skeleton Hill (Hanna 1980:54), and reported in site form W-12: "This region, as well as Lower California, has had to be watched and patrolled for years after heavy rains to take advantage of peeling cliff exposures of burials" (Rogers 1920s, W-12). Rogers began his work at W-12 in 1929 and reports: "[I]ts steep talus produced scattered human remains everywhere and on the rim. Fragments of burials were still in situ . . . in subsequent years . . . we were able to locate and excavate three complete skeletons. The Littoral [La Jollan] II burials all had at least one metate over them and two had a cairn of metates, whole and broken, over them . . . The deepest burial was at 6ft. depth. Two that were in the grey basal sand were mineralized with calcite" (Rogers 1920s, W-12). He also reports: "The first occupation here was on a ridge of marine coarse grey sand, which paralleled the coast at an elevation of 325 ft. This has all been destroyed by recession of the sea cliff margin . . . Back of this site is a second ridge 350 ft. to 375 ft. . . . Its base is red marine crag upon which rests a thin bedded, lime-indurated Littoral I midden capped with a thick bedded Littoral II midden, which, because of years of cultivation and erosion, has been reduced to an unknown degree" (Rogers 1920s, W-12). Artifacts on file with the Museum of Man and probably collected by Rogers include manos, metates, one *Olivella* sp. bead, two bipointed bone tools (gorges), and two donut stone fragments (Hector 2007).

The data recovery program conducted by Roth and Berryman (1996) for the Eberlin portion of SDI-4669/W-12B (located adjacent and northwest of the Chancellor's House, W-12A) included the excavation of 48 1x1 m units and 38 trenches (see Table 4). This study produced 31 manos, 7 metates, 1 biface, 16 hammerstones, 4 cobble tools, 42 cores, 35 scrapers, 6 flake tools, 1,766 debitage, 5 worked bone, and shell (2,508.5 g/16 species). A radiocarbon sample taken on shell produced a date of 7800 B.P. (Roth and Berryman 1996).

The CSUN excavation of 12 2x2 m units was conducted in 1976 (see Table 4). However, no report of findings was produced. Roth and Berryman (1996) reviewed CSUN's data sheets and reported that their findings at the Eberlin Property (W-12B) were similar to CSUN's 1976 work at W-12A. CSUN's study produced 35 scrapers (ovoid/oval, domed/convex, flake end, flake side, and scraper plane), 2 San Dieguito bifaces, 32 manos, 3 metates, 8 round stone balls, 2 stone bowls, 18 hammerstones, 24 cobble tools, 2,637 debitage, 20 flake tools, 14 cores, 4 burials (including a double burial), and selected shell (Tivela stultorum, Chamidae, Mytilus, and Astraea undosa) (Roth and Berryman 1996).

Burials at the Chancellor's site include 25 documented as a result of the San Diego Museum of Man's work, 4 from the 1976 CSUN excavation, and 13 as a result of TMI's excavation at the adjacent Eberlin Parcel (Roth and Berryman 1996). The total of 42 burials from SDI-4669 does not include the 35 human bone entries in the CSUN catalogue.

Burial SDM-16709 was reported as: "Male . . . Flexed on right side—head to west, metate covering head . . . Body surrounded by whole and broken metates" (Hector 2007:14). Burial SDM-16709 was radiocarbon dated (uncorrected) to 8360 B.P. and 8470 B.P. (Bada and Masters 1978; Ike et al. 1979:526). Unique to this site is not only the high number of burials, but the sitting burial and the double burial. The sitting burial, removed under the direction of Tuthill (San Diego Museum of Man curator) from the construction of the Chancellor's House patio in 1950, was described as buried in a sitting position, with knees under the chin. Remains of a string of stone and shell beads were found near the head. The male individual was estimated to be 40 to 50 years of age and 5'10" to 6' tall (San Diego Union 1950).

The People—Characteristics, Lithics, Dating, Language, Ethnohistory, and DNA

Often, little is said about the people of which the artifacts, faunal remains, rock features, and burials represent. However, based on previous excavation work and the report on Kumeyaay Cultural Affiliation prepared for the National Register nomination by Wilson (2001), a discussion is provided below.

Rogers (1920s site form) refers to an early SD occupation in the LJAA. However, other researchers, such as Shumway, Warren, Moriarty, Pigniolo, and Masters report little, if any, San Dieguito evidence at LJAA sites that would support an early SDCP occupation. The artifactual and faunal remains, burials, and continuous radiocarbon dates support an Early Holocene occupation by a coastal people (LJCP) who settled in the LJAA and continued to occupy this region throughout the Holocene. Also, Moriarty reported that both he and Rogers found "no stratigraphic break between the La Jolla and the Diegueño [Kumeyaay] at the Spindrift site [SDI-39/W-1] . . . It appears that the process of amalgamation between the two cultures [La Jolla and Diegueño] covered a relatively long period, beginning about 3000 B.P." (Moriarty 1966:23).

Lithic Ability

Emma Lou Davis, in reference to the La Jollan people and lithic ability stated: "La Jollan campers did not go to the pains of making any fancy stone tools since a clam is delicious raw or popped open by having been tossed into a small fire. Hence, La Jollan stone work looks rough and uninstructed . . . The people were far too knowledgeable to waste their efforts needlessly. However, when occasion demanded, they could knap sophisticated bifacial knives out of rough porphyritic cobbles. This required great skill. They also understood platform preparation, the fabrication of polyhedral cores, and (when occasion demanded) selection of fine grained basalt or metavolcanics for more elaborate tools . . . La Jollan knappers knew exactly what they wanted out of a cobble as well as the most economical way of getting it. Their cobble craft is as fine a cultural signature as were the heat-treated chalcedony and exquisite pressure flaking of Classic Clovis folk over in the desert . . . they knew how to slice up a beach rock as though it were a loaf of rye bread. La Jollan stone work . . . was both competent and surprisingly subtle" (Davis et al. 1969).

Physical Characteristics—Double Burial Descriptions and Analyses

Burials were the traditional treatment of the dead from ca. 10,000 to 1,300 years ago. During the Late Period (ca. 1300 to historic contact) the dead were cremated, thereby providing no skeletal evidence to compare human remains from the earliest of times to the present Kumeyaay. However, Hunt, (personal communication with Wilson 2001) states: "The skeletal remains from 8000–2000 years B.P. are distinct from the ethnohistoric Kumeyaay people . . . [and] similar to . . . Spirit Cave (Nevada), Minnesota woman, and Kennewick man" (Wilson 2001:13).

Hunt identifies "the earliest Archaic Period skeletons as long-headed [dolichocephalic], shorter, and heavier-boned than . . . from the ethnohistorical period . . . [with] a shift toward more rounded skulls from 3000 to 1300" (Wilson 2001:13). Jantz and Owsley hypothesize early population movements around the Pacific Rim with a generalized morphology still seen in such modern groups as Polynesians and Ainu (Jantz and Owsley 2000:13). "However, a more recent study found the skull and facial morphology to have a variety of traits, including many used in forensic anthropology that would be termed 'Asian' and/or 'Native American' . . . Currently, the La Jolla burials [double burial] have been designated as culturally unidentifiable" (Mayes 2010:138). For the Scripps Estates site, dated from 8450 to 4310, burials were reported as having considerable skull variation with "both brachycephalic (short-headed) and dolichocephalic (long-headed) types . . . Some skulls have thick bones, but others have more typically thin bones . . . the people, whatever their race, were of moderate stature and apparently were reasonably free of vitamin-deficiency diseases" (Shumway et al. 1961:127).

Mayes (2010:137–138) described the double burial as follows: "[T]hey were interred in one grave, head to toe, on their sides in a flexed position (knees up), one facing east, the other facing west. The . . . male in his mid- to late twenties, lived an active lifestyle. He was not a large man, but his overall appearance is that of a robust or strong man. He was right-handed, with prominent muscle attachments in the elbow and wrist area from a repetitive lock-and-thrust action, such as the use of an atlatl, or spear thrower, indicating that he was a hunter. His teeth are worn evenly, suggesting a high-protein diet. A bony nodule located in the right ear, called an auditory exostosis, is a variation that is often observed in the skulls of individuals who have spent a considerable amount of time in cold water . . . His older companion, a female, in her late thirties to early forties, tells a somewhat different story. Her legs and arms are strong, with an emphasis on the upper arms carrying out repetitive behaviors. In addition to this are signs of occupational stress in the dentition. Her enamel crowns are completely worn down to the roots of the teeth, which, in turn, are polished and in some cases have observable striations across and down the exposed surfaces, very likely from some form of fiber strands having been pulled across the teeth. However, rather than having been worn in an even plane, the teeth are worn at odd angles opposite to one another, a pattern of occupational stress observed on the dentition that is often attributed to basket making . . . The shape of the fully developed impacted tooth is that of a prominent shovel-shaped [incisor of the Sino-American type]. This trait, considered by researchers as a quintessential Native American dental trait . . . These observations . . . documented in 2008 through a CAT-scan image . . . [and] Isotope analysis indicated a heavily marine-based diet from the sea and estuaries."

Radiocarbon Dating of Double Burials

As a result of Dr. Owsley's (Smithsonian Institution) analysis, a radiocarbon date on human bone for the double burials produced an uncorrected date of 8690, when calibrated provides a 2-sigma date range of 9740–9545 cal B.P. with a 95 percent probability (see Table 1). Seven uncorrected radiocarbon dates for the Chancellor's House range from 8690–7680 B.P., with one Tivela stultorum (Pismo) sample dated to 1140 B.P.

Language

In addition, Golla (2007:78) states: "The Hokan phylum is the oldest linguistic relationship among western North American languages that can be established by normal comparative linguistic methods. The time depth of the relationship is on the order of 8,000 years ago . . . and the languages are scattered as classificatory isolates or in subfamily cluster of closely related languages from the California-Oregon border to southern Mexico. The restricted territories of the California Hokan isolates . . . suggest that they are the eroded remnants of formerly widespread language groups." The Kumeyaay in San Diego County are one of the remnants of this formerly

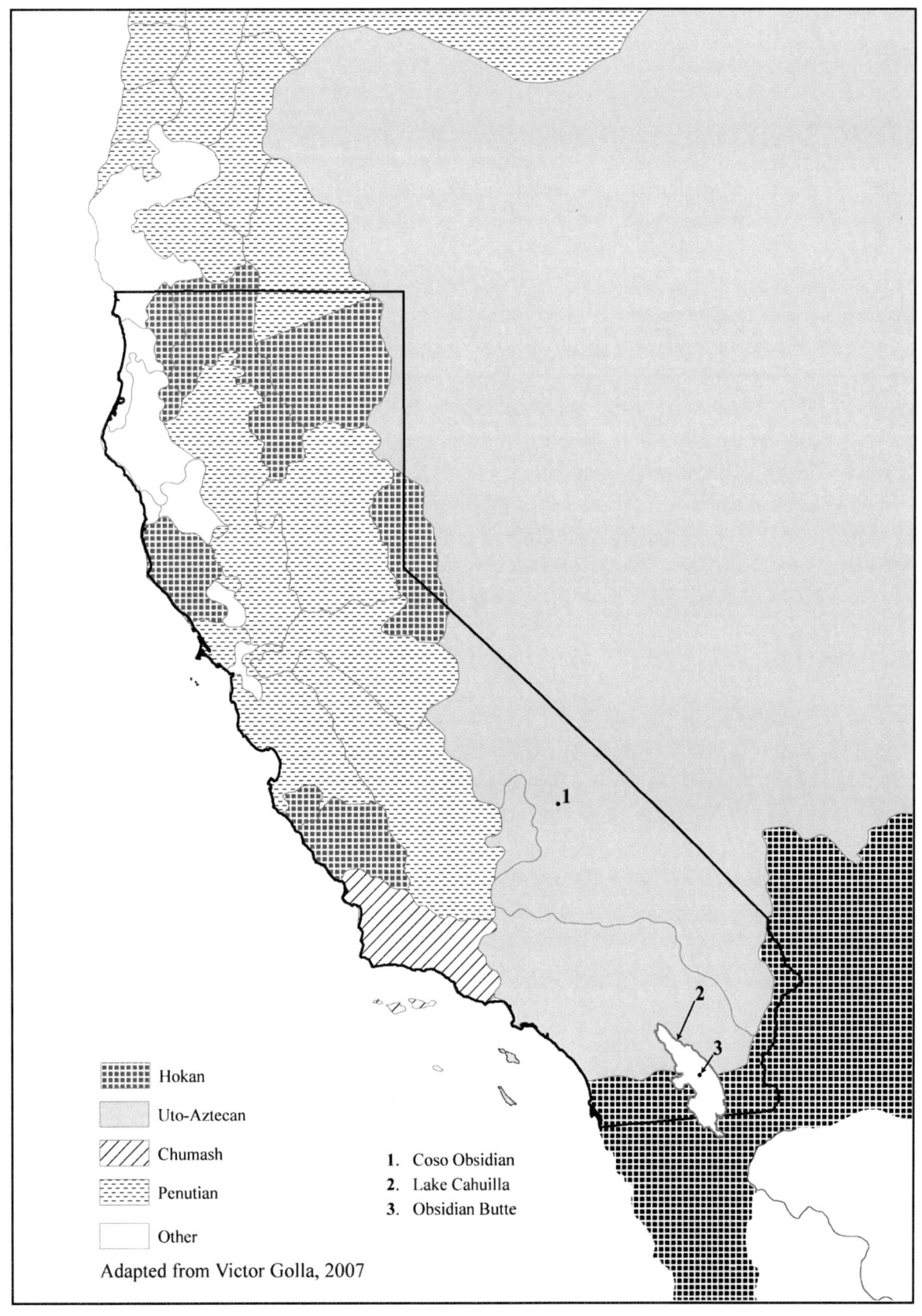

Figure 10. Linguistic Western Groups, Obsidian Sources and Lake Cahuilla

widespread language group and as such, may be directly related to Early Holocene peoples in a much broader context to include Oregon, California, Great Basin, and Mexico (Figure 10).

Ethnohistoric and Historic Accounts

Kumeyaay elders state that they have been here since time immemorial. Kroeber (1925:789) provides an ethnographic account of an origin tradition for Yuman/Kumeyaay that suggests origin from the ocean: "[A]dd the fact that the two brothers, the creator and his death-instituting opponent, are born at the bottom of the sea, and that the younger emerges blinded by the salt water."

DNA and Most Likely Descendent

Most Likely Descendent questions include: Do the artifacts associated with these sites represent SDCP or LJCP? And, is there a Most Likely Descendent (MLD) to present-day people? These questions could best be answered by DNA, given the 10,000+ years of an unwritten record. However, DNA is not always available from human remains for a number of reasons; and, the Kumeyaay choose to not allow DNA analysis because it is a destructive procedure. DNA, when allowed, has proven to be an effective method for identifying MLD. Evaluating MLD through other means is for the most part simply conjecture and not easily proven one way or the other. Mayes (2010:151) states: "[G]enetic studies, which many groups hesitate to employ, show relationships between Paleoindian remains and living Native American populations. This is an important factor in determining the descendents of First Nations. That the stories of these ancient emissaries will be lost in the political entanglements of today is a great concern … at almost ten thousand years old, the University House Burials are important to all Native Americans."

Chancellor's House National Register Status

The National Register of Historic Places (NRHP) for the William Black House (Chancellor's House) and archaeological site SDM-W-12 Locus A (SDI-4669) forms were prepared by Dalhberg, Schmidt, and Carrico in 2007 and accepted for placement on the NRHP in 2008 (#08000343). The NRHP site boundary is the Chancellor's House property and not the entire archaeological site, which would include SDM-W-12 Locus B and additional portions of house lots in the immediate area. It should be noted that all of the sites within the LJAA south of the Chancellor's House SDI-4669 to Spindrift SDI-39 are contributing elements to the story of the people who lived here over the past 10,000+ years (see Figure 8).

Summary

The environmental setting ca. 10,000 years ago was cooler and wetter than present and the shoreline (-35 m) was adjacent to both La Jolla and Scripps submarine canyons. By 6000 B.P. the shoreline (-5) had moved away from the submarine canyons, and sand transport after this time changed the setting for beaches, lagoons, and associated marine resources; and, sand transport may have closed off the canyons north of Spindrift to flushing ocean water and therein the loss of shellfish, thereby causing abandonment/depopulation of the Pleistocene marine terrace sites north of Spindrift ca. 5000 B.P.

First People had their choice of locations and a coastal location adjacent to resource-rich submarine canyons, a bay and lagoon, and protected on the east by coastal hills that provided an excellent location for the LJAA occupants. It should be noted that all of the LJAA sites are situated adjacent to the coast and focused on ocean/coastal resources.

A good representation of Early and Middle Holocene (ca. 9000–3000 B.P.) occupation are those sites situated on the Pleistocene marine terraces adjacent and north of Spindrift. Cultural material recovered and believed to best represent this Early and Middle Holocene occupation are shown on Table 4 (summary for all LJAA sites without Spindrift). Artifacts include: bifaces (1%); scrapers (18%); choppers (4%); cobble tools (2%); hammerstones (7%); cores (9%); groundstone (42%); *Olivella* beads (6%); stone balls (17); pitted cobbles (3); donut stones (9); discoidals (2), bone tools (10); crescents (2?); and burials.

Given the radiocarbon dates and burials, the Spindrift site SDI-39 was occupied throughout the Holocene. However, given the artifacts recovered, this site appears to best represent the Late Period occupation with arrow points (15%), scrapers (1.5%), cobble tools (6%), hammerstones (8%), cores (17%), groundstone (30%), bone tools (10%), flake tools (5%), an arrow shaft straightner, a clay pipe, ceramics (527), and cremations (15) (see Table 4).

Present condition of these important sites is poor, given: the loss of coastal bluffs due to sea level rise; loss of sites to early commercial and residential development, as reported by Rogers of the 1926 steam shovel destruction of W-2 at La Jolla Shores; residential and commercial development of the Spindrift site SDI-39/W-1; and residential and commercial development of SDI-11075, Scripps Estates SDI-525/W-9, and the Chancellor's site SDI-4669. The site in the best condition is Middle Midden SDI-4670/W-5, within a designated protected area. It should be noted that an excavation was conducted at SDI-4670 using 25 2x2 m units, but no report of finding was completed (Hanna 1980; and Roth and Berryman 1996).

LJAA is an excellent candidate for First People, given the Early Holocene occupation beginning ca. 9740–9545 cal B.P., the protected setting, rich coastal resources (e.g., submarine canyons, lagoon, and bay), and concentrated Early and Middle Holocene occupation. Cultural material from LJAA sites and the analysis of the double burial identify a range of activities including use of coastal resources, milling, and basketry for these early settlers.

In addition to Early to Middle Holocene LJAA sites discussed in Chapter 2, is the San Dieguito Plateau, a region that also has Early to Middle Holocene sites and is an excellent example of occupation during this time period. The San Dieguito Plateau, discussed in Chapter 3, includes Windsong Shores SDI-10965, Harris Site SDI-149 and a number of sites Rogers identified as San Dieguito. The Harris Site interpretation by Rogers and Warren, as well as sites on the San Dieguito Plateau played an important role in the development of the chronology for SDC.

CHAPTER 3

Rogers' San Dieguito Plateau: Dating San Dieguito and Warren vs. Rogers' Chrononology

Rogers: San Dieguito Plateau Sites

If the Harris site is not a habitation site, and the primary purpose of the Harris site is to manufacture Stage 3 bifaces for transport to habitation sites, then where are these artifacts being transported to? Rogers (1929) answers this question in his *The Stone Art of the San Dieguito Plateau* paper where he discusses the Scraper-Maker (a term later replaced with San Dieguito) types of artifacts and location for their camps and villages. The artifacts that define these Scraper-Maker sites "may be grouped under three generic types: (1) scrapers, (2) knives, and (3) ceremonial stones [crescents]; and they are numerically common in the order named. The first-named type of artifact so far out-numbers the other two types that it often constitutes the sole evidence of a Scraper-Maker site.…To the people who produced this industry I have given the provisional name of Scraper-Makers, after the most numerous and distinctive of their stone implements. Their camp and village sites are found only on mesas and ridges.…The material utilized for chipping by the Scraper-Makers is of two different sources, but both are in the immediate region. The most readily usable material was the extensive stratum of ancient river gravel that caps the greater part of the coastal plateau . . . composed of fine-grained, igneous rocks . . . The second source was in the eruptive rocks of the Coast Range. Where the San Dieguito River cuts through this range [includes Harris site and Rancho Cielo Quarry] several large bodies of latite and felsite [fine-grained metavolcanic] are exposed, and it was from such material that the finest chipped work was fashioned. These rocks are fine-grained and uniform in texture, have a conchoidal fracture, and flake well" (Rogers 1929: 457-461).

Rogers identified four loci for the San Dieguito Plateau (also referred to as the Encinitas Grant Plateau), each with at least one village and small campsites, located within "an area of about one hundred square miles" (Rogers 1929:454, Figure 1:455). The San Dieguito Plateau (SDP), on the basis of Rogers' Figure 1 (Rogers 1929), as well as Rogers' field work and more recent studies, appears to minimally extend from just east of Agua Hedionda and Batiquitos lagoons (Locus 1), south to the heads of San Dieguito and Peñasquitos lagoons (loci III and II, respectively), and east to Locus IV, Scraper-Maker site SDI-8330 in Escondido. The San Dieguito Plateau includes rolling coastal foothills east of the lagoons and west of the coast range, and Rogers' Scraper-Maker site SDI-8330/W-240. The San Dieguito Plateau and north SDC sites with crescents are shown on Figures 11 and 12.

Pigniolo (2013) in reviewing Rogers' San Dieguito Plateau loci, noted the association of his Scraper-Maker sites in proximity to Santiago Peak Volcanics. He also noted that parent stone of a certain size and quality (e.g., Santiago Peak Volcanics) was necessary to produce the bifaces, scrapers, and crescents as opposed to local beach quartzite and porphyritic cobbles, which both Rogers and Warren associated with La Jolla (LJCP) tools. Therefore, the stone materials are local beach quartzites and porphyritic cobbles in the Shell-Midden area (lagoon/coastal areas), and Santiago Peak Volcanics located within or adjacent to the San Dieguito Plateau and Scrapers-Maker loci I–IV.

Rogers' site form for W-181, in reference to the San Dieguito Plateau, states: "First settled by SD [San Dieguito] …This is a very concentrated occupation … Beginning at W-181 and extending to the [south] west on a general

46 *First People: A Revised Chronology for San Diego County*

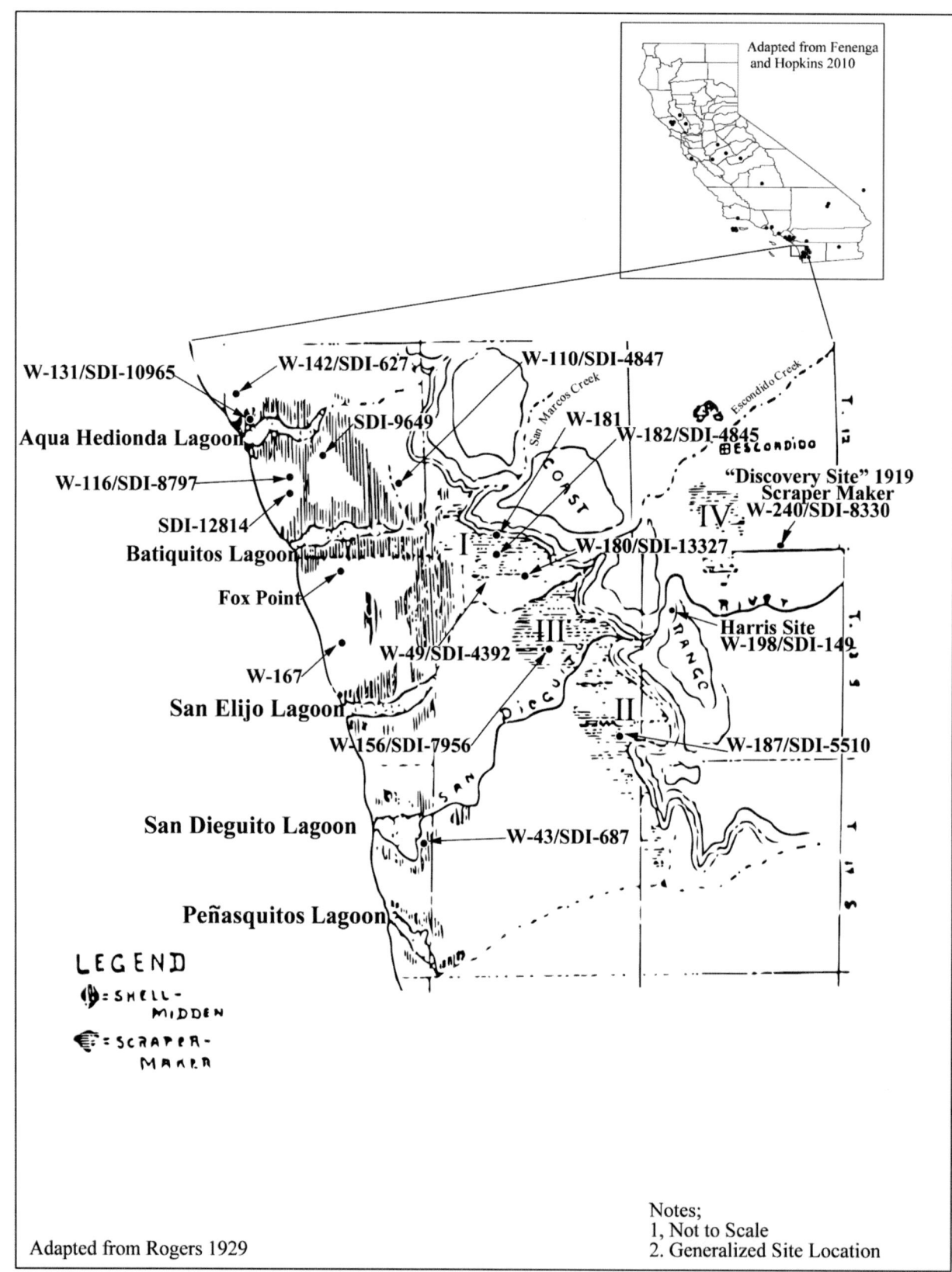

Figure 11. Generalized Distribution of Crescents in California (upper right); and, the San Dieguito Plateau Loci I, II, III and IV Showing Sites with Crescents.

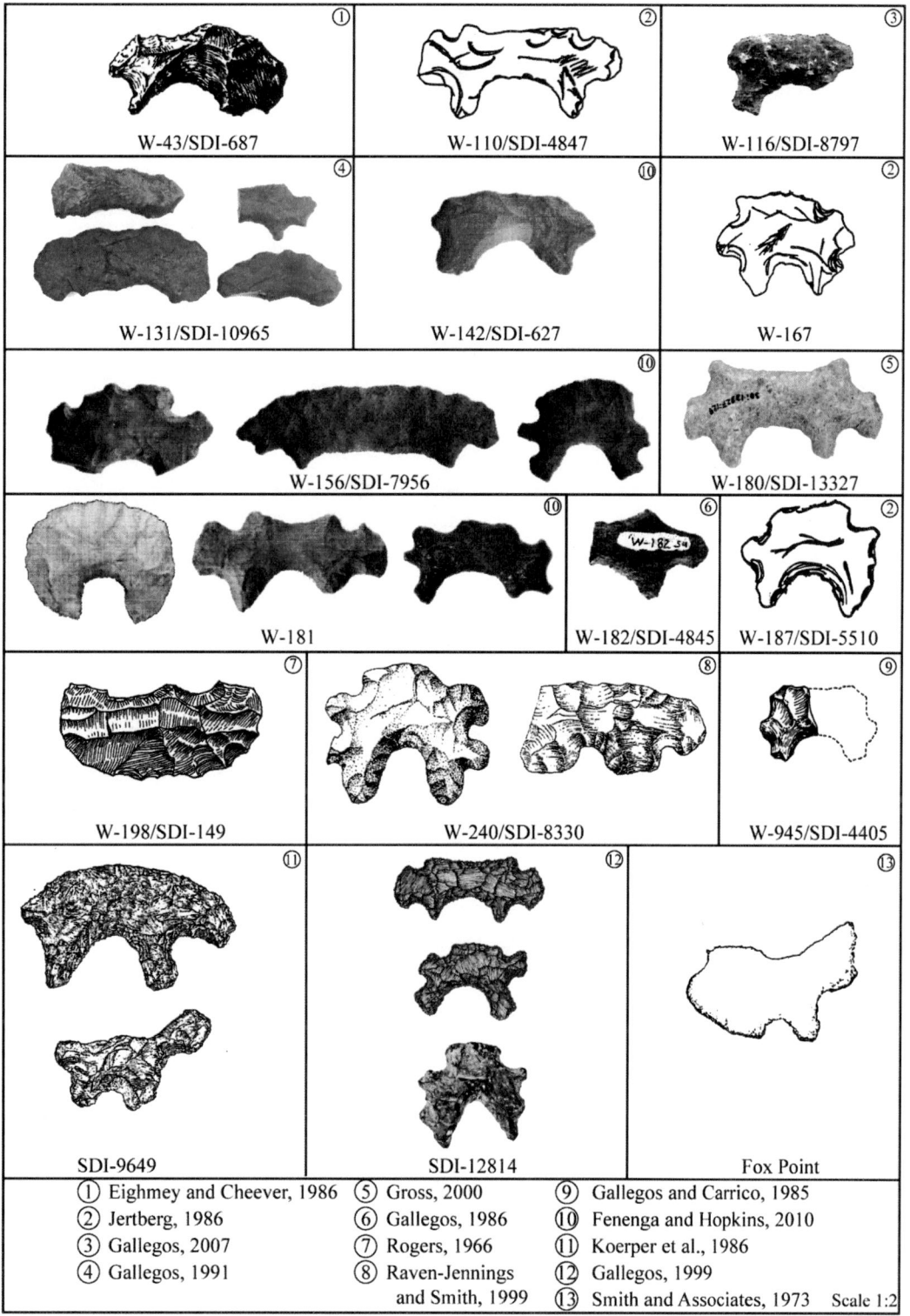

Figure 12. Selected Crescents from the San Dieguito Plateau and North San Diego County Sites.

elevation to W-182 [SDI-4845] and beyond it to the end of the Mesa is continuous evidence of SD-II [San Dieguito] material. This is a total distance of 1-3/4 miles. As a matter of fact, there is no part of the Encinitas Grant Plateau [San Dieguito Plateau] where felsite flaking cannot be found and it is the center of the greatest concentration of SD occupation in San Diego County" (Rogers 1920s, W-181).

However, Rogers' San Dieguito Plateau sites have been interpreted as either having complete tool kits or as mixed SDCP and LJCP sites/tool kits, given the consistent findings of milling tools, multipurpose cobble tools, scrapers, bifaces, crescents, burials, *Olivella* sp. spire-removed beads, and faunal remains of shellfish and small to large mammal bone. Rogers follows the traditional Abandonment Model of initial SD occupation and then abandonment, followed by LJ, and then Yuman occupation. Selected sites within Rogers' SDP Locus I, as well as the Scraper Hill site in Locus IV are discussed below. The Harris site and Rancho Cielo Quarry are located between Locus III and Locus IV, and have been previously discussed. Artifact illustrations for selected SD sites within the SDP are shown in Rogers (1966). Radiocarbon dates for selected sites within the San Dieguito Plateau are provided in uncorrected measured age on Table 6 and shown on Figures 11 and 13. Table 7 provides site summaries for San Dieguito Plateau sites discussed below.

San Dieguito Plateau, Locus I
Rancho Park North/Great Western Site SDI-4392/W-49

Radiocarbon dates using six samples from Levels 5–13 produced dates from 8280–8010 B.P. Early Holocene Levels 5–13 produced bifaces, crescents, scrapers, cobble tools (choppers, hammerstones), milling tools, four *Olivella* sp. spire-removed shell beads, bone tools, shell (33,708 g of primarily lagoon species), and small to large mammal bone (see Table 7).

Kaldenberg (1982:198-199) on the basis of his work at W-49A, which included his master's thesis (1976) under Dr. Ezell and his later publication on Rancho Park North, states: "Perhaps the most important scientific discovery as a result of this research has been that the San Dieguito, a people of the PaleoIndian Tradition, must now be construed as generalized hunters and gatherers much the same as were their more recent successors, the Kumeyaay. It is also strongly suggested that the San Dieguito people became the La Jolla people through the addition of a developed milling tool kit which enabled them to forage with greater efficiency. It is also suggested that the La Jolla peoples did not push their San Dieguito predecessors out of the littoral zone but were the same people simply changing their mode of adaptative interaction to include a reliance upon a new technology to augment that of the old. With this understanding I feel that it will now be possible to examine coastal sites in San Diego County without negating the hypothesis that the "manufacturers" of these middens were the La Jolla people and not the San Dieguito. Further research should show us that the San Dieguito and La Jolla people were one and the same, simply exploiting different eco-zones at various seasons and leaving behind a technology at a site corresponding not to temporality, but to spatial reality. Rather than being construed as a Paleo-Indian mode, the coastal San Dieguito manifestation probably should be conceived as a behavioral aspect of the more generalized hunting-gathering-fishing pattern of human behavior which dominated the Far South West for approximately 10,000 years." Kaldenberg, as per this discussion, identifies his position as following the Transformation and Non-transition models.

Ezell, discussing the SDC chronology, states: "I had subscribed to the triad described by Rogers for most of my life as an anthropologist. Not only that, I had supported that scheme during all the time I was on the faculty at San Diego State; thus, I imbued generations of students with that view to varying extent. Our interpretations of what was found at the Great Western Site, as presented by Kaldenberg in his master's thesis (1976), followed that same Procrustean tactic of trying to make the data fit an already accepted scheme" (Ezell 1987:17).

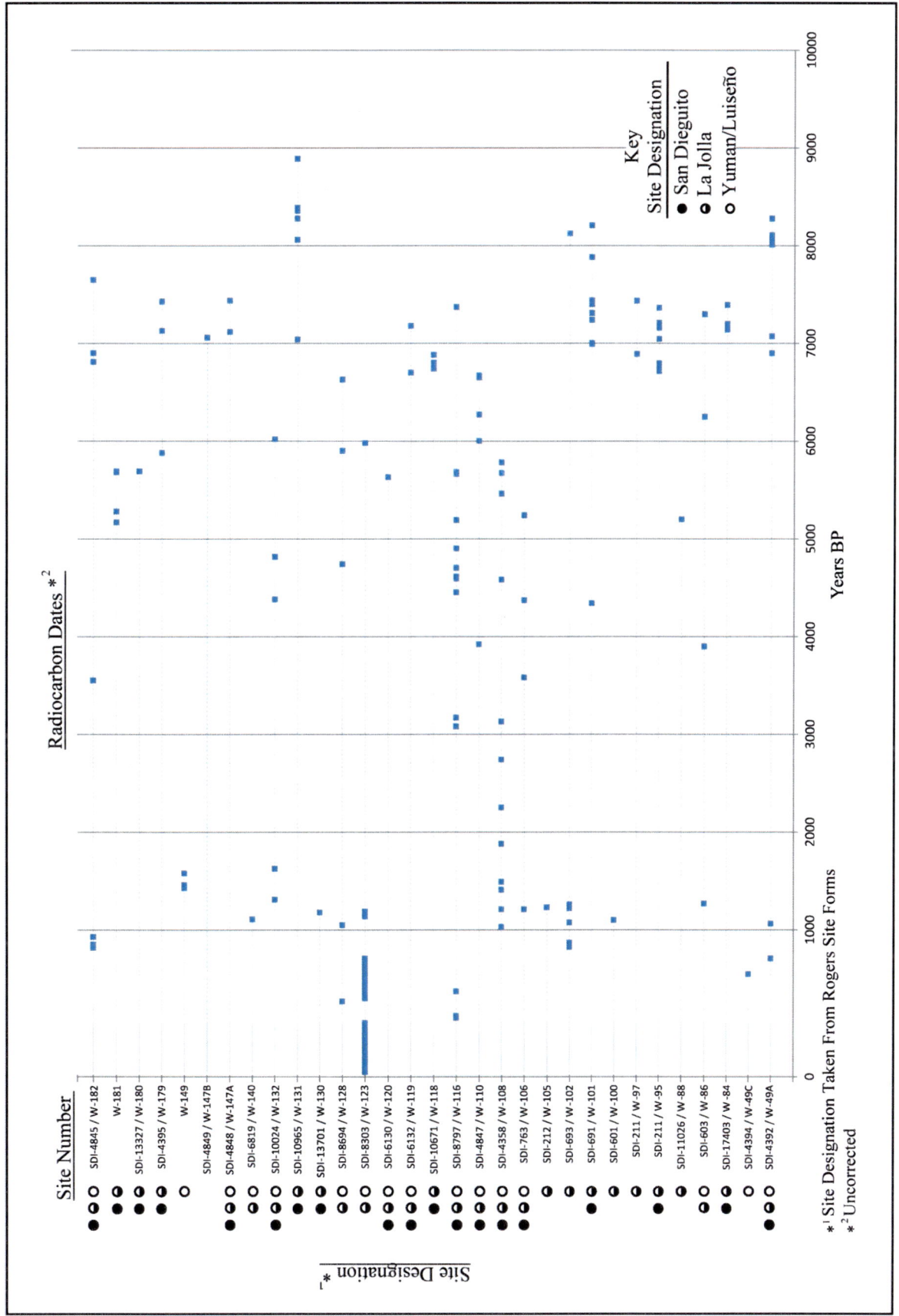

Table 6. Radiocarbon Dates for Rogers' Sites near Agua Hedionda and Batiquitos Lagoons and San Dieguito Plateau Locus I.

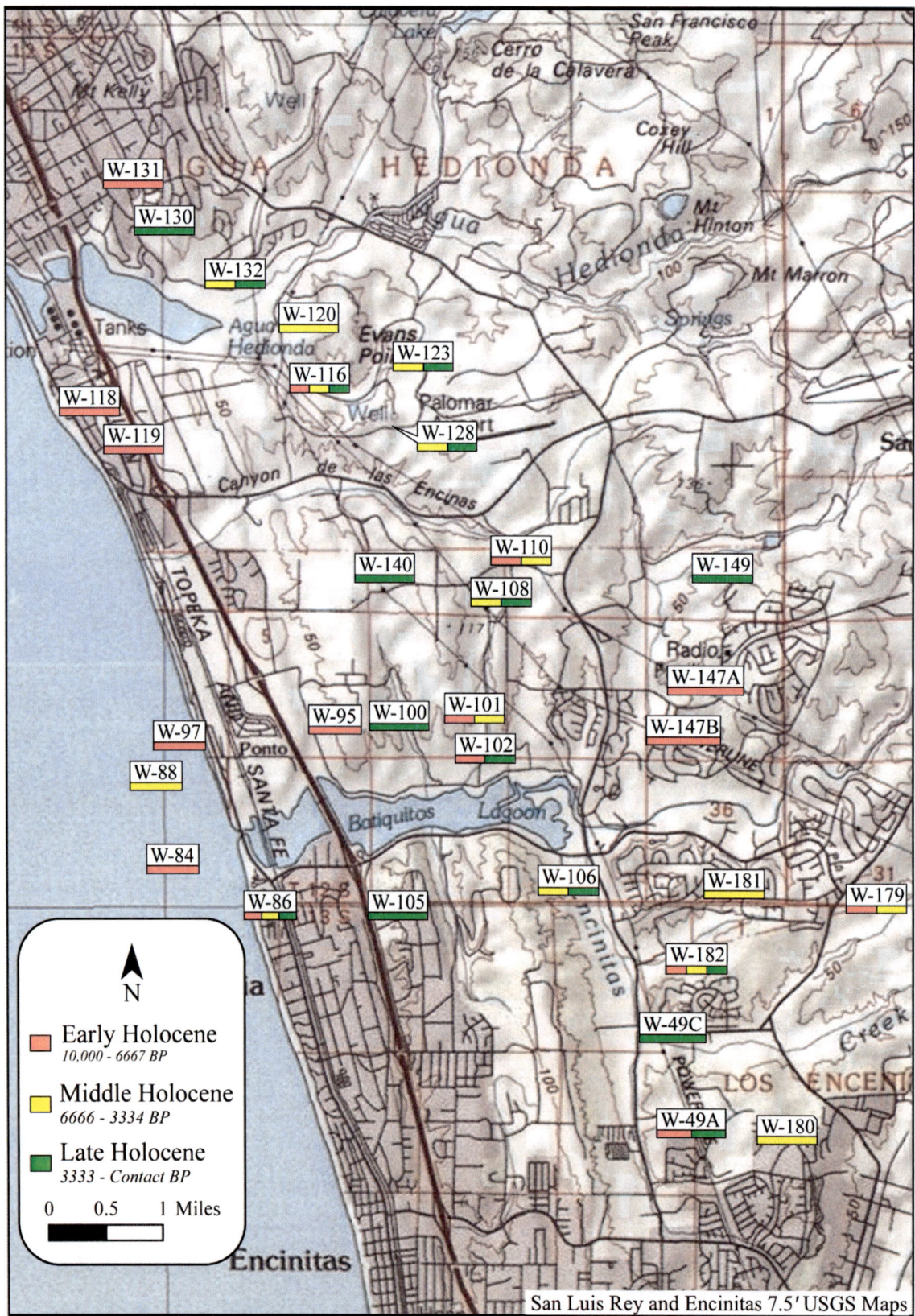

Figure 13. Agua Hediona, Batiquitos Lagoon and San Dieguito Plateau Locus I sites Recorded by Rogers with Radiocarbon Dates.

Cultural Material	SDI-149 C.W. Harris Site Locus I E-Stratum		Locus II		Rancho Park North Levels 3-4		SDI-4392, W-49A Levels 5-13		SDI-4395, W-179 Center Hill		SDI-13327, W-180 Air Field Site		W-181 North Hill		SDI-4845, W-182 Rogers Ridge L-6		SDI-4405, W-945 The La Costa Site		SDI-8330, W-240 Scraper Hill		San Dieguito Plateau Total**	
	Count	Percent	Count	Percent	Count	Percent	Count	Percent	Count	Percent	Count	Percent	Count	Percent	Count	Percent	Count	Percent	Count	Percent	Count	Percent
Biface/Knife/Point	90	44.8%	13	68.4%	4	1.9%	11	2.3%	3	1.3%	23	13.7%	24	23.1%	4	1.6%	6	7.2%	107	11.7%	182	7.5%
Crescent	2	1.0%		0.0%	1	0.5%	0	0.0%	0	0.0%	1	0.6%	1	1.0%	0	0.0%	1	1.2%	4	0.4%	8	0.3%
Scraper	97	48.3%	5	26.3%	74	35.6%	170	35.9%	55	23.6%	32	19.0%	16	15.4%	34	13.2%	10	12.0%	177	19.4%	568	23.3%
Chopper	0	0.0%		0.0%	7	3.4%	14	3.0%	5	2.1%	2	1.2%	1	1.0%	5	1.9%	0	0.0%	7	0.8%	41	1.7%
Hammerstone	9	4.5%		0.0%	3	1.4%	12	2.5%	20	8.6%	2	1.2%	13	12.5%	31	12.1%	32	38.6%	48	5.3%	161	6.6%
Core	3	1.5%		0.0%	45	21.6%	100	21.1%	99	42.5%	29	17.3%	17	16.3%	26	10.1%	5	6.0%	169	18.5%	490	20.1%
Utilized/modified Flake	0	0.0%	1	5.3%	60	28.8%	161	34.0%	10	4.3%	53	31.5%	11	10.6%	79	30.7%	7	8.4%	302	33.0%	683	28.0%
Debitage/Flake*	0	0.0%		0.0%	1500		2837		1796		21314		1509		6688		810		22568		59022	
Mano	0	0.0%		0.0%	10	4.8%	0	0.0%	36	15.5%	18	10.7%	12	11.5%	65	25.3%	17	20.5%	89	9.7%	247	10.1%
Metate	0	0.0%		0.0%	3	1.4%	0	0.0%	4	1.7%	3	1.8%	6	5.8%	12	4.7%	4	4.8%	7	0.8%	39	1.6%
Groundstone	0	0.0%		0.0%	0	0.0%	0	0.0%	0	0.0%	5	3.0%	2	1.9%	0	0.0%	1	1.2%	3	0.3%	11	0.5%
Pestle	0	0.0%		0.0%	0	0.0%	4	0.8%	0	0.0%	0	0.0%	1	1.0%	0	0.0%	0	0.0%	1	0.1%	2	0.1%
Shell Bead	0	0.0%		0.0%	0	0.0%	0	0.0%	1	0.4%	0	0.0%	0	0.0%	1	0.4%	0	0.0%	0	0.0%	2	0.2%
Bone Tool	0	0.0%		0.0%	1	0.5%	1	0.2%	0	0.0%	0	0.0%	0	0.0%	0	0.0%	0	0.0%	0	0.0%	2	0.1%
Total*	201	100.0%	19	100.0%	208	100.0%	473	100.0%	233	100.0%	168	100.0%	104	100.0%	257	100.0%	83	100.0%	914	100.0%	2440	100.0%
Total Shell (gms)	0				14019		33708		7829		21482		168g		36728		4139		0.6		96,059	
Total Bone (gms)	0				NA		NA		NA		21.9		1.5g		230		9.15		19.8		277.95	
Resources:	Rabbit, Deer		Chione		Shellfish, fish, rabbit, bird, deer				Shellfish, fish, rabbit, bird, deer		Shellfish		Shellfish		Shellfish, fish, rabbit, deer, crab 2 Coso Obsidian		Shellfish, Ray, rabbit, crab		Casa Diablo Obsidian			
Number of 1x1m Units	Trench		Trench		59		59		38		35		26.5		32 Units, Locus 6		10					
Rogers Site Type	SD				SD, LJ, YIII		SD, LJ, YIII		SD, LJ		SD, trace LJ		SD, LJ		SD, trace LJ and Y				SD		ca. 5400 to 8280 B.P.	
C-14 Dates, Years B.P.	8490, 8490, 9030		4720 B.P.		6900, 7075, 8040		8010, 8060, 8030, 8280, 8110 B.P.		7130, 7430, 5880 B.P.		5690		5400		6810, 6900, 7650		6140, 6900, 7070					
Notes:			Elko Point										13 ceramics						1 donut stone 1 Atlatl weight			
Burial	None		None		None		1 partial		None		None		None		Rogers - 1 crescent 1 partial		Hearth, w/bifaces None		None			
Source	Warren et al. 1998		Warren 1966		Kaldenberg 1976, 1982		Kaldenberg 1976, 1982		Bull 1976 Waters 1972		Gross 2000		Hanna 1991		Gallegos 1986		Gallegos & Carrico 1985		Summary Table for Previous Work by Raven-Jennings, Smith 1999			

*Excludes Flakes/angular waste/debitage, arrow points, and ceramics

**Total W/O SDI-149

Table 7. San Dieguito Plateau Site Summaries.

Moratto, discussing Rancho Park North, states: "Rancho Park North seems to have been occupied most intensively from circa 8300 until 8000 B.P. by people who subsisted on shellfish, fish, and plant foods, augmented by small game. Technically and formally, their lithic toolkit is linked to that of San Dieguito, suggesting that the Paleo-Coastal Tradition was not far removed from its WPLT antecedents. Economically, however, the PCT is distinguished by an emphasis on coastal resource" (Moratto 1984:106).

Center Hill Site SDI-4395/W-179

Radiocarbon dates using three bulk shell samples produced dates of 5880, 7130, and 7430 B.P. Rogers (1920s, W-179) reported: "[F]irst visited by SD ... people as a temporary campsite but over a long period. Archaeology is scattered over large area typical of this kind of camping ... The apex ... is capped with a small area of Lit. II [La Jolla] occupation."

Waters (1972) reports that the site is 3.6 km (1.4 mi) from Batiquitos Lagoon, on a knoll top (84 m) above Encinitas Creek. The midden covers 800 sq m with a depth of 50–80 cm with the majority of materials recovered from 0–50 cm, and no visible stratigraphy noted. In all, 34 1x1 m units were excavated producing 297 whole and fragmentary groundstone (251 manos, 42 metates, 3 discoidals, 1 reamer); 1 *Olivella* sp. spire-removed shell bead; 2 worked bone; flaked stone tools (82 choppers, 83 scrapers, 6 gravers, 8 knives, 1 broken biface preform); 178 hammerstones; 15 teshoa flakes; and 2,464 debitage with some hematite. Late Period ceramics (51) and one pipe fragment in the upper 15 cm were also reported. All bifaces are of fine-grained metavolcanic material except for a point tip of chalcedony. The bifaces are generally described as having convex edges and thin lenticular cross sections, with a rounded or pointed tip and a rounded or blunted base, and all but one shows heavy patination. Waters (1972:10) reports that the flakes are secondary resharpening flakes with few primary or cortex flakes, therefore preliminary quarry and production of tools was occurring somewhere else with only finished tools and useable flakes being brought to the site, and only resharpening of tools occurring on site. A bulk sample of *Chione* sp. shells from the 40–50 cm level produced a date of 5880 ±125 (Gak-4711). Faunal includes rabbit (jackrabbit and cottontail), wood rat, mule deer, deer mouse, fish, bird, and shell. Waters reports 29 shellfish species with *Argopecten*, *Chione*, Mytilus, Ostrea, and Tagelus dominating. Given the high amount of shellfish (7,829 g) recovered, and high number of milling tools, Waters suggests a heavy dependence on shellfish, with gathering and milling of plant foods.

Waters (1972), a student of Dr. Ezell at SDSU, used the traditional Abandonment Model, identifying the SDCP as the first occupants, who left behind heavily patinated scrapers, choppers, and knives, followed by LJCP. Dr. Ezell revised his Abandonment Model views after the completion of the Rancho Park North project, ca. 1980s to generally follow the Transformation and Non-transition models.

Bull (1976), also a student of Ezell's, tested site SDI-4395 using 19 1x2 m units placed across the site. Bull (1976) reports there was "no evidence—based on the classification system used—of typological change over time. Groundstone artifacts are present throughout the depth of the site as are teshoa flakes, pushplanes, flakes, and debitage." And suggests the potential for human and bioturbation displacing materials. Artifact and ecofact results were similar to Waters (1972) and two shell samples provided radiocarbon dates of 7430 and 7130 B.P. (see Table 7). Bull (1976:93) states: "It is not possible at this time to determine whether we are dealing with two or more, distinct culture groups, or a single group adapting to slightly different environs. Both of these explanations could account for the variation perceived within the region." Bull in 1976 identifies both Model 1 Abandonment (two or more distinct culture groups), and Model 5 Non-transition (single group adapting to slightly different environs) as potential explanations for the varied tool kit recovered from SDI-4395. By the 1980s, Bull identified his position on mixed tool kits as Non-transition (Bull 1987).

Scraper-Maker Hill Site SDI-13327/W-180

Rogers' (1920s, W-180) site form for Scraper-Maker (SM) Hill reports: "With regards to area this is the largest SD site known, and scattered evidence in a marginal position covers 10 acres with a central area of 5 acres with more concentration. To the east on the plateau can be found a continuous occurrence of felsites [fine-grained metavolcanic] flakes for ½ mile . . . On the apex . . . is an 8" veneer of mixed Lit. II [La Jolla] and Y-III [Yuman] occupation."

The data recovery excavation of 35 1x1 m units and previous test work by Gross (2000) produced milling tools, bifaces, a crescent of Piedra de Lumbre (PDL) chert; scrapers, choppers, flake tools, and cores (see Table 7). Materials for the 21,314 debitage included 93 percent metavolcanic with the remaining materials: quartz, quartzite, PDL, chert, chalcedony, jasper, and three obsidian (one sourced to Coso); faunal included *Chione* sp., *Argopecten* sp., and *Chama* sp. shell (21.9 g); and 20.4 g of large mammal bone (Gross 2000).

Gross followed the traditional Abandonment Model with SDCP as First People, then LJCP occupation. Gross's tool classification system was based on the types defined by Warren and True (1961) for the San Dieguito component of the C.W. Harris site SDI-149 and by Warren et al. (1961) for the LJCP/Archaic (Gross 2000:56). The La Jolla/Archaic is generally defined by crude cobble tools, especially choppers and scrapers, and also includes manos and metates, burials, and a coastal resource orientation of shellfish and fish. As a result of this analysis, Gross (2000:56) states that 53.6 percent of the artifacts were best classified under the San Dieguito typology [SDCP] (e.g., bifaces, scrapers, and crescents), 32 percent attributable to the LJCP typology, with the remainder 14.5 percent in an unclassifiable category. Therefore, the site assemblage primarily fits Rogers' description of San Dieguito, with La Jolla and some Late Prehistoric. A recent date on charcoal, as well as recent historic materials from 0–40 cm led Gross to state: "[D]isturbance of the sediments was evidenced in the stratigraphy and the distribution" (Gross 2000:53). One bulk shell sample produced a date of 5690 B.P. (Gross 2000).

North Hill Site W-181

Radiocarbon dating using one bulk shell sample produced a date of 5400 B.P. Rogers' (1920s, W-181) site form states: "First settled by SD . . . very concentrated occupation . . . Beginning at W-181 and extending . . . to W-182 and beyond . . . is continuous evidence of SD-II material . . . is the center of the greatest concentration of SD [San Dieguito] occupation in San Diego County."

Results of Hanna's test and data recovery program (surface collection, STPs, and hand excavation of 26.5 1x1 m units and controlled grading) are shown on Table 7. Cultural material recovered includes bifaces, a crescent, cores, scrapers, hammerstones, and milling tools. The 1,509 debitage was primarily of local metavolcanic material, with five quartz, 33 chert/chalcedony, and two obsidian. Faunal included 168 g of lagoon shell (*Chione* sp. and *Argopecten* sp.) and 1.5 g of unburned bone (Hanna 1991). Hanna states: "Most of the items classified as bifaces would fit within broadly defined stylistic types attributed to the San Dieguito Complex, although a few might be considered La Jollan or even Late Prehistoric/Proto-historic" (Hanna 1991:53). A hearth excavated by Hanna (1991) was described as roughly circular in planview with fire-affected rocks mostly lining the base. Within and adjacent to the hearth were charcoal, shell (*Argopecten* sp. and *Chione* sp.), and three bifaces, one utilized flake, one hammerstone, and 13 debitage. A shell sample from the hearth was dated to 5400 B.P.

Hanna (1991:77-80) states: "This study's findings contradict the orthodox cultural chronology model . . . It has been demonstrated that the material culture inventory at W-181 remained essentially similar over a span of some 4,650 to 5,300 years. Such continuity indicates a mutual association of elements that orthodox perspectives consider temporally distinct, including a 'La Jolla' cobble/core-tool industry; a 'San Dieguito' scraper-and-biface industry with crescentics and large, thin, double-convergent, bifacially worked blades . . . a ground stone assemblage with items that are variously attributable to the 'La Jolla Complex' and 'Encinitas Tradition' or the Late Prehistoric/Proto-historic period; an exploitation of floral and faunal resources in lagoonal-estuarine and coastal sage scrub/chaparral environments ... long term continuity in the material culture of W-181 included a generalized subsistence strategy involving exploitation of both lagoonal-estuarine and terrestrial resources. The location of W-181, as a temporary camp, is seen to express optimization between various subsistence possibilities within a district that incorporated Batiquitos Lagoon, the Encinitas Grant Plateau [San Dieguito Plateau], and hilly areas to the east. Specific resources probably included various seeds, roots, and tubers; small-to-medium sized mammals ... various avian and reptilian species; and lagoonal shellfish (mostly *Argopecten* spp. and *Chione* spp.). Habitation was brief, repetitive, and possibly seasonal." Hanna (1991:80) summarizes his work by stating: "Since the earliest known use of W-181 was circa 5400 B.P., after the region had already been occupied some 3,000 to 4,000 years, a fully diversified hunting-gathering toolkit and short-term habitation pattern should be exhibited by cultural debris from its initial period. This would account for the co-occurrence of 'San Dieguito' and 'La Jolla' elements [cultural patterns]." Hanna's statement above supports the Non-transition Model.

Rogers Ridge Site SDI-4845/W-182

Radiocarbon dates for Locus 6 using three bulk *Chione* sp. shell samples produced the dates of 6810, 6900, and 7650 B.P. (Gallegos 1986). Rogers (1920s, W-182) site form states: "SD ... were the first campers here, living in their characteristic manner of scattering out. In time the more popular spots on the mesa gained the greatest concentrations of occupational debris ... Later Lit. II [La Jolla] people came into the area but formed no middens except on the low terrace at W-48. After them W. Diegueño [Yuman] camped over the area leaving only traces of occupation here and there." Surface artifacts collected by Rogers and curated at the San Diego Museum of Man include: 221 artifacts identified as bifaces, crescents, scrapers, hammerstones, cores, and milling tools.

Gallegos (1986) identified SDI-4845/W-182, Locus 6 as primarily an Early Holocene occupation site with some Late Period arrow points and ceramics (see Table 7). Fieldwork produced: one partial burial, one *Olivella* sp. spire-removed bead, bifaces/knifes (1.5%), scrapers (13%), milling tools (30%), choppers (2%), hammerstones (12%), cores (8.5%), flake tools (30% including scraper, knife, composite, and drill), and debitage including two Coso obsidian. Faunal included 36,729 g of primarily lagoon shell (e.g., *Argopecten, Chione,* Mytilus, and Ostrea), 230 g of bone (small to large mammal), and 2.3 g fish bone (e.g., sheephead, bat ray, and rockfish).

Gallegos (1986:6–3) states: "SDI-4845, Locus 6 compares well with other north San Diego County Early Period sites ... The common thread between these sites includes dates circa 7,000 years B.P., large leaf-base bifaces/knives, cresentics, milling tools, spire-lopped beads, number of core cobble tools, large amount and variety of shellfish, and flexed burials ... [and] all of these sites are situated on a knoll or ridge adjacent to a semi-permanent stream." Gallegos in 1986 supported the Non-transition Model.

San Dieguito Plateau Locus IV-Scraper Hill Site SDI-8330/W-240

Only one site, SDI-8330/W-240, was identified by Rogers as within Locus IV. This site was recorded by Rogers on Christmas Day 1919, and was referred to by Rogers as "Scraper Hill" and the original "Discovery Site" of the San Dieguito culture (Rogers 1966:184).

Given the general absence of shell and bone, no radiocarbon dates have been produced for this site. However, shell from site SDI-20662, located approximately 100 m north, produced a date of 7130 B.P., 2-sigma calibration 8020–7820 cal B.P. (Beta 312855) (Gallegos 2012).

Rogers' (1920s, W-240) site form states: "Small camping groups of SD-II people visited this area first and probably only seasonal. This condition prevailed for hundreds of years." Chase (1980) postulated wetter conditions ca. 10,000 B.P., and proposed that a natural dyke created a series of ponds and marshes adjacent to the site. Emma Lou Davis and Jane Lenker described this site as one-quarter mile in size with shallow deposits on the slopes and ridge tops.

Fieldwork included: 1) Rogers' 1919 site recording and artifact collection; 2) Emma Lou Davis and Jane Lenker (1969–1980) collection of surface artifacts; 3) excavations and collections conducted by Palomar College/O'Neill in 1976–1977; 4) Malies and Knutson 1976; 5) Seibert 1978; 6) Berryman S. 1979; 7) Chase 1980; 8) Berryman J. 1985; 9) Berryman S. 1985; 10) Berryman and Berryman 1988; and 11) Raven-Jennings and Smith 1999.

Raven-Jennings and Smith (1999:5.0–14) compiled a summary of previous surface and subsurface work at SDI-8330 (see Table 7). The makeup of this collection is bifaces (11.5%), crescents (0.5%), scrapers (19.5%), hammerstones (5%), cores (18.5%), utilized flakes (33%), and milling tools (11%). In addition, one possible atlatl weight, one donut stone, one spokeshave, and obsidian sourced to Casa Diablo was recovered.

Raven-Jennings and Smith (1999:7.0–1,2,7,9) states: "As defined by Rogers and those who adopted his triculture chronology for this area, the San Dieguito Complex is most often characterized as a hunting-oriented lifeway ... The hallmark artifacts of the San Dieguito Complex are crescents, bifacially flaked knives, and well-to-exceptionally flaked scrapers. These hallmarks were all identified at W-240 ... The age of Site W-240 remains an enigma, as are most sites attributed to the San Dieguito Complex. The standard reasoning is that the sites are too old to retain any midden and are usually positioned in non-depositional environments (e.g., mesas and ridges), rendering dating by scientific methods unfeasible ... [It should be noted that only 0.6 g shell and 19.8 g bone were recovered from the excavation of 175 cubic meters] ... In general, the validity of the contrast between an earlier 'San Dieguito' hunting-oriented strategy and the later Archaic shellfish and plant (seed) oriented strategy has been increasingly challenged. Koerper's (Koerper et al. 1986) work at Agua Hedionda revealed a similar, diverse range of species taken in both San Dieguito and later Archaic time periods, indicating that hunting, fowling, fishing, shellfish collecting, and plant food gathering were all important throughout time ... In the San Dieguito ... [p]hase, the hunting of medium and large game was supplemented by the gathering of plant foods and marine resources (Warren and True 1961; Moriarty 1966: Kaldenberg and Ezell 1974). Data from Windsong Shores (Gallegos and Carrico 1984), Rancho Park North (Kaldenberg 1982), Newport Bay (Koerper 1981), and Lake Elsinore (Grenda 1997) also suggest continuity in patterns between the San Dieguito and La Jolla Complex on the basis of a shared, varied economy. Differences are attributed to adaptations to different primary ecozones (i.e., terrestrial versus coastal) and its consequences for the availability of subsistence and lithic resources ... If W-240 dates to the Middle Archaic Period, the entire argument derails. Maybe there was not a marsh teeming with Pleistocene megafauna, but rather a seasonal wet spot attracting short-term resource extraction, much like the conditions present today. This would better account for the ephemeral but extensive nature of the site. Far from debunking Site W-240's place in San Diego's prehistory, this interpretation represents a return to its interpretive roots. Malcolm Rogers' first impressions ... W-240 is an ephemeral camp where milling and tool production took place..." The previous discussion supports the Non-transition Model.

J. Berryman 1985:5–6 states: "Materials recovered from Scraper Hill again point to a heavier reliance on gathering activities ... The milling assemblage recovered from this site are well defined and exhibit heavy use. Many of the manos and metate fragments recorded for Area 3 were found lying next to more 'typical' San Dieguito-like tools (scraper planes, knife blades, etc.), indicating that the entire assemblage is single component and not resultant from inter-mixing by later inhabitants ... Based on the excavation results from this area, a subsistence model for W-240 must involve the collection of vegetal materials, small game and water fowl that were present along the mesa tops. The lack of bone, butchering areas or well-defined hearths from any of the excavation units ... does not support the contention that 'big-game' hunting or megafauna existed in the study area ... A more likely model is that small pond-related animals, such as migratory birds, turtles and possibly fish were gathered from the 'marsh' or wetter areas. Plants associated with such habitats, particularly reeds and seed plants, would have been the prime reason for exploiting such resources. This would help explain the large number of milling stones and metates recovered throughout the entire assemblage."

Berryman and Berryman (1988:58) states: "As early as the 1960s, researchers have suggested that the site was bracketed by a marsh on the northern and southern perimeter. It was thought that this marsh was what attracted prehistoric peoples to this specific area. Big-game animals unable to free themselves from the mud and marsh bottom and could be easily hunted. This subsistence pattern fit perfectly into the accepted idea that the San Dieguito people were big game hunters who moved from area to area following game trails and large herds. Early definitions of site patterns and analysis of tool kits obtained from 'type sites' perpetuated this view, resulting in commonly held beliefs becoming scientific 'fact' . . . Investigations at the site have failed to identify areas where any form of hunting or butchering took place . . . A more realistic viewpoint of early lifeways at W-240 has to be considered . . . Data collected from the Batiquitos Lagoon [region] suggests that differences in tool kits currently defined for the San Dieguito and La Jolla are merely cultural adaptations to different environments rather that lithic debris from two separate groups of people (Gallegos 1985 [1987])."

San Dieguito Plateau Summary

It should be noted that there are two schools of thought in interpreting the data from the same kinds of sites within the San Dieguito Plateau. These researchers opinions are represented by their excavations and reports, discussed above from 1972 to 2000. The first group follows the Abandonment Model and separates SDCP from LJCP cultural material and therein identifies an Early Holocene SDCP occupation, followed by abandonment, and then LJCP occupation. The second group of researchers do not see a temporal gap for site occupation and activities conducted, and therein use the radiocarbon dates and cultural material recovered to discuss SDCP and LJCP as a single occupation with a wide range of activities (i.e., hunting, fishing, shellfish collecting, plant/seed collecting and processing, cooking, tool making, and burial of the dead) conducted on the San Dieguito Plateau. This second group generally follows the Non-transition Model and interprets the lithic assemblage to include finely made bifaces, crescents, and scraping tools, along with milling, and cobble and flake tools, thereby identifying a wide range of activities by one people over a long period of time (e.g. 9000 to 4000/3500 B.P.)

Rogers: Shell-Midden People, Materials, Occupation Areas, and North County Lagoons

Rogers (1929) identified the Shell-Midden (LJCP) occupation areas "to be found not only on the coast, but as far as four miles inland. In elevation they range from tidewater to two hundred and fifty feet [76.2 m] above sea level . . . They are invariably located on mesa rims adjacent to sanded-in sloughs, which indent the local coast and extend inland often for several miles. Judging from the contents of the middens, these sloughs formerly supported an abundant molluscan fauna . . . The surface finds from these middens include manos, metates, hammerstones, teshoa-flakes, and a great amount of split stone, but no chipped stone artifacts which may be recognized as finished implements" (Rogers 1929:456–457). Using Rogers (1929), the areas for Shell Midden (La Jolla) occupation are adjacent to north SDC coastal lagoons (Agua Hedionda, Batiquitos, San Elijo, San Dieguito, and Peñasquitos) (see Figure 11). The environmental setting for these lagoons includes the rise in sea level and flooding of coastal river valleys ca. 9,000 to 4,000/3,400 years ago, creating rich lagoonal resource areas for shellfish, fish, birds, small to large mammals, and plant foods. The lagoons appear to be productive throughout the period from ca. 9000 to ca. 4000/3400 B.P. This period, ca. 4000 to 3400 years B.P., based on the research by Miller (1966) and Gallegos (1985) supports rapid siltation of Batiquitos Lagoon. The loss of lagoonal resources led to depopulation of the area adjacent to the lagoon, as demonstrated by the few archaeological sites dated ca. 3500–1600 B.P. In concert with the siltation model is Emory's work (1960:23) wherein he states: "Once on the beach [sand, gravels and cobbles], whether derived from streams or sea cliffs, the sediments come under the influence of waves. Before being lost to the sea, the sand and heavier material is moved along the shore for greater or lesser distances. It is in this manner that the gravel beach was deposited across the mouth of Batiquitos Lagoon [thereby blocking the mouth of the lagoon and contributing to lagoon siltation]." The loss of lagoonal resources for North County lagoons ca. 4000–3400 B.P. signaled the end of an era for La Jolla/Archaic occupation at these lagoons. However, use of lagoonal resources post 3500 B.P. to historic contact is demonstrated at Peñasquitos Lagoon, La Jolla Spindrift site, San Diego Bay, and the Tijuana Estuary where conditions for shellfish and fish were good to excellent throughout the Middle to Late Holocene.

Although there are a range of sites from small shell processing camps to habitation sites adjacent to these lagoons, a good example of LJCP occupation is SDI-603 (W-86), excavated by Crabtree, Warren, and True (1963). This site was initially recorded by Malcolm Rogers (1920s, W-86) as a Lit II (LJCP) with the "usual number of cobble hearths . . . metates are common . . . tool content is low . . . burial was lying on its left side in a flexed position with the head probably facing north east . . . No artifacts were found in association" (Rogers 1920s, W-86). Artifacts recovered from SDI-603, Stratum 3 and Stratum 4 by Crabtree et al. are: 2 bifaces, 32 scrapers, 67 hammer/choppers, 4 cores, and 48 manos, as well as lagoon shell (primarily Mytilus, *Argopecten* sp., *Chione* sp., and Ostrea) with associated dates 6250 and 7300 years B.P. (Crabtree et al. 1963; Warren et al. 1998:II, 49–52). Crabtree et al. (1963:343) conclude: "The material from SDI-603 suggests a long period of intermittent occupation with as great a degree of conservatism in the artifact inventory as has been described for the New World. The basic pattern present in the earlier portion of the occupation (some 6000 to 7000 years ago) did not alter significantly in the 3000 years that followed . . . There is continuity throughout—no sudden shifts, no 'new people.'" This description of LJCP is similar to Shumway et al. (1961:98) for the Scripps Estates site SDI-525, and follows the traditional Abandonment Model (e.g., initial SDCP occupation then abandonment, followed by LJCP and abandonment, followed by Yuman/Kumeyaay).

Dating of Rogers' San Dieguito Plateau and Lagoon Sites

Rogers recorded a number of sites within the area he identified as the San Dieguito Plateau, as well as a second area he identified as Shell-Midden (LJCP). The LJCP area includes North County lagoons from Agua Hedionda to Peñasquitos (see Figure 11). For the Agua Hedionda Lagoon, Batiquitos Lagoon, and San Dieguito Plateau Area I, Rogers recorded 19 sites as containing a SD component (see Figure 13 and Table 6). Radiocarbon dating of Rogers' SD sites produced a range of dates from ca. 3000 B.P. to Windsong Shores, dated to 8890 B.P. (2-sigma corrected date, 9930–9580 cal B.P.) (see previous discussion and Tables 1 and 2).

Given this Early to Middle Holocene range of radiocarbon dates for Rogers' SD sites, it appears that Rogers had a much broader time frame for what he identified as SD (see Figure 13 and Table 6). It should be noted that much of Rogers' work was conducted prior to radiocarbon dating. This broader range of Rogers' SDCP is also evident in his work at the Harris site, wherein he discussed a second locality, discovered in a section of the lime-cemented conglomerate that had been torn up exposing what Rogers describes as "an underlying stratum of sand containing marine shells and felsite flaking. Upon inspection it proved to be a San Dieguito III camp site which had miraculously escaped destruction while the heavy burden of cobbles was being washed over it" (Warren 1966:5). This stratum was named Locus II within the San Dieguito River channel (see Figure 6). Locus I, a result of the 1926 flood, was identified in 1928 by Rogers and both loci I and II were excavated by Rogers in 1938 with publication of Rogers' work posthumous in 1966 (Warren editor 1966). The presence of a granite dike and bedrock at the bottom of the channel served to trap water and provide the magnet that drew people to this location for over 9,000 years.

Warren's artifact descriptions for both Harris site loci I and II were based on the typology proposed by Warren and True (1961). Artifacts reported at Locus I E-Stratum (both Rogers and Warren identified this as SDCP) include 49 scrapers, 32 knives, four projectile points, one eccentric flake, one crescent (amulet), two cleavers, one chopper, and one core (Warren 1966:14–15, Table 1). Artifacts from Locus II (only Rogers identified this as SDCP) included: five scrapers, 10 knives and knife blanks, two projectile points, one round based knife, and one triangular perforator (Warren 1966:15–16, Table 1). One of the two points from Locus II was typed as "similar to Elko eared" (Warren 1966:16). One *Chione* sp. shell sample (LJ-136), collected in 1938 and submitted by Rogers in 1959 for radiocarbon dating, produced a date of 4720 ±160 B.P. Hubbs et al. (1960:220) reports: "*Chione* and *Argopecten* . . . made up 98% of the shells . . . found in limited number . . . Included also were a few pieces of the warm-water cockle Laevicardium elatum . . . Shells were in a sandy layer . . . below a concrete-like layer and before erosion was under ca. 5 m of valley fill . . . from the same sand layer Rogers took artifacts . . . notched points, etc., regarded by him [Rogers] as characteristic of what he has termed San Dieguito III" (Hubbs et al. 1960:220, Figure 14).

Rogers considered Locus I E-Stratum and Locus II coeval on the basis of geological grounds (Warren 1966:18). Warren argued for Locus I E-Stratum as solely representing the San Dieguito component and the radiocarbon date for Locus II as erroneous (Warren and True 1961:260) or "an intrusion of a culturally distinct group into an area already occupied by the La Jolla population" (Warren 1966:18). The differences here are important, as Rogers believed that Locus I E-Stratum and Locus II (Locus II) are both San Dieguito, while Warren identified only Locus I E-Stratum as SD. If both Locus I E-Stratum and Locus II are SD, then a long tradition (ca. 10,000–4000/3500 B.P.) of finely worked stone tools (SDCP) is recognized in perhaps the beginning and ending phases. However, if only Locus I E-Stratum is identified as SDCP, then a much smaller and tighter time frame (ca. 10,000–8000 B.P.) is used to identify the SD Harris site occupation and the tradition of finely worked stone tools. Also, using Rogers' broader SDCP timeframe, terms such as Pauma Complex, inland La Jolla, and intrusions from the desert (presently used to explain the finding of SD-like tools associated with younger than 8000 to 10,000 year radiocarbon dates) would not be necessary. Warren states that the "Pauma Complex, defined by True (1958) from the Pauma Valley area, while containing some San Dieguito traits appears to have much closer affiliation with the coastal La Jolla material, which suggests that it is a related inland complex" (Warren et al. 1961:262). True's Pauma Complex includes crude chipped stone implements, grinding tools, scrapers, biface knives/points and Elko points, with True stating that the chipped stone implements "reveal similarities to the San Dieguito complex" (True 1958:255). There is a difference in bifaces from Locus I E-Stratum and Locus II, but overall the patterns may represent the continuation of a lithic tradition of finely worked stone tools started over 9,000 years ago and continuing throughout the Early and Middle Holocene. This long tradition fits with both True's Pauma Complex, La Jolla Inland Hunting Tradition, and Rogers' San Dieguito Plateau sites. Brott (in Davis et al. 1969:9) supports the 4720 B.P. date and states: "We do not share his (Warren's) conservatism here, because the specimen was kept in closed containers in a basement laboratory. The specimen probably was not contaminated enough to alter greatly the date it yielded. Furthermore, artifacts stylistically similar to those found in Locus 2 [II] are found in La Jolla shell middens (Moriarty 1966), with corresponding dates. It is quite possible that we are uncovering the Hunting Mode or the Male-activity Mode of the La Jolla Pattern."

In support of Rogers' radiocarbon date for Locus II is the finding of an Elko point from SDI-532/4935A (a campsite within the Harris site National Register District), similar to the one Rogers recovered from Locus II. Carrico added: "Locally this style is generally considered, to be contemporaneous with, if not actually associated

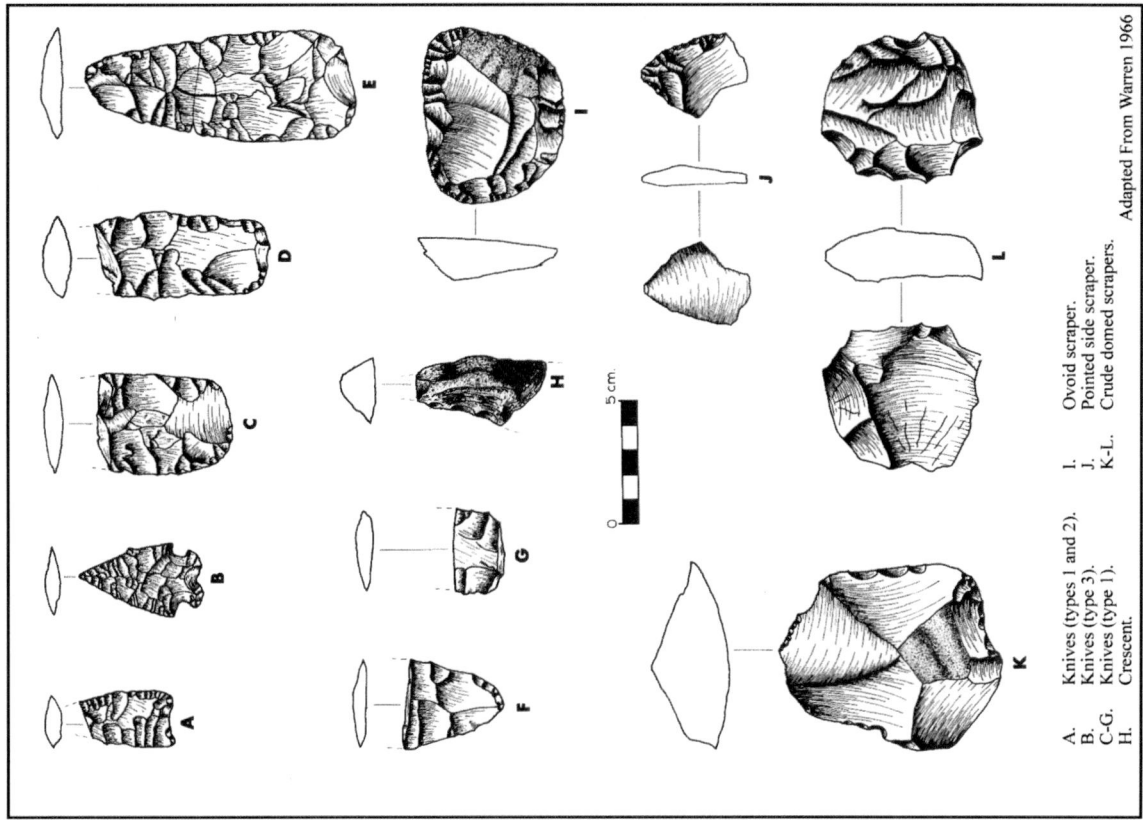

Harris Site, Locus II

A. Knives (types 1 and 2).
B. Knives (type 3).
C-G. Knives (type 1).
H. Crescent.
I. Ovoid scraper.
J. Pointed side scraper.
K-L. Crude domed scrapers.

Adapted From Warren 1966

Harris Site, Locus I E-Stratum

A-G. Knives (types 1 and 2).
H. Knives (type 3).
I. Knives (type 1).
J. Crescent.
K. Eccentric Flake.
M-N. Projectile point (type 1).
O. Projectile point (type 3).
P. Knife blank

Adapted From Warren 1966

Figure 14. Harris Site Artifacts: Locus I E-Stratum and Locus II

with, La Jollan period assemblages" (Carrico et al. 1991:7–34). The artifact assemblage for site SDI-532/4935A includes the Elko point, scraping tools, hammerstones, cores, debitage, manos, metates, and bone and shell. These artifacts represent hunting, vegetal processing, and food preparation activities, all of which would be associated with a La Jolla Complex site (Carrico et al. 1991:8–22).

Another site supporting the Elko date, SD-like artifacts, and the tradition of finely worked stone tools containing bifaces (knives/points and Elko points) is the Cactus Street site SDI-11424. This site, situated adjacent to a spring on Otay Mesa (Figure 15a), was dated using charcoal and shell from 7240 to 3380 B.P., with the majority of dates between 4690–3380 B.P. (Kyle et al. 1997). Artifacts recovered as a result of a testing program include 15,090 debitage, 48 bifaces, with 262 flake tools, 252 cores, 353 cobble tools, two abraders, 36 milling tools, and two *Olivella* sp. spire-removed beads. In all, 197 of the core/cobble tools are scrapers (including adze, scraper plane, and scraper), and these may be woodworking tools. It should be noted that another hallmark of the SDCP, as defined by Rogers, are scraping tools, wherein his first name for San Dieguito was Scraper-Maker. However scraping tools are not unique to a specific time and are found across Otay Mesa, dating from ca. 9000+ B.P. (Remington Hills site SDI-11079) to at least 3380 B.P. (Cactus Street site SDI-11424). It should be noted that no crescents were recovered from SDI-11424 or from Otay Mesa (OMPA) in general.

Fine-grained metavolcanic material, in cobble and boulder form, is available from the surface of Otay Mesa and from veins within the Santiago Peak Volcanic formation in the San Ysidro Mountains. Bifaces were primarily produced from local surface cobble materials and include all five stages of production: Stages 1 (early stage) through Stage 5 (finished knife or dart point) with: Stage 1, n = 23; Stage 2, n = 6; Stage 3, n = 5; Stage 4, n = 3; and Stage 5, n = 7 (1 Elko). Schroth and Flenniken (1997) conclude: "The occurrence of all five biface stages in the collection suggests that biface production was an important activity. . . . The breakage patterns exhibited by the Stage 5 bifaces are primarily damage from impact and use, and even some of the Stage 4 breakage may be from impact. Certainly point replacement appears to have been carried out, but the frequency of Stage 1 and Stage 2 bifaces to the finished points suggests that most of the production was geared to producing the early stage bifaces. These probably were carried away from the site to be used: as tools; to produce thin flakes for other tools: and, to ultimately be transformed into atlatl points or knives, as attrition, resharpening, and reduction for flake tools decreased their size (Schroth and Flenniken 1997) . . . similar to the Stahl Site (Schroth 1994)." Using protein residue analysis, two bifaces tested positive for deer, and one biface tested positive for agave. Faunal remains include shellfish taken from rocky, sandy, and lagoonal habitats as well as bird bone and small to large mammal bone.

The San Dieguito Plateau site SDI-4405 (the La Costa site) was radiocarbon dated 6140 ±80, 6900 ±120, and 7070 +100 (Beta 11105, 11106, 11107) (Gallegos and Carrico 1985). This single deposit locality within site SDI-4405 produced a hearth, radiocarbon dates, and a number of artifacts primarily within four adjacent units. Artifacts associated with this feature include four large bifaces, one crescent, two *Olivella* sp. beads, nine scrapers, six cobble tools, 19 hammerstones, five cores, 15 manos, and one complete metate (see Table 7 and Figure 15b). Faunal materials include: 3,583 g of shell (primarily *Chione* sp. and *Argopecten* sp., 92 percent), crab claw fragments, and 6.25 g of small to large mammal bone. This collection fits well with a complete tool kit (Non-transition Model) and faunal remains for the inhabitants of the San Dieguito Plateau circa 7000–6000 B.P.

Crescents, (also referred to as crescentics, eccentric crescentics, amulets and ceremonial stones) identified as one of the hallmarks of the SDCP, are found at a number of Rogers' San Dieguito Plateau sites: Harris site SDI-149 Locus I E-Stratum; Rancho Park North SDI-4392/W-49A; Scraper-Maker Hill SDI-13327/W-180; North Hill W-181; Rogers Ridge SDI-4845/W-182; Scraper Hill SDI-8330/W-240; as well as the Agua Hedionda sites Windsong Shores SDI-10965/W-131 and the Allan O. Kelly site SDI-9649 that produced the California State Artifact, a bear-shaped eccentric crescentic (Gallegos 1991; Koerper et al. 1986) (see Figure 12).

Figure 15a. Bifaces from Cactus Street Site SDI-11424.

Taken from Kyle et al. 1997

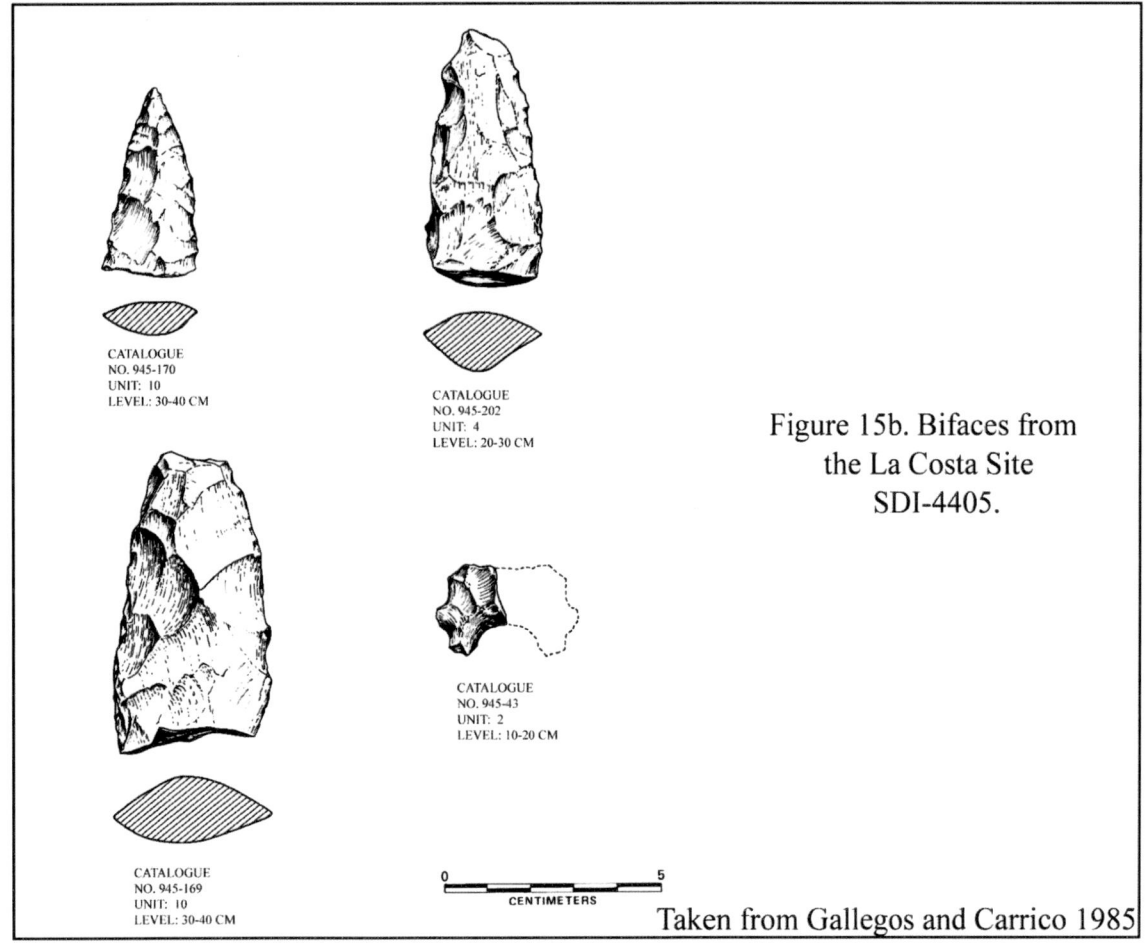

Figure 15b. Bifaces from the La Costa Site SDI-4405.

Taken from Gallegos and Carrico 1985

Figure 15. Bifaces from Cactus Street SDI-11424 and La Costa Site SDI-4405.

Jertberg (1986) identified 32 crescents in SDC, primarily located south of the San Luis Rey River valley and north of Peñasquitos Lagoon (see Figures 11 and 12). Crescents are generally identified as dating over 7000 B.P. (Fenenga and Hopkins 2010). However, the Legoland site SDI-12814, located near Agua Hedionda, produced a number of radiocarbon dates taken on charcoal from hearths resting on the Pleistocene marine terrace. These dates documented the hearths and all cultural materials including five crescents not older than 4460 B.P. years ago (Gallegos et al. 1999) (Figure 12). For crescents, identified as part of the SDCP, this may be the youngest dated site with crescents, or perhaps these artifacts were taken from earlier sites and reused at SDI-12814. However, given the number of crescents, this was not a random act. What is noticeable is the number of crescents within the San Dieguito Plateau and the absence of crescents within the Otay Management Plan Area. The OMPA is an area of approximately 10,000 acres situated east of the Pacific Ocean, north of the US-Mexico border, east of Otay Mountain, and south of the Otay River valley. This area includes over 300 archaeological sites dated from 10,000 B.P. to historic contact (Gallegos et al. 1998) (see Figure 7). The OMPA does have SDCP bifaces and scrapers but not the crescent. Scrapers are also referred to by Flenniken as steep edge unifacial tools (SEUTs).

Ezell, discussing the recording of sites using the Harris "type site" and chronology states: "As workers after Rogers attempted to relate an increasing number of sites in southern California (and beyond) to the assemblage found at the Harris Site, the framework proposed by Rogers became ever more entrenched in our (often unstated) set of premises. Consequently, a growing number of sites came to be identified as either San Dieguito with-a-difference, or as something other than San Dieguito" (Ezell 1987:16). This was especially true with sites containing SD finely worked stone tools, cobble tools, milling tools, and radiocarbon dates younger than 8000 B.P.

Rogers vs. Warren: San Dieguito Cultural Pattern

Rogers and Warren had different views of the San Dieguito cultural pattern. On the basis of dating and reviewing Rogers' SD sites, it is apparent that Rogers had a more generous time frame and view of what should be included into SDCP with respect to finely made finished tools that included bifaces (knives/points), crescents, scrapers, and Elko points, given that he included both Harris site Locus I E-Stratum, and Locus II. These loci represent a lithic tradition started over 9,000 years ago and continued to ca. 4,000 years ago with minor changes in the lithic assemblage over a long period of time. Warren had a more defined view, focusing on what was recovered from Locus I E-Stratum, dated ca. 10,000 to 8,000 B.P. and generally associated with inland/Great Basin WPLT/WSPT. It should be noted that neither Rogers nor Warren included cobble-based tools, milling tools, burials, or coastal resources of shellfish and fish into the SDCP. However, more recently Warren has included milling tools, into his SDCP (Warren et al. 1998).

Hanna's master's thesis (1982) provides a better understanding of Malcolm Rogers' strong personality through the following interviews with his staff, fellow workers, and researchers: "He was quite careful and his field methods were for that time, I think, quite good ... He made many changes ... He was continually trying to adjust his chronology and he changed his terminology a number of times" (Hanna 1982:173). However, of interest to chronology is the comment by Informant 4 stating: "Rogers simply sorted his material 'to fit his notions.' Corroboration is provided by two informants, who describe Rogers' 1959 and 1960 review of the Campbell's collections at the Southwest Museum and William J. Wallace's collections at the University of Southern California ... In both instances, Rogers laid the artifacts out and proceeded to group them according to his 'complexes,' 'industries,' and formal types. The artifacts were primarily flaked and ground lithic specimens. Rogers' groups did not match the stratigraphic sequence of artifacts which had been recovered from carefully excavated deposits.... This is described by one informant ... as follows: We had excavated a rockshelter ... It was a stratified site, or appeared to be, and we had all the artifacts laid out on long tables by levels. Malcolm Rogers took a look at it and he said,

'Well, this item doesn't belong here' and that sort of thing ... He was going on typology alone and not paying any attention to the fact that they clustered together and when you had them in a certain level, obviously they had to be of certain age. That's all it amounted to: and you couldn't convince him. The one thing that stands out in my mind was, there were some great milling stones that were quite deep down in the cave deposit. He said, 'No, those had to come way up high because you didn't get milling stones that early" (Hanna 1982:375).

In all, 71 sites in SDC have been identified by Rogers as SD or sites with a SD component. Whereas, Warren's recorded San Dieguito sites, from 1966 to 1998, only included the Harris site SDI-149 Locus I E-Stratum. More recently, Warren et al. (1998) identified four additional San Dieguito sites (SDI-9956, SDI-6087, SDI-4937, and Gladishill) on the basis of type and number of artifacts (Table 8). Except for the Gladishill site, sites SDI-9956, SDI-6087, and SDI-4937 are similar to the Harris site Locus I E-Stratum containing primarily bifaces (33%–43%) and scrapers (33%–43%), but also contain a few milling tools (4%–7%) (Table 8). Whereas the Gladishill site is 59% scrapers, 24% milling tools, and 16% bifaces. Warren et al. (1998:II-44) states: "The Gladishill site looks like a San Dieguito site with fewer bifaces, greater number of unifaces and a heavy (for San Dieguito) emphasis on milling equipment." The Gladishill site is located in Valley Center and was recorded by True and Bouey (1990). The surface collection produced 2,121 artifacts with most (n = 1997) being debitage, with only 124 identified as formal tools. Analysis of the debitage suggested mostly percussion flaking, biface production was not important at this locus, and that little or no primary tool manufacture took place on site (True and Bouey 1990). Formal tools are primarily scrapers (n = 57), which are divided into domed (9), irregular domed (25), heavy irregular flake scrapers (12), thumbnail scraper (1), and scraper planes (4). Bifaces included cutting (9) and projectile points (5). The remaining artifacts and ecofacts included worked flakes (18), one core, one core hammer, one plane/grinder, one shaped schist disc, groundstone (19 manos and one metate) and two shells (possible abalone and clam). In True's general discussion he states: "[T]his site appears to be the first site from the Valley Center region which is clearly dominated by artifacts with apparent San Dieguito affiliations. San Dieguito elements are known from sites in the larger area, but typically they are represented by isolated or small members of San Dieguitolike artifacts in assemblages dominated by Milling Stone-related artifacts. . . . The presence of Milling Stone elements in what appears to be direct association with a substantially pure San Dieguitolike assemblage is of particular interest. This relationship has long been a bone of contention and represents one of the most important interpretational issues related to the San Dieguito pattern. Many surface manifestations of San Dieguito sites have Milling Stone elements in what appear to be direct association or in immediately adjacent contexts. Because of this, some scholars are convinced that milling elements are a proper part of the San Dieguito inventory. In contrast, the data from the Harris site seem to support a separation of the two, with San Dieguito being the earliest of two clearly defined components. . . . Second, any attempt to deal with these contextual relationships requires some definition of San Dieguito as a cultural entity: what it is or is not, and how it relates to the larger regional and area prehistory" (True and Bouey 1990:24).

Except for the Harris site Locus I E-Stratum, none of these additional sites have been radiocarbon dated to verify Warren's revised Initial Period of 10,500–8000 B.P. (Warren et al. 1998:II-26). Sites SDI-9956, SDI-6087, and SDI-4937 identified by Warren et al. (1998) as SDCP are comparable in types of artifacts, but may simply represent special-use tool production activity sites and not a full representation of an Early Holocene WPLT/WSPT habitation site, such as Windsong Shores SDI-10965 or San Dieguito Plateau sites. Defining the Harris site SDI-149 as being neither a quarry nor a habitation site, but a workshop with temporary campsites where Stage 3 tool production activities were conducted as part of the production cycle of stone tools provides a better understanding of this site and its placement in time.

Cultural Material	SDI-149 C.W. Harris Site				SDI-9956		SDI-6087		SDI-4937		Gladishill		San Dieguito Summary	
	Locus I E-Stratum		Locus II										Total**	Total**
	Count	Percent	Count	Percent	Count	Percent	Count	Percent	Count	Percent	Count	Percent	Count	Percent
Biface/Knife/Point	90	46.88%	13	72.22%	100	43.10%	18	33.33%	17	36.96%	14	15.91%	239	39.05%
Crescent	2	1.04%	0	0.00%	5	2.16%	0	0.00%	0	0.00%	0	0.00%	7	1.14%
Scraper	97	50.52%	5	27.78%	100	43.10%	18	33.33%	16	34.78%	52	59.09%	283	46.24%
Hammer/Choppers	0	0.00%	0	0.00%	4	1.72%	11	20.37%	0	0.00%	0	0.00%	15	2.45%
Core	3	1.56%	0	0.00%	6	2.59%	5	9.26%	11	23.91%	1	1.14%	26	4.25%
Mano	0	0.00%	0	0.00%	17	7.33%	2	3.70%	2	4.35%	21	23.86%	42	6.86%
Total*	192		18		232		54		46		88		612	

* Does not include debitage

Number of Units	Trench	Trench	
C-14 Dates, Years B.P.	8490, 8490, 9030	4720 B.P.	
Notes:		Elko Point Locus II was added for comparative purposes and was dated to 4720 B.P.	

			No Dates	No Dates	No Dates	Surface Collection No Dates Shellfish: Abalone Clam
Site Type: San Dieguito	Warren	Rogers	Warren	Warren	True, Warren	
Source	Warren et al. 1998	Warren 1966	Warren et al. 1998	Warren et al. 1998	True & Bouey 1990	

Note:
Only one of Warren's five San Dieguito sites has been dated.

**Locus II, Component not included in totals

Data for sites SDI-149 Locus I E-Stratum, SDI-9956, SDI-6087, SDI-4937 taken from Warren et al. 1998
Selected cultural material listed followed Warren et al. 1998.

Table 8. Site Summaries for Warren's San Dieguito Sites.

As Rabbi Erv Herman (personal communication 1994) once said, "And you're right too." Rogers, as based on his identification of sites on the San Dieguito Plateau and Harris site Locus I E-Stratum and Locus II may have been right when he identified the San Dieguito Tradition of finely worked stone tools continuing from ca. 10,000 to 4,000 B.P. in San Diego County. And, Warren is right in identifying the SDCP tool kit to WPLT. However, the Western Pluvial Lakes Tradition ended in the Early Holocene when the Pleistocene Lakes dried up, leaving behind a record of finely made stone tools and occupation near Great Basin lakes dating over 8,000 years ago in the Great Basin/California interior. The biface tradition has a very long history in the West, and only starts and stops in areas dependent on the presence/absence of water and the need to move from drying inland locations to locations with water and resources that sustain life. It appears that this tradition of finely made stone tools (e.g., San Dieguito Plateau) continued into the Middle Holocene/Archaic and perhaps the Late Holocene.

Summary

Rogers' view of San Dieguito was different from Warren's in that Rogers believed that both Locus I E-Stratum (dated ca. 10,000–8000 B.P.) and Locus II (dated ca. 4720 B.P., and containing an Elko point) were San Dieguito. Whereas Warren only identified Locus I E-Stratum dated to the Early Holocene as San Dieguito and did not accept Locus II as SD given the presence of the Elko point and radiocarbon date of 4720 B.P. Given that Rogers identified 71 sites (19 in north SDC) as having a SD component, and Warren identified five sites as San Dieguito, it is apparent that Rogers had a broader temporal and artifact type definition for San Dieguito; and, Warren had a more narrow temporal and artifact type range for San Dieguito. The differences between the Harris site to the San Dieguito Plateau Locus I sites are discussed below.

The Harris site both Locus I E-Stratum and Locus II primarily contain bifaces and scrapers (90+ percent). San Dieguito Plateau sites also contain San Dieguito bifaces, crescents and, scrapers, but also contain milling tools, cobble tools, shell, hearths, and burials that Rogers, Warren, and others identified as mixed SDCP and LJCP sites. Rogers did most of his recording of sites prior to radiocarbon dating, and only after the 1960s have sites on the San Dieguito Plateau been radiocarbon dated. By viewing the dates for Rogers' San Dieguito sites, it is apparent that Rogers had a longer time frame for his San Dieguito than Warren. The inclusion of the Gladishill site by Warren et al. (1998) into his San Dieguito sites provides the inclusion of milling as a major component along with bifaces, scraping tools, and shell into his acceptable San Dieguito sites. With the stronger milling component and therein more complexity, the Gladishill site is more similar to sites on the San Dieguito Plateau than the Harris site Locus I E-Stratum or Warren's San Dieguito sites SDI-9956, SDI-6087, and SDI-4937 (see Table 7). As shell was recovered from the Gladishill site, radiocarbon dating is important for the placement in time for this site.

As previously discussed, the Harris site is identified as a workshop with temporary camping where Stage 3 tool production activities were conducted. The San Dieguito Plateau sites are habitation sites and the probable destination for bifaces and scraping tools made at the Harris site. If the San Dieguito Plateau sites are viewed as single component habitation sites, then artifacts and ecofacts from these sites represent a wide range of activities conducted to hunt, fish, collect, and process lagoon and coastal foothill plant and animal resources dating from ca. 9000–4000/3500 B.P. and represent Early to Middle Holocene occupation.

The Harris site SDI-149 Locus I E-Stratum is primarily represented by bifaces (45 percent) and scrapers (48 percent). A contrasting and perhaps a more realistic view of SD occupation on the San Dieguito Plateau circa Early and Middle Holocene is shown on Table 7 summary totals without the Harris site. The composition of San Dieguito Plateau sites without the Harris site are: utilized flakes 28%, scrapers 23%, cores 20%, milling tools 12%, bifaces 7.5%, hammerstones 6.6%, choppers 1.7%, crescents 0.3%, shell beads 0.2%, bone tools 0.1%, and burials. Faunal and flora remains include lagoon shell, fish bone, small to large mammal bone, and milling tools representing processing of plant foods.

Warren (Warren et al. 1998) proposed five models to explain the initial occupation and the following occupations, as well as LJ and SD cultural patterns within the same space and time. All of these models are based on SD as First People. The first three models assume two separate cultural phases by two populations. The last two models assume two cultural phases by one population. These models include:

Abandonment (Model 1) —*The SDCP peoples left the area before the LJCP arrived.*

Comment: Given the continuous radiocarbon-dated archaeological sites for the past 10,000+ years in SDC, abandonment cannot be supported.

Displacement (Model 2)—*The LJCP rapidly displaced the SDCP cultural pattern by force or competition for resources.*

Comment: This hypothesis would be difficult to prove or disprove unless DNA identified a change in people. It is interesting to note that only burials are identified with the LJCP. No human remains/burials are identified to the SDCP. However, there is no evidence (e.g., multiple burials with cause of death due to atlatl, knives, or clubs) representing warfare that would have caused displacement. Also, LJCP sites have been radiocarbon dated equal to, or earlier than, SDCP sites.

Acculturation (Model 3) —*The SD and LJ cultural patterns were present in SDC at the same time, and through a process of acculturation the SDCP changed to the LJCP.*

Comment: This hypothesis does not account for the continuation of SDCP within the San Dieguito Plateau dated from ca. 9000–4000/3500 B.P. The acculturation model may be better explained through amalgamation of SD and LJ people, with coastal areas represented by the efficient use of local cobble tools required for coastal resources; and San Dieguito Plateau representing the use of milling and cobble tools of local materials; and bifaces, scraping tools, and crescents primarily of fine-grained metavolcanic material for coastal and inland/foothill resources.

Transformation (Model 4) —*The SDCP became the LJCP through adaptation to the coastal environment.*

Comment: This assumes SDCP as First People who adapted to coastal resources and changed their tool kit to efficiently collect and process primarily shellfish and fish. Early Holocene LJAA sites show little evidence of a basal SDCP and a transformation.

Non-transition (Model 5) —*The SDCP and LJCP represent two modes of behavior [cultural pattern] within a single culture system.*

Comment: If this single culture system is represented by both SDCP and LJCP tools, and the use of these tools reflects coastal and/or inland plant and animal resources sought and processed, then Non-transition is a viable model. Another form of Non-transition to explain the LJCP and SDCP assemblages is presented by McDonald and Eighmey (1998:III-16) wherein they state: "[A] lithic industry that appears to be focused more on utilization of materials procured closer to residential base [or use location] [and] the manufacture and transport of large bifaces and bifacial cores is retained. . . . These two patterns of reduction debris, the 'expedient local' [LJCP] and the 'specialized logistical' [SDCP] . . . may in fact delineate two or more sets of toolkits; those which are not curated and are used for general tasks and left on site [LJCP], and those which are maintainable and are transported from site to site [SDCP]" (Bamforth 1991). This would leave a campsite with a complete "expedient local" cobble-based tool kit, and an incomplete "specialized logistical" tool kit wherein formal tools such as bifaces and crescents are curated and moved to the next task locality/campsite.

All five models proposed by Warren discussed above assume SDCP as First People arriving by an inland route. However, given the work by Erlandson and others, a coastal initial occupation is possible and added here as models 6 and 7 with LJCP as First People.

Model 6 (Non-transition LJCP First People) identifies the LJCP as initially occupying the La Jolla Archaeological Area, given the deep La Jolla and Scripps submarine canyons, which would have been accessible with lower sea level, especially 12,000 to 8,000 years ago. In Model 6, the LJCP may have added SDCP tools for the purpose of better exploiting and processing inland resources.

Model 7 (Amalgamation) also identifies the LJCP as First People probably in the La Jolla Archaeological Area, but with an intrusion into SDC by a people as represented by SDCP leaving the Great Basin drying lakes (e.g., Lake Mojave and Silver Lake) ca. 10,000 to 9,000 years ago and settling in north SDC as represented at Agua Hedionda (Windsong SDI-10965 and UCLJ-M-15), and the Harris site (SDI-149 Locus I E-Stratum). Model 7 is more complex but would be a better fit to explain the cultural assemblage and amalgamation of LJCP and SDCP (e.g., milling tools, cobble tools, flake tools, bifaces, scrapers, crescents, *Olivella* sp. spire-removed beads, hearths, burials, and faunal remains of shell, fish bone, and small to large mammal bone) found at sites situated just east of Agua Hedionda, Batiquitos, San Elijo, and San Dieguito lagoons, an area identified by Rogers as the San Dieguito Plateau (Rogers 1929). The San Dieguito Plateau appears to represent multiple modes of behavior (LJCP and SDCP) to best hunt, collect, and process a wide range of coastal and foothill/inland resources, beginning ca. 9000+ B.P. and continuing this tradition to ca. 4000/3500 B.P.

Also, the people (as represented by SDCP and LJCP) may have been related, as the earliest language proposed for California is Hokan, and this is the same language stock used by the Yuman/Kumeyaay. The SDC coastal people, if related to inland people using the same language or closely related language, would have traded and traveled to interior Great Basin/desert lands on a regular basis. For example, coastal to inland trade and travel is documented by *Olivella* sp. spire-removed beads found on Early Holocene SDC sites, as well as sites in the Great Basin (Oregon, Washington, Nevada, and Utah) to the Channel Islands (Fitzgerald, Jones, and Schroth 2005); also, obsidians and cherts have been traded to the coast from the eastern Sierras/Great Basin region.

Chapters 1-3 provided discussions on the Early and Middle Holocene occupation of SDC. Chapter 4 discusses the Late Holocene beginning ca. 3500, and the Late Period occupation (ca. 1300 B.P. to historic contact).

CHAPTER 4
Late Holocene and Late Period Occupation

The previous chapters focused on Early and Middle Holocene occupation in SDC, primarily within the Maritime and Coastal climate zones, an area that makes up less than 10 percent of SDC. However, during the Early and Middle Holocene, this coastal region may have been the most productive biological area for plants, shellfish, fish, birds, and mammals, given the submarine canyons, open and flushing lagoons, and coastal river valleys. At the end of the Middle Holocene and during the Late Holocene, there is a change in land use, as a number of north SDC lagoons (e.g., Agua Hedionda, Batiquitos, San Elijo, and San Dieguito) silted in, and with this resource loss, the Late Period (1300 B.P. to historic contact) occupants changed their settlement pattern and resource focus and adapted to this environmental change by increasing use of plant and animal resources, not only in the Maritime and Coastal climate zones, but across San Diego County including Interior, Transitional and SDC Desert climate zones, with increased habitation and land use near oaks and grassland resources.

Climate and Setting

The end of the Middle Holocene ca. 4000–2500 B.P. was a period of cooler temperatures and higher rainfall (West et al. 2007), followed by a dry period from 2800–1850 cal B.P. (Mensing et al. 2013), followed by the Medieval Climatic Anomaly (warm period) from 1200–750 cal B.P. (Mensing et al. 2013), and then the Little Ice Age ca. 750–150 B.P. (West et al. 2007). More threatening to north SDC's LJCP population's coastal way of life was the stabilization of sea level ca. 4000–3000 B.P. and lateral sand and cobble transport blocking lagoon mouths, and the resulting filling of lagoons with silt and the concomitant loss of lagoon resources of shellfish and fish as documented by Miller's core study at Batiquitos Lagoon and Byrd's work at San Elijo Lagoon (Byrd et al. 2004; Gallegos 1985; Miller 1966; Warren and Pavesic 1963). The combination of lagoons closing followed by a dry period is reflected by the near absence of archaeological sites at Agua Hedionda, Batiquitos, San Elijo and San Dieguito lagoons ca. 3500–1580 B.P. The opening of lagoons ca. 1580–1000 B.P. may have been caused by increased rainfall and flooding to the level necessary to open the mouths of these lagoons. Given radiocarbon dated sites adjacent to Batiquitos Lagoon, it appears that this lagoon was open from ca. 1580–505 B.P., and San Elijo was open from ca. 1050–650 B.P. However, Peñasquitos Lagoon and Tijuana Lagoon did not close, and along with San Diego Bay and Spindrift in La Jolla, these areas demonstrate continuous occupation throughout the Late Holocene. It should be noted that sites W-5, W-9, and W-12 within the LJAA appear to have been abandoned ca. 5,000 to 3,000 years ago along with the loss of rocky shore shellfish population. San Diego Bay, the largest natural bay in Southern California, was created ca. 6000 B.P. by sand transport and wave shadow effect around Point Loma, as well as by Tijuana River sand transported north along the Silver Strand Beach that together created the bay, leaving the mouth of the bay protected from closure by the shadow effect of Point Loma (Masters 1988:4–18). The Middle Holocene creation of San Diego Bay increased marine resources that continued through the Late Holocene, and likely made up for the loss of north SDC lagoon resources. However, ca. 1,500 to 1,000 years ago, the north SDC lagoons reopened to function as shallow lagoons/mudflats, but not at the level of productivity during the Early and Middle Holocene. Around this same time (ca. 1500–1000 B.P.), Northern Uto-Aztecan (NUA) appear in north SDC, having expanded south from the areas presently referred to as the Los Angeles Basin and Orange County.

Another major environmental event during the Late Holocene was the Colorado River flooding of the Imperial Valley. This resulted in the creation of Lake Cahuilla, a freshwater lake approximately 161 km long by 56 km wide (115 by 35 mi.) when full to the 12 m (40 ft.) shoreline. This lake, located approximately 129 km (80 mi.) east of San Diego Bay, and adjacent and east of SDC, provided excellent habitat for shellfish, fish, birds, and various mammals. Flooding created at least one full lake stand ca. 2600 B.P. and ca. 1250 B.P. (Waters 1983); and filled at least three times between ca. 750–250 B.P. (Laylander 1997). The presence of a lake in the desert the size of Lake Cahuilla, ca. 1250 B.P., could well have been the attraction for the NUA/Takic moving south into the Imperial Valley. A lake this large and rich in food resources also brought the Kumeyaay east from SDC to the lake, as well as Yumans from the Colorado River area to exploit shellfish, fish, birds, mammals, and plants (see Figure 10). The last full stand of Lake Cahuilla is dated to ca. A.D. 1700 (250 B.P.) (Laylander 1997).

Northern Uto-Aztecan-Takic Movement into Southern California

Sutton (2009) proposed a model of Takic language prehistory deriving from Northern Uto-Aztecan (NUA) moving into the western Mojave Desert, the southern Sierra Nevada, and perhaps the southern San Joaquin Valley ca. 5000–3500 B.P. By ca. 3500 B.P., the NUA branched out and moved into Southern California/Los Angeles Basin, southern Channel Islands, and Orange County. This intrusion replaced the existing Millingstone (Hokan, proto-Yuman) populations (north of SDC) (Sutton 2009:65). Circa 2500–1500 B.P., cremation and large mourning features appear; and, by ca. 1500–1000 B.P., the Gabrielino language diffused south and becomes the foundation for Luiseño, Cahuilla, and Cupeño (Sutton 2009:68). Kennett et al. (2007) hypothesizes the expansion of NUA on very dry conditions in western North America between 6,300 and 4,800 years ago. In addition to the NUA expansion west, Penutian groups were moving south into the northern San Joaquin Valley ca. 3500 B.P., pushing or absorbing both the NUA and Hokan groups to the south (Moratto 1984:560; Sutton 2009). Due to the value of oaks/acorns ca. 5000 B.P., Krantz (1978:64) identified the "acorn revolution" in Northern California, with Penutian pressure reaching the Takic Kitanemuk in the Tehachapi Mountains ca. 2000 B.P., causing them to "overrun their neighbors for a considerable distance to the south." Therefore, the causal factors for NUA movement have been hypothesized as drought in the western North America during the Middle Holocene and the attraction of oak resources; as well as, a people (NUA) coming from the desert and being more efficient and outcompeting for island and coastal resources of Southern California (Cochran 1965:87). The effects in the central part of California, affected the Hokan/Yuman in the northern, central, and southern portions of California, with both the Penutians and NUA enlarging their territories and Hokan/Yuman/Kumeyaay lands becoming smaller and more fragmented.

Even in a major drought, SDC had sufficient water and resources to sustain life, and was more hospitable than the hotter, drier desert. The movement by Takic speakers into San Diego County may have been the overall result of drought and the attraction of grasslands, oaks, and acorns. Christenson (1990:301) reports that basic nutritional requirements could be met using only acorns and rabbits (rabbits and hares). By the Late Holocene-Late Period, acorns were a primary food resource for both the Luiseño and Kumeyaay.

NUA Expansion, Obsidian Trade, Bow and Arrow, and Takic/Luiseño Movement into SDC

During the Early to Middle Holocene, high-quality obsidian from the Coso Volcanic Field (southeastern side of the Sierras) was the primary source for SDC obsidian (see Figure 10). Specific obsidian sources include: Sugarloaf, West Sugarloaf, Mono Craters, Mono Glass, Casa Diablo, Fish Springs, and Mt. Hicks. This obsidian trade network may have been in place as early as 10,000– 9000 B.P., given the obsidian recovered from Windsong Shores site SDI-10965, dated to 9930–9580 cal B.P. containing both Coso obsidian and Casa Diablo obsidian, and Remington Hills site SDI-11079 dated 10,625–10,250 cal B.P. with Coso obsidian. The end of north-south obsidian trade into SDC may coincide with NUA expansion into the southern Sierras and Los Angeles Basin ca. 5000–3500 B.P. The time period 1500–1000 B.P. for the movement of Luiseños into north SDC appears to fit well with the archaeological record, along with the introduction of the bow and arrow. Yohe's (1998:28) research identifies the bow and arrow as diffusing into the Mojave Desert from the north ca. 1500 B.P. (uncorrected dates: 1360 ±70/UCR2535; and 1400 ±70/UCR2324). NUA expansion into north SDC could account for the introduction of the bow and arrow; increased use of acorns; and the loss of Sierra/Coso obsidian trade.

Languages and Boundaries

The Hokan phylum is the oldest of the North American languages, and is found in subclusters from Oregon to southern Mexico (Golla 2007:78) (see Figure 10). Hokan is the language of the Kumeyaay (also previously referred to as Diegueño and Yuman) and most of SDC is represented by Kumeyaay Ipai in the north/central, and Kumeyaay Tipai in the south (Figure 16). Late Holocene-Late Period Kumeyaay occupation is documented for most of SDC, however Luiseño occupation may have influenced its southern neighbor as early as 3,000 years ago; and, Luiseño villages are present in north SDC after ca. 1300 B.P. Kroeber (1925) defines the northern boundary for the Kumeyaay and southern boundary for the Luiseño (Uto-Aztecan/Takic) between Agua Hedionda and Batiquitos Lagoon and this boundary continued east from the ocean to the desert. The northern boundary for the Kumeyaay Tipai begins near San Diego Bay and generally follows the San Diego River valley. Shipek (1993) identifies the southern boundary for the Kumeyaay in Baja ca. 100 miles south of the US-Mexico border.

Late Period: Site Type, Density and Distribution

In the Late Period, the number of sites appears to increase suggesting a more intensive occupation. This could be the result of more recent sites not buried by silt and sediment, as opposed to Early and Middle Holocene sites being buried and therein masked/hidden from the archaeological record. This hypothesis of SDC being more intensively occupied, especially in the inland areas during the Late Period, cannot be quantified. However, radiocarbon-dated sites, as well as sites containing Late Period time markers of ceramics and arrow points, generally supports this view (Figure 17). In addition, the 2008 SDG&E Sunrise Powerlink Northern Corridor survey 250 km long (155 linear miles) across north SDC provides a view of site type and site density from the coast to the desert (Noah and Gallegos 2008). The record search and survey for this study began at the coast (Peñasquitos Lagoon); continued east/northeast through coastal foothills and Peninsular Range; continued adjacent to the Anza-Borrego Desert State Park, and then turned south, ending in the Imperial Valley. (IV) The Class I record search for the San Diego coast to the desert portion of the study area (148 sq mi.) produced 754 archaeological sites and a general perspective of site types and density across San Diego County. The results of the SDC record search identified the following site type percentages: Bedrock Milling (23%), Lithic Scatter (12.9%), Isolate Find (12.6%), Temporary Camp (12.2%), Artifact Scatter (6.2%), Habitation (5.6%), Roasting Pit (4.9%), Ceramic Scatter (3.7%), Rock Feature (2.9%), Shell Midden (1.1%), Rock Shelter (0.5%), Quarry (0.5%), and Trail (0.1%) (Figure 18). Many of these sites reflect Late Period occupation.

Modeling provides a tool to better understand site patterning across SDC. For this study, modeling used climate zones (SDC Natural Resource Shape File) as a general proxy for variables to evaluate the relationship of site types to landform, geology, and biology, included maritime, coastal, transitional, interior, and SDC and Imperial County desert zones (Figure 19). Site types dominating each climate zone are: (a) Temporary Camp and Shell Midden in the Maritime Zone; (b) Temporary Camp and Habitation in the Coastal Zone; (c) Bedrock Milling,

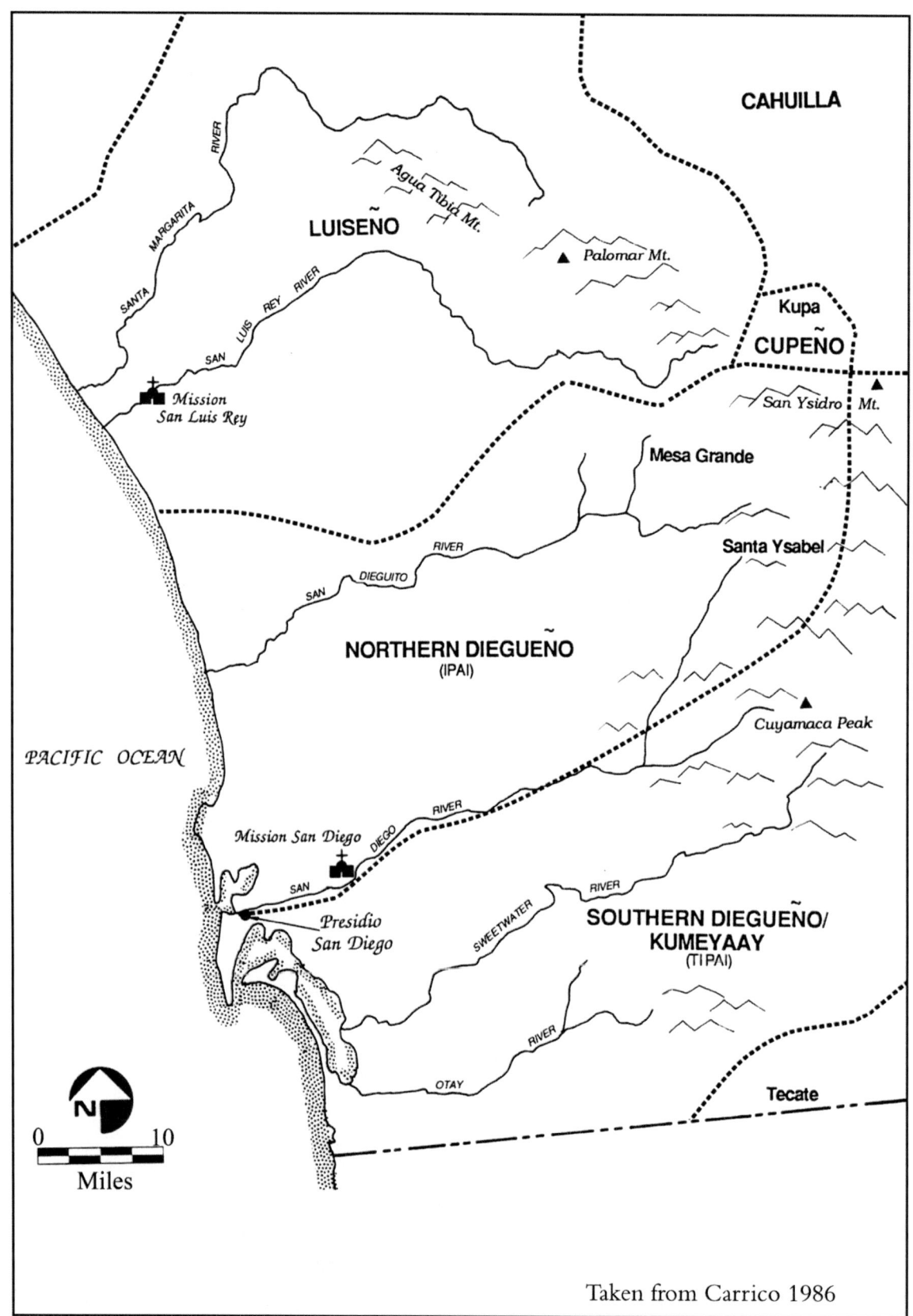

Figure 16. Kumeyaay and Luiseño Boundary Map.

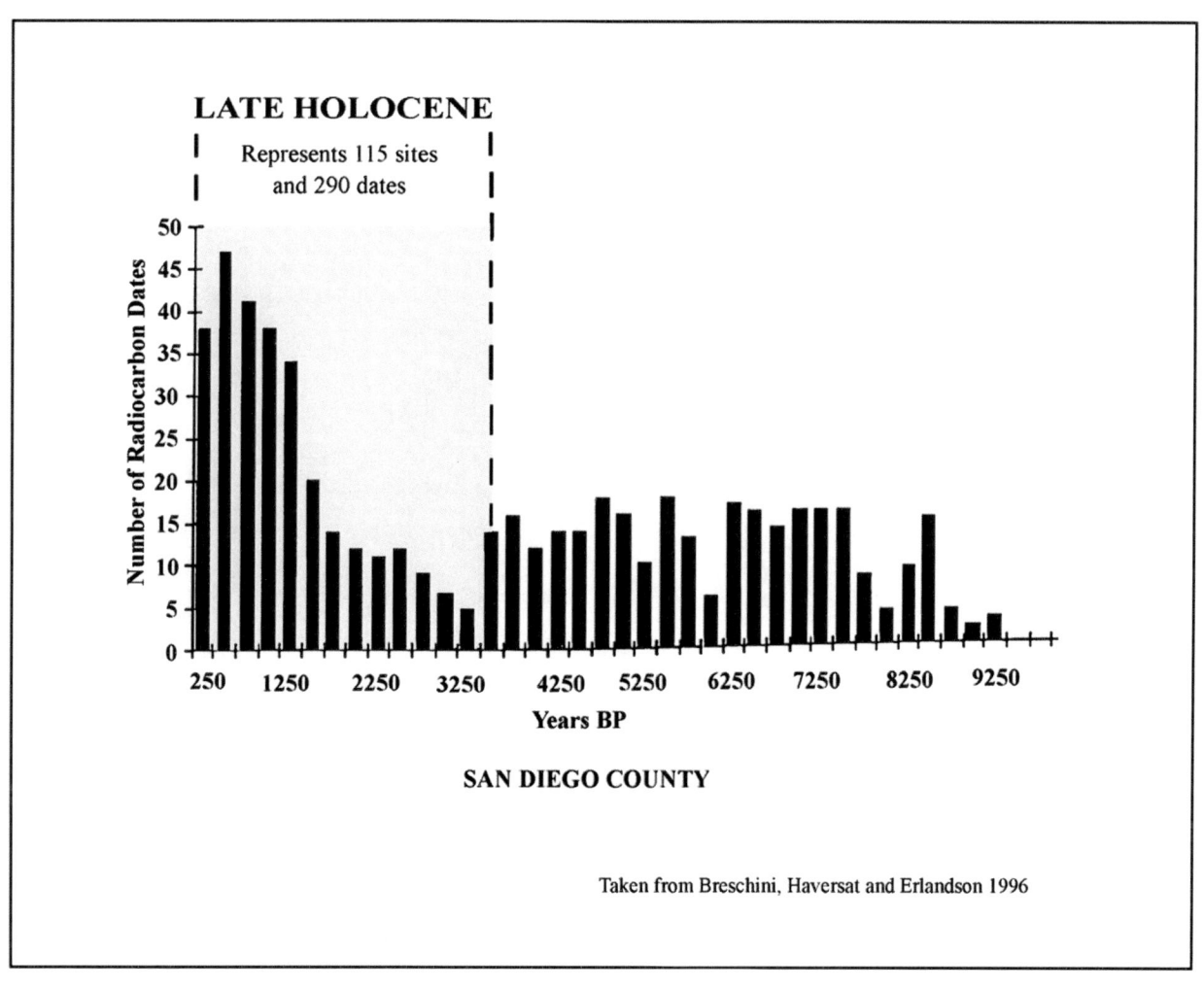

Figure 17. Late Holocene Radiocarbon Dated Sites in San Diego County.

Figure 18. Site Type and Artifacts.

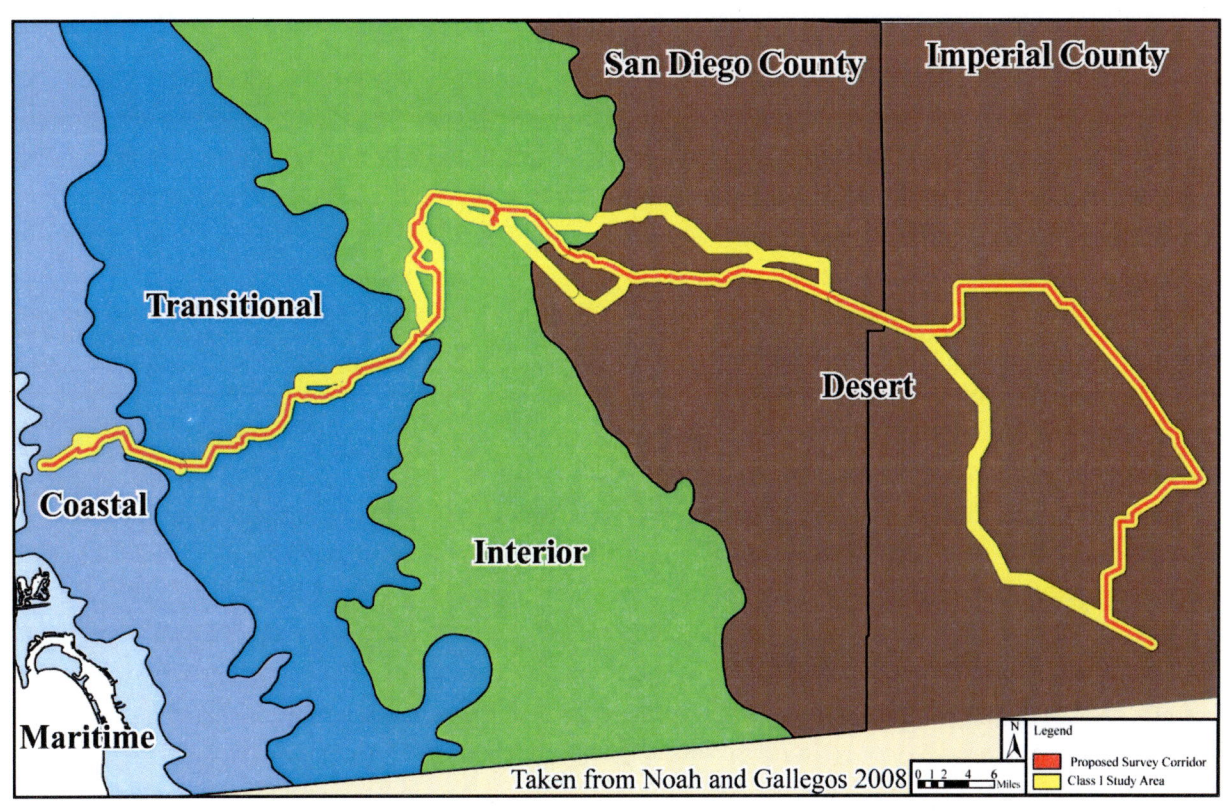

Figure 19. Climate Zones for San Diego County with Record Search and Inventory Corridors.

Habitation, and Temporary Camp across the Transitional and Interior; and (d) Bedrock Milling, Temporary Camp, Roasting Pit, Ceramic Scatter, and Rock Feature within the SDC Desert Zone. Lithic Scatters, Artifact Scatters, and Isolates are found across SDC. The dryer Imperial County Desert Zone produced Artifact Scatters, Isolates, Temporary Camps, Lithic Scatters, and Rock Features, identifying transient use of this region, except for those areas with present or past water sources (e.g., springs, Lake Cahuilla). Using the survey corridor study results to estimate site density, by climate zone, produced the following estimated site density per square mile: Coastal 24; Transitional 23; Interior 35; and SDC Desert 80 (Noah and Gallegos 2008:Table 7-2).

It should be noted that much of the previous discussion about the Early and Middle Holocene occupation was focused on the maritime and coastal zones. For the Late Holocene, Late Period sites are numerous and appear to dominate all climate zones, especially with Bedrock Milling and Habitation sites in the Transitional and Interior zones. It appears that many of the inland bedrock milling features and habitation sites are primarily related to Late Period occupation and acorn processing.

Resource Intensification

Resource intensification during the Late Period has been reported by a number of researchers, and is defined by Broughton (1997:846) as "a process by which the total productivity or yield per areal unit of land is increased at the expense of declines in overall caloric return rates or foraging efficiency." Byrd and Raab (2007:223) interpret Broughton's statement as "the result of consuming increasing quantities of lower-ranked, less-productive food species." Resource intensification also resulted from loss or reduction of higher-ranked foods, such as rocky shore and lagoon shellfish and fish due to sand transport and the corresponding loss of rocky and/or lagoon habitat. Examples of resource intensification in SDC during the Late Holocene include: (a) the use of Donax open-coast shellfish; (b) increased milling of plant seeds/nuts in inland locations; (c) numerous fire hearths at Torrey Pines, likely used to heat Torrey pine cones to facilitate the removal of pine nuts; (d) agave roasting pits (used for baking agave hearts in subterranean pits) identified in the SDC desert zone, and radiocarbon dated to the Late Period (770–100 B.P.) (Bastian 1977; Cheever and Gallegos 1988); (e) use of ceramic vessels for storage; and (f) the introduction of the bow and arrow, providing efficiencies in both hunting and warfare. Mealey, placing the Torrey Pines fire hearths in time states that "most have been found to be Late Prehistoric . . . [and] there is a nice sequence of dates ranging from around 2000 years B.P. to present" (Mealey 2006:13).

Also, Byrd and Raab (2007:223–224) report that during the Late Holocene "plant resource exploitation was focused on species requiring higher handling costs, particularly grasses (Poaceae) (Reddy 1999) . . . [and that] 'Fire followers' (plants that thrive in open areas created by regular fires) are represented to varying degrees at Late Holocene coastal sites." This suggests that intentional burning took place to improve cultivation of selected native plants during the Late Holocene. Byrd and Raab (2007:224) and Rosenthal et al. (2001) identify the Late Period Luiseño settlement pattern for Camp Pendleton as composed of major residential bases, with smaller short-term residential camps and limited activity sites.

Christenson (1990:286) reports that when considering Late Period site placement, site location was based on water, geology, slope, landform, and vegetation with the top priority being acorns, grasses, and rabbits. In addition, the burning of grasslands produced greater quantities of grass seeds and better forage for animals. Christenson (1990:297–299) identified the settlement pattern as consisting of large habitation sites for acorn gathering; small habitation and large processing sites occupied for short periods; and small processing sites, which she identifies as the most numerous.

Late Period Villages, Cultural Materials and Traditions

The time period from ca. 3500–1500 B.P. is notable for the siltation and depopulation of north SDC lagoons, and for the increase in sites/population (especially in inland areas) after 1500 B.P. (Figure 20).

For the Kumeyaay, the congregation at permanent water locations and the foundation for the Late Period village may have started as early as 3,000 years ago, given the earliest radiocarbon dates from Ystagua SDI-4609 (2890 B.P., 320–330 cm) (Carrico and Gallegos 1989); La Rinconada de Jamo SDI-5017 (2860 B.P., 140–150 cm) (Winterrowd and Cardenas 1987); Sabre Springs SDI-6669 (2950 B.P.) (Laylander 1989); Cosoy SDI-11767/12126 (2750 B.P.) (Smith 1986); and Las Chollas SDI-17203 (2270 B.P., 140 cm) (Brodie et al. 2014). Luiseño village formation in north SDC is difficult to discern, given the possible previous use by Kumeyaay and more recent use by Luiseño peoples. However, the earliest dates for two Luiseño village sites in north SDC: SDI-5353 (Agua Hedionda, 1290 B.P.) (Koerper et al. 1986); and SDI-8303 (Agua Hedionda, 1040–840 cal B.P.) (Gallegos 2007) suggest that Luiseño village formation began ca. 1300-1000 B.P.

The change in land use is also noticeable for the Otay Management Plan Area where Early and Middle Holocene sites are situated at the foothills, on the mesa, adjacent to springs and river valleys, and near the Tijuana Lagoon (Gallegos et al. 1998). However, during the Late Period, land use is dominated by three major village sites (Otai, La Punta, and Milejo), and all are adjacent to river valleys and reliable freshwater (see Figure 7) (Gallegos et al. 1998).

By 1,300 years ago (Late Period), changes include: the introduction of the bow and arrow and arrow shaft straightener; use of more variety of stone for tools (e.g., use of Obsidian Butte obsidian, chert, and quartz for arrow points); finely made pressure-flaked bifaces; increased number of milling tools including manos, metates, mortars, and stone bowls; an increase in milling, especially of acorns in inland locations with water, grasslands, granitic rock, and oaks; ceramics for seed storage, water vessels, and smoking pipes; villages with large concentrations of people at dependable water sources; introduction of fishhooks; and cremation of the dead.

Spanish Accounts

Father Crespi stated: "All the port is well populated with a large number of Indians, too clever, wide-awake, and business-like for any Spaniard to get ahead of them" (Bolton 1926). Palou reported: "Both the beach and the vicinity of the mission are very well populated . . . and there are more than twenty large villages [within 25 miles], one of them being close to the mission [Cosoy]" (Bolton 1926). Reported by Fages in 1769, the village of Cosoy was estimated to have 25 families (Engstrand 1975).

Cultivated Fields

Shipek (1989), on the basis of Spanish accounts, believed the Natives enhanced production of certain plants through burning and water diversion. In 1772, Father Jayme reported that Spanish soldiers turned their horses into the Native's fields (Jayme 1920:39). And Juan Crespi reported Sorrento Valley "to be nothing less than a cultivated cornfield or farm, on account of its mass of verdure (large-leafed calabashes and thickets of wild roses)" (Palou 1926, II:111).

Fishing

Fishing, from shore and by boat using nets and bone fish gorges, was conducted throughout the Holocene. Father Junipero Serra reported "rafts made out of tules and formed like canoes with which they ventured far out to sea" (Engelhardt 1920). Only a few shell fishhooks have been recovered from Late Period villages. Fish vertebrae recovered from the village of Ystagua identified sardine, shark, sheephead, tuna, and bass, representing

78 First People: A Revised Chronology for San Diego County

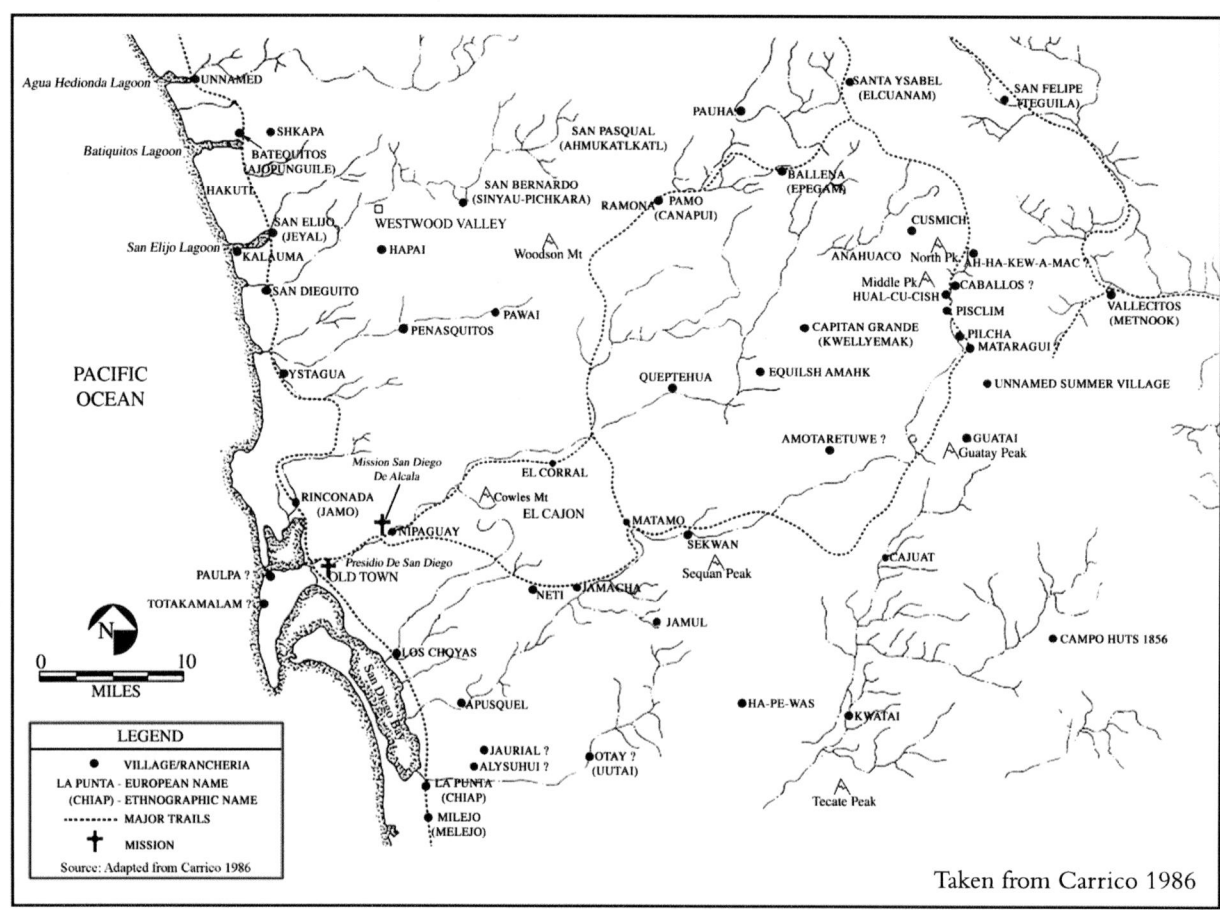

Figure 20. Late Period Village Locations.

varied habitats and a well-developed fishing technology (Carrico and Gallegos 1989). Shell fishhooks may have been introduced from contact with island or coastal people to the north.

Rogers Late Period/Yuman Contribution

Rogers may be best known for his work at the Harris Site; his San Dieguito - La Jolla - Yuman chronology; and, his association with the San Diego Museum of Man. But, his work was more extensive with surveys and site recordings across the California desert and into Arizona, Nevada, Utah and Baja California, as well as his Late Period/Yuman publications: *An Outline of Yuman Prehistory* (Rogers 1945) and *Yuman Pottery Making* (Rogers 1936). Rogers' work provided in many cases the baseline record for a wide range of sites, features and artifacts to include pictographs, petroglyphs, burials cremations, ceramics, trails and trail shrines, rock rings, quarries, and the recording of 72 Lake Cahuilla shoreline sites in the 1920s.

Features

Features include brush house structures, stone enclosures, sweathouses, small cooking hearths, roasting pits, granary bases, and bedrock milling, pictographs and petroglyphs. Roasting pits were circular rock-lined pits that varied in size, heated by fire to roast/bake agave hearts.

Rock Art

Rock art, somewhat rare in SDC, includes both pictographs (painting on rock) and petroglyphs (etching on rock) with most if not all SDC rock art dating to the Late Period. Rock art styles include: Diegueño, Rancho Bernardo, and La Rumarosa (Hedges 1970, 1973, 1979; Hedges and Hamann 1987).

Cremation

After 1300 B.P., cremation was the common practice for both the Luiseño and Yuman/Kumeyaay. This practice may have been introduced from the north, as Gamble and Russell (2002:123) "identified the earliest cremations dated to 2600 B.P. at Encino Village (CA-LAN-43) within Gabrielino territory"; or from the east as suggested by Rogers (1945). Hypotheses for the change from burial to cremation include: cremations may have been adopted for religious reasons; or due to higher populations congregating at permanent water sources for control of disease.

Ceramics

Rogers provides one of the earliest records in *Yuman Pottery Making* (Rogers 1936), wherein he documents types of pots, pipes, implements (i.e., rattles, scoops, plates); as well as designs, pottery making tools used, methods, and the amount of time needed to complete manufacture. Rogers (1936:4) reports that only women, engaged in pottery making, usually during summer months using primarily local materials. Rogers (1936:5) also reported that bad luck and failure was identified to "the clay does not like her" [and] "success... construed inversely. This belief is consonant with the general Yuman ideology wherein inanimate materials are endowed with animate faculties."

Moriarty (1966) reports the introduction of pottery into SDC ca. 1270 B.P.; however, May (1976) proposed a date of ca. 960 ±80 B.P. (LJ-3296); and J. Berryman (1981) proposed a date of 1220 ±110 (UCR-877). Griset's work with ceramics and radiocarbon dating supports the introduction of ceramics circa 1350–1151 B.P. (A.D. 600–799) (Griset 1996). Ceramics were likely introduced into SDC Kumeyaay from the east (Rogers 1936,

1945) and later diffused to the Luiseño/Takic. Kumeyaay/Yuman vessels include utilitarian water and seed storage, pots, bowls, and clay smoking pipes.

Arrow Points

Yohe (1992, 1998) suggests the introduction of the bow and arrow into California ca. 1500 B.P. And, Koerper et al. (1996) suggests ca. 1250 B.P. for the introduction of the bow and arrow into Orange County, which is also reasonable for SDC. Common arrow point types in SDC are the Cottonwood Triangular and the Desert Side-notched. Cottonwood and Desert Side-notched (DSN) points have been identified as a boundary marker on the basis of the high use of Cottonwood Triangular and low use of DSN points in Luiseño territory, as opposed to the higher use of DSN points in Kumeyaay lands, especially Tipai. This distinction was noted by Rogers (1945) and True (1966) and further refined by Pigniolo (2004). Pigniolo, using data from 95 sites across San Diego County, documents the percent of sites with Cottonwood Triangular and DSN points. His findings identify not only a difference between Luiseño and Kumeyaay Ipai, but also a difference between Kumeyaay Ipai and Tipai, suggestive of cultural Kumeyaay differences between this Hokan language nation. Carrico pointed out another difference in political unity in the sacking of the San Diego Mission in 1775, where only the Tipai took part in the revolt and the killing of Father Jayme, while the Ipai did not participate in the revolt (Carrico 1986).

Obsidian

Relatively recent volcanic activity at the north end of the Salton Trough, ca. 2480 ±470 created two obsidian-bearing lavas: Red Island and Obsidian Butte (Schmitt et al. 2012). Given the date for the creation of the Obsidian Butte source (Schmitt et al. 2012), all obsidian from this source is younger than ca. 2480±470. This obsidian source was probably known to Native Americans during the early part of the Late Holocene, but perhaps due to poor quality of material, use was questionable for large bifaces (e.g., atlatl points). It was not until the introduction of the bow and arrow and the need for smaller arrow points ca. 1500 B.P., which was more amiable to the use of Obsidian Butte obsidian, did this resource become highly valuable, sought out, and traded. It should also be remembered that this highly sought obsidian resource was not available when Lake Cahuilla was present (See Figure 10). Given the model of "three separate cycles of full lake-stands and then desiccation through evaporation, between circa cal A.D. 1200–1700 [750–250 cal B.P.]" (Laylander 1997, 2006), this resource was available roughly 50 percent of the time between A.D. 1200–1700. In addition to Obsidian Butte obsidian (located approimately 140 km/87 mi. from San Diego Bay), obsidian from San Felipe, Mexico, has also been identified at San Diego sites (McDonald et al. 1993; Robbins-Wade 1990; Winterrowd and Cardenas 1987).

Lithic Technology

Schroth and Flenniken (1997) identified a number of lithic reduction strategies at SDC sites. These include: (a) biface reduction, (b) split-nodule core reduction, (c) small blade core reduction, (d) bipolar core reduction, and (e) nodule reduction. Selection of technique was based on type of material, morphology of parent material, and the intended tool.

For the purpose of representing lithic tool production throughout the Holocene, Flenniken et al. (1998) reviewed and compared lithics from eight radiocarbon-dated SDC coastal and inland archaeological sites. These sites included the Early Holocene Harris site SDI-149 Locus I E-Stratum; Middle Holocene lagoon/coastal sites SDI-211/W-95, SDI-525, SDI-691, and SDI-4608c; and Late Period sites SDI-4609 village of Ystagua, and habitation site SDI-13504 (located adjacent and west of the Harris site).

Flenniken's work (Flenniken et al. 1998) resulted in identifying lithic reduction constraints due to both availability and form of raw materials. Early to Middle Holocene sites (SDI-211, SDI-525, and SDI-691) situated near the ocean and cobble resources contain almost 100 percent cobble reduction debitage. While the Late Period village of Ystagua SDI-4609, situated adjacent to a freshwater stream just east of Peñasquitos Lagoon, contained over 60 percent cobble reduction debitage. Flenniken et al. (1998:IV-37) reports that "evidence of biface finishing, but not production, was found at the Late Period sites," especially Ystagua. While the Harris site SDI-149 located approximately 10 miles east of the ocean near a fine-grained metavolcanic quarry, contained only 30 percent cobble reduction debitage. Flenniken et al. (1998:IV-37) reports that "flintnappers brought large flakes to the Harris site from nearby quarries and then proceeded to work these into biface blanks, probably for off-site transport." Flenniken et al. (1998: IV-38) identified the following basic trends: (a) cobble core reduction has been the most common on-site technology for SDC habitation sites for all of its prehistory; (b) Early to Middle Holocene coastal sites have very little in the way of on-site bifacial reduction; (c) Late Period sites typically have some evidence of biface refinishing; (d) teshoa flakes identified as one of the hallmarks of the LJCP are nearly absent from early coastal sites; (e) lithic manufacturing (through time) appears to represent the same range of flake production that occurs at many other sites in SDC; and (f) no biface reduction, maintenance, or retooling debris was noted on early coastal sites; however, bifaces were not absent from the tool kit.

For the Early Holocene coastal sites, as well as the Harris site, Flenniken et al. (1998:IV, 38-41) states: "In both cases it appears very likely that we are not viewing a complete picture of a technological system, but simply a component of it. Until we approach regional site patterns with this possibility in mind we are likely to have an incomplete picture of the cultures which produced these sites . . . In respect to later periods, the Late Prehistoric sites in this sample exhibit not so much different lithic reduction techniques but a wider range of them at a given site. The proportions of debitage classes of all the late period sites are very similar with the exception of pressure flaking debris, which only occurs in Late Prehistoric components." Flenniken et al. (1998:IV-41) further states: "[O]ver the course of San Diego history . . . subtle differences [are noted] in the emphasis on various reduction techniques, debitage types, and tool forms over time. . . . In doing this we have found that many of the variations in these assemblages can be explained as simple and direct responses by relatively mobile groups with limited access to better raw materials to the vagaries of local toolstone. The degree to which these patterns manifest themselves are indicators of a group's reliance on 'expedient' tools at a given location as well as the range of activities in which they were engaged . . . much of the lithic assemblage variation used to characterize these sites in archaeological taxonomies is attributable to differences in the suites of on-site activities and is manifested in the proportions of the tools and debitage and not, as is sometimes supposed, in their general form and method of manufacture."

For large bifaces, reflective of the Early and Middle Holocene, large boulders or excellent quarry veins of fine-grained metavolcanic, chert or obsidian are necessary. For small arrow points, however, poorer quality obsidian from Obsidian Butte will suffice as did PDL, and local metavolcanic cobbles and vein-quarried materials. For scraper tools, cobbles are perfectly suited, as they can be split and flaked, leaving a sharp edge and a cortex backside protecting the hand. In most cases, local granitic and sandstone were used for milling tools.

In addition, Flenniken's lithic technology and replicative analysis identified the use of core cobble tools to rejuvenate groundstone implements at site SDI-10148, dated 2250–800 B.P., within the San Diego River valley (Flenniken et al. 1993). As core cobble tools demonstrating battering are necessary to rejuvenate groundstone implements, then these battered core cobble tools are not signatures of LJCP, but are simply tools necessary for maintaining milling tools used throughout the Holocene.

With respect to lithic technology distinguishing SD, LJ, and LP cultural patterns, Becker and Iversen (2004:268) state: "[F]laked stone artifact types and sizes are thought to help distinguish San Dieguito, La Jolla, and Late Prehistoric Periods: Points/knives, cores, and scrapers...However the same lithic artifact types are found throughout each time period...While typological differences may exist between the different periods, there is currently a lack of evidence to make such claims, and from the perspective presented here, the lithic assemblages currently appear to be remarkably homogenous rather than distinctive, except for...small points such as Desert Side-notched and Cottonwood Triangular."

Summary

Changes from the Early and Middle Holocene to the Late Period include the direction of obsidian trade from north-south (southern Sierra/Coso) to east-west (Imperial Valley/Obsidian Butte); introduction of the bow and arrow; use of more varied stone materials; increased use of inland resources; introduction of ceramics; cremation of the dead; and resource intensification. These changes to some appear to reflect a change in people; however, given the over 8,000-year time depth for the Kumeyaay's Hokan language, there is the potential for one people occupying SDC over a very long period of time. These Late Period changes may simply be the result of the influence of Uto-Aztecan/Takic (Luiseño/Cahuilla); Yuman influence from the Colorado River; and local adaptation and innovation to changing environmental conditions during the Late Holocene.

Chapters 1-4 provided a discussion on Late Pleistocene-Early Holocene setting for First People and potential locations for Early Holocene archaeological sites; a discussion of the La Jolla Archaeological Area and why this would be a likely area for First People; Early to Middle Holocene San Dieguito Plateau sites and temporal range for occupation, as well as site type and Rogers' and Warren's definitions for San Dieguito; and a discussion on Late Holocene and Late Period occupation. The chronology provided in Chapter 5 is based on these previous chapters.

CHAPTER 5
Chronology and Discussion

A chronology for SDC is provided below and shown on Table 9 with a discussion on time periods, nomenclature, cultural material, and environmental setting over the past 12,000 years. The chronology for San Diego County (SDC) should be viewed as a continuum and is divided here into time periods to generally identify cultural material, sites, and people's adaptation to a changing environment. Time periods are divided into: Early Archaic (12,000–9000 B.P.), Middle Archaic Phase I (9000–7500 B.P.), Middle Archaic Phase II (7500–3500 B.P.), Late Archaic (3500–1300 B.P.), and Late Period (1300 B.P. to historic contact). The term "Archaic" follows Willig and Aikens's (1988:5) definition as a broad-spectrum economic pattern.

Environmental Setting, Subsistence and Radiocarbon Dating

Environmental change including the effects of sea level rise and stabilization, sand transport and climate greatly affected the setting and therein affected the local population throughout the Holocene. The setting for the coastal region and occupants was positively affected by the rise in sea level, which flooded coastal canyons to create rich marine habitats including submarine canyons and lagoons during the Early and Middle Holocene. By the Middle Holocene sand transport changed rocky habitats to sandy beach habitats, and helped to create San Diego Bay. By the Late Holocene ca. 3500 B.P., sea level stabilized and north SDC lagoons silted in, therein negatively affecting shellfish and fish populations and the human population that relied on lagoon resources. Periods of cool-wet and warm-dry affected plants, animals, and local inhabitants throughout the Holocene. During the Late Period, adaptation and innovation included the bow and arrow for hunting, ceramics for storage, cremation of the dead, resource diversity and intensification, as well as the formation of villages at reliable water sources.

The setting for the inland region is best described by Jones and Beck (2012:118) as: "Shifts in subsistence, mobility, and industrial patterns of desert foragers were well underway between 9500 and 8320 cal B.P....These included decreases in the sizes of wetland habitat and corresponding expansions of xerophytic plant associations across valley floors, and, at higher elevations, replacement of steppe grassland by desert shrub communities with attendant decreases in large game animal populations . . . these biotic changes appear to have encouraged use of a broader suite of plant and animal foods, accommodated by longer residential stays within resource patches and probably use of smaller territories. Substantial increases in the numbers and kinds of groundstone tools mark a significant new reliance on small seed resources, and new elements of basketry technology suggest heightened investment in collecting, transporting, and storing these foods. In contrast to these diversifying trends, chipped stone technology simplified, with expansion of the expedient component of toolkits".

The absence of consistency in radiocarbon dating and reporting over time (e.g., old vs. new labs and reporting procedures), the use of bulk samples vs. AMS single item dating and calibration correction methods have contributed to differences in dating results and therein problems in comparing dating results. For this reason, radiocarbon dates are used here as general reference points, to provide a framework for the chronology presented.

Early Archaic (12,000–9000 B.P.)

The Early Archaic includes the earliest SDC sites ca. 12,000–9000 B.P. These Early Holocene sites represent the initial occupation and include: Remington Hills SDI-11079, Del Mar Man SDI-10940, Harris site SDI-149

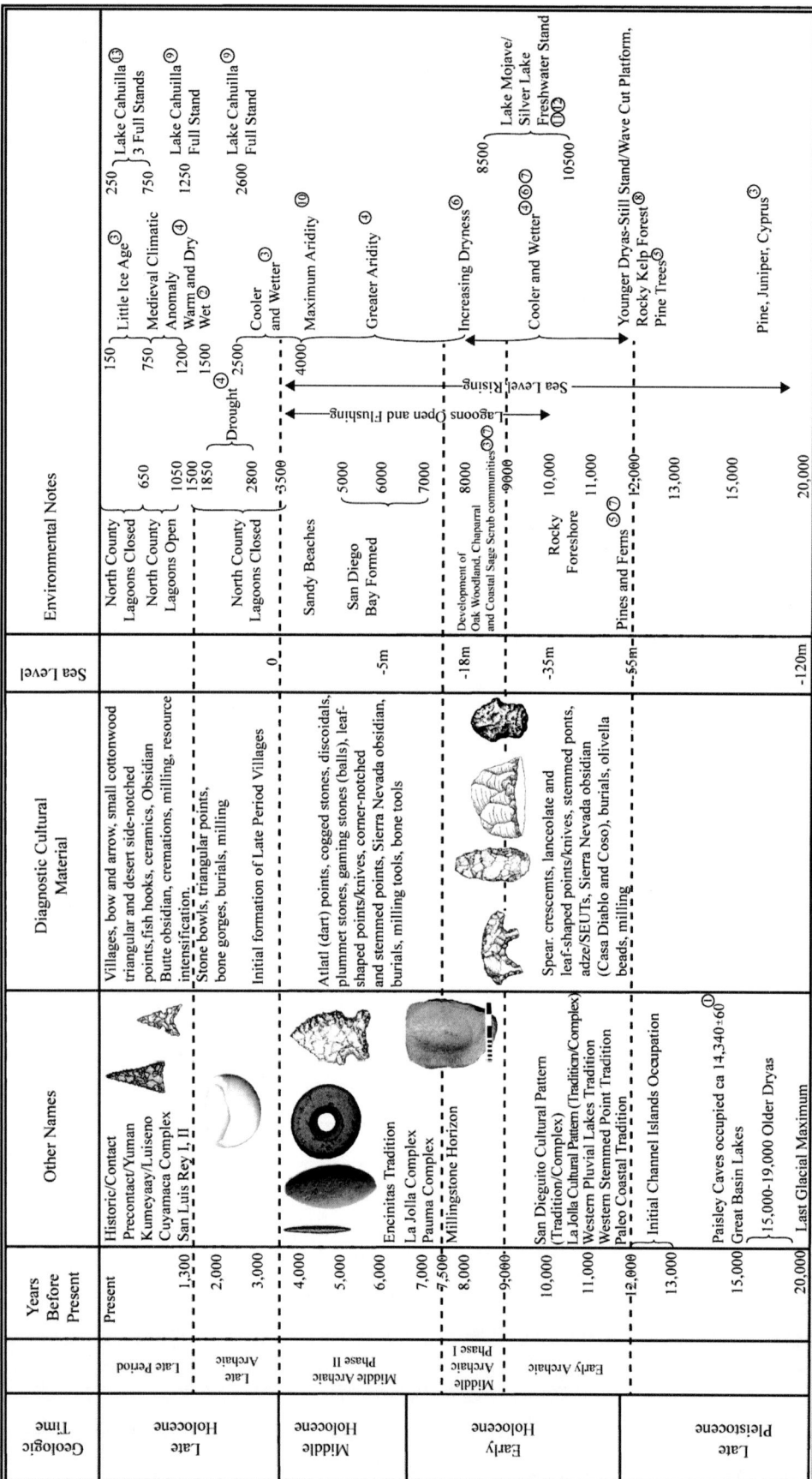

Table 9. A Chronology and Culture History for San Diego County.

Locus I E-Stratum, Agua Hedionda UCLJ-M-15, Windsong Shores SDI-10965, Spindrift SDI-39, and the Chancellor's House SDI-4669 (see Figures 3–5 and Tables 1–3).

First People may have arrived by land or by sea; and except for the Harris site, all of the Early Archaic sites have a coastal orientation and are situated adjacent to a lagoon and/or a submarine canyon. The arrival by the sea option include those Early Holocene sites situated directly on the coast, with few formal tools and a predominance of local cobble tools. These sea option sites are Remington Hills, Spindrift, Chancellor's House, and the Del Mar Man site. The arrival by the land option would likely identify a people leaving the drying Great Basin lakes and entering SDC. The candidates for the land option are those sites that have been identified as San Dieguito or San Dieguito-like (e.g., those sites with more formal tools such as knives, points, scrapers, and crescents). The three candidates for the land option are Windsong Shores SDI-10965, UCLJ-M-15 basal level, and the Harris site SDI-149 Locus I E-Stratum.

Land Option

The Harris site SDI-149 Locus I E-Stratum is situated in the San Dieguito River channel, approximately 10 miles east of the coast and adjacent to quarry material (e.g., Rancho Cielo). This site was previously discussed in Chapter 1 and, on the basis of lithic analyses (Cook 1985; Flenniken et al. 1998; Knell 2010) the Harris site is identified as a lithic workshop with temporary camps, primarily for the production of Stage 3 bifaces for the ultimate purpose of transport to local habitation sites (i.e., San Dieguito Plateau sites). Given the radiocarbon date of 11,190–9325 cal B.P., and the presence of primarily bifaces (45 percent), scrapers (48 percent) and two crescents, this site appears to serve as a specific use site, linking SDCP to Early Holocene WPLT/WSPT Great Basin occupation, especially to Lake Mojave and Silver Lake artifact assemblages.

As no archaeological report was completed for UCLJ-M-15, the validation of this site as San Dieguito or transitional rests on the radiocarbon date of 9020 ±500 (11,190–9325 cal B.P.), and Moriarty's statement (1967:555) identifying the basal level (130–170 cm) as containing "[f]airly large amounts of small felsite flakes . . . and the base of a large projectile point . . . The technique and pattern appeared similar to those of San Dieguito material, a resemblance confirmed by laboratory comparison with San Dieguito material recovered from the type site [Harris site]."

More interesting is Windsong Shores SDI-10965, dated 9930–9580 cal B.P., wherein finely made points, knives, scrapers, and crescents representing SDCP/WPLT/WSPT, as well as the use of lagoon shellfish and fish, mammals (primarily rabbit with some large mammal), and plant resources is documented adjacent to the mouth of Agua Hedionda (see Figures 3 and 5). Windsong Shores SDI-10965 is the best candidate for identifying a people (SDCP) who left the shoreline of drying inland Early Holocene Great Basin lakes (e.g., Lake Mojave and Silver Lake) and moved to a north SDC lagoon shoreline; and hypothesized here as amalgamating with an earlier coastal people (LJCP) creating an LJ/SD cultural pattern found on the San Dieguito Plateau. Adaptation to coastal resources by SDCP would have been minimal as inland Great Basin lakes also supported shellfish and fish for early peoples. Also, given that the Hokan phylum is one of the earliest languages that may have once covered a large portion of the Great Basin (Golla 2007), the people at La Jolla (LJAA) and at Windsong Shores may have been distant relatives, generally speaking the same language, thereby making amalgamation possible.

Sea Option

Remington Hills, Spindrift, Chancellor's House, and the Del Mar Man site all have a coastal orientation and suggest a people focused on ocean/coastal resources and therein may have a Kelp Highway lineage. Also, these sites are generally similar in makeup with cobble tools of local materials, scrapers, milling tools, faunal remains of shell and fish bone with some mammal bone, *Olivella* sp. shell beads, burials (except for Remington), a few bifaces, and few if any crescents.

On the basis of radiocarbon dates and environmental setting there are two localities for the initial occupation of SDC. These are Remington Hills SDI-11079 and LJAA sites (e.g., Spindrift SDI-39 and the Chancellor's House SDI-4669). For both of these localities, a submarine canyon "sweet spot" would have been accessible and near the 12,000–10,000 B.P. shoreline. The Remington Hills site has four of the earliest radiocarbon dates beginning 10,625–10,250 cal B.P., all taken on *Olivella* sp. spire-removed beads. Remington Hills, Tijuana Lagoon, and Otay Mesa (see Figure 7) as a whole (Otay Management Plan Area) represents continuous Holocene occupation, but this site/area lacks the density of cultural material, with burials as represented by the La Jolla Archaeological Area. The LJAA is an occupation area over two miles long situated along the La Jolla shoreline (from La Jolla Bay to Chancellor's House/UCSD) dating as early as 9740–9545 cal B.P. (see Figure 8).

Given the radiocarbon dates and the idyllic setting of La Jolla Submarine Canyon, Scripps Submarine Canyon, La Jolla Bay/lagoon/estuary, caves, and freshwater springs, the most likely candidate for the initial occupation is the La Jolla Archaeological Area (LJAA), especially in the area of the Spindrift site. This "sweet spot" was especially favorable from ca. 12,000+ to 8000 B.P., as the coastline did not move far from the edge of the submarine canyons, even as sea level rose, due to the submarine canyon's depth and steepness (see Figure 2). The LJAA has the best potential for earlier finds than the earliest date reported for the Chancellor's House of 9740–9545 cal B.P., given the submarine canyons and archaeological sites/artifacts on land and reported offshore. However, with the rise in sea level and loss of land between the submarine canyons and shore, these earlier sites may be underwater or destroyed due to wave action and/or development. Such as the development reported by Rogers for the 1926 steam shovel destruction of W-2: "The site was completely demolished and with it probably the most important prehistoric station in southern California" (Rogers 1920s W-2; 1926).

Development and therein all or partial site loss is reported for sites SDI-39/W-1, W-2, SDI-11075, SDI-525/W-9, and -SDI-4669/W-12. In addition, Pleistocene marine terrace cliff failure and possible loss of earlier portions of important Early Holocene sites has been demonstrated at the Chancellor's House SDI-4669/W-12 where burials were reported falling off the cliff (Rogers 1920s, W-12); and at SDI-11075 with the loss of a major portion of the site due to cliff failure, leaving 1.83 m of truncated midden dated to 7530 B.P at the cliff edge.

The landform for the LJAA is oriented to the ocean with La Jolla Bay, submarine canyons, and lagoon, and is protected on the east by the adjacent coastal hills which rise to over 250 m; and due to past geologic events does not have a setting similar to north SDC lagoons created with the rise in sea level ca. 9000 B.P. If the First People arrived via the Kelp Highway ca. 12,000 to 10,000 years ago in the La Jolla area, and these people were primarily oriented towards ocean and coastal resources of shellfish and fish, with some use of plants and small to large mammals, then the tool kit of local cobbles and sandstone materials may have changed little over thousands of years and would not need to be extensive or elaborate for collecting and processing coastal resources. Also, tools made of wood, and fiber for nets or baskets would not be represented in the archaeological record, given the fragileness of these artifacts.

A view of these early settlers is provided by Mayes (2010) who describes the double burial at the Chancellor's House SDI-4669, dated 9740–9545 cal B.P. as follows: "[T]he male shows evidence of atlatl or spear throwing, as well as auditory exostosis, a result of considerable time in cold water; with the female having strong arms from carrying out repetitive behaviors such as milling, and dental wear suggesting use of teeth for basket making or other fiber use. The diet, on the basis of a CAT-scan indicated a marine-based diet" (Mayes 2010:137–138). This is not the description of a simple gathering people, but of a people who could carry out a variety of tasks and could orient to the most favorable ocean or land resources as needed.

Trade and travel during the Early and Middle Archaic is demonstrated by Coso, Casa Diablo, Mt. Hicks, Mono Craters, Mono Glass, and Fish Springs obsidian recovered from Early and Middle Holocene SDC sites as well as the influences in atlatl point types through time; the wide distribution of crescents from the Great Basin to Channel Islands to San Diego County; and the presence of *Olivella* sp. spire-removed beads from coastal to Great Basin/desert regions.

Middle Archaic (9000–3500 B.P.)

The Middle Archaic from 9000–3500 B.P. should be viewed as a continuum from the Early Archaic and is divided into Phase I (9000–7500 B.P.) and Phase II (7500–3500 B.P.) for discussion purposes. LJCP sites during the Middle Archaic are similar in content, with artifact additions to the assemblage over time. Burials dated from ca. 10,000–3500 B.P. are usually flexed with metates, in many cases capping the burial. Middle Archaic sites east of the coastal zone usually have little if any shell, plant or small to large bone representing diet or burials, and this may be the result of lack of preservation due to soil chemistry.

Radiocarbon dates based on the shell species for La Jolla Bay and Pleistocene terrace UCSD sites identified the coastal habitat for shellfish circa 9000 B.P. as primarily rocky with the local inhabitants preferring *Mytilus* shellfish. However, by ca. 5430 B.P. the habitat began to change to sandy as demonstrated by *Tivela stultorum* (Masters 2006) (see Table 5). With the loss of rocky shellfish, it appears that sites such as Scripps Estates SDI-525; Chancellor's House SDI-4669; Middle Midden SDI-4670; and SIO Upper Cliff site SDI-11075 were either depopulated or abandoned ca. 5,000 to 3,000 years ago. The site occupants may have been accessing adjacent steep coastal canyons containing rocky habitat shellfish, until sand transport (beginning ca. 5000 B.P.) blocked canyon mouths, followed by siltation and loss of the shellfish habitat. However, for the Spindrift site, radiocarbon dates document continuous occupation over the past ca. 10,000 years, with rocky habitat, lagoon, and sandy habitat overlapping in time.

Occupation during the Middle Archaic is best reflected by the health of SDC lagoons. For north SDC lagoons, the rise in sea level ca. 9000–3500 B.P. created healthy and flushing lagoons producing shellfish and fish until sea level stabilized followed by blockage of lagoon mouths and siltation of lagoons ca. 3,500 years ago. Occupation and special use sites are situated adjacent to the lagoons and primarily reflect the 9000–3500 year occupation. For the period 3500–1500 B.P., few archaeological sites are recorded adjacent to north SDC lagoons.

East of the north SDC lagoons (Agua Hedionda, Batiquitos, San Elijo, and San Dieguito) is an area identified by Rogers (1929) as the San Dieguito Plateau (see Figure 11). Sites identified by Rogers on the San Dieguito Plateau contain both SDCP tools (e.g., finely worked bifaces, scrapers, and crescents) and LJCP cobble tools, milling tools, burials, and *Olivella* sp. spire-removed beads. These sites are generally dated to the Middle Archaic (see Table 6). Archaeologists interpreting these sites either assume that these are mixed SDCP and LJCP sites (multicomponent) following the traditional Abandonment Model and therefore the artifacts need to be sorted to understand SDCP vs. LJCP; or, these are single deposit sites representing two modes of behavior within a single cultural system, demonstrating a wide range of tools to best acquire and process coastal and inland plant and animal resources (Non-transition Model).

The San Dieguito Plateau sites likely represent two modes of behavior and the need for a varied tool kit to best exploit the rich coastal and inland resources over a long period of time. In addition, we are dealing with site types, wherein sites adjacent to lagoons (ca. 9000–3500 B.P.), may have the simplest of assemblages for the purpose of collecting and processing shellfish and therefore do not define a complete cultural pattern. More complex coastal habitation sites, also located near lagoons may contain burials, milling tools, bone tools, beads, and some finely made tools of fine-grained metavolcanic material. Also, certain activities may be either male or female (e.g., gathering and processing shellfish; collecting and milling of plant foods; woodworking; making of stone tools; and hunting, which may include cutting, cooking meat, and cleaning animal skins), and therefore a tool kit as represented at a task-specific site (e.g., shellfish processing, milling station, or lithic acquisition/quarry or lithic reduction site) will not have the same cultural assemblage (diversity or density) as a habitation site. It should be noted that the end of the Middle Archaic, with the closure of north SDC lagoons and concomitant loss of lagoon resources, is also the end of LJCP and SDCP sites adjacent to lagoons and on the San Dieguito Plateau as well as the distinctive SDCP signature of finely made large bifaces, scraping tools, and crescents (see Figures 11, 12 and 15).

It should also be noted that Rogers and Warren had different viewpoints on SDCP with respect to what should be included in a SDCP tool kit and therein the time frame for these early people. Rogers was more inclusive and included both Locus I E-Stratum (dated ca. 10,000–8000 B.P.) and Locus II, dated 4720 B.P. with an Elko point (see Figures 6 and 14); and Rogers identified 71 sites in SDC (19 sites within or adjacent to the San Dieguito Plateau) with a San Dieguito component (see Table 6). Whereas Warren was more limiting in his selection of San Dieguito sites and artifacts, initially identifying only the Harris site Locus I E-Stratum dated ca. 10,000–8000 B.P.; and therein keeping SDCP more in line with Pleistocene-Holocene Great Basin shoreline finds (e.g., Lake Mojave and Silver Lake) ca. 9,000 to 11,000 years ago. More recently, Warren has added four SDC sites to his SDCP based solely on the basis of types of artifacts with no supporting radiocarbon dates (Warren et al. 1998). These four sites may simply represent additional lithic workshops and not represent the range of SDCP activities found at sites on the San Dieguito Plateau (see Tables 7 and 8). However, it should be noted that the Gladishill site is more similar to the San Dieguito Plateau sites than to the Harris site Locus I E-Stratum. This difference in viewpoints affected both the SDCP time frame and sites/regions represented by SDCP occupation for both Rogers and Warren, as well as those that followed.

Windsong Shores SDI-10965, UCLJ-M-15 basal level, and the Harris site Locus I E-Stratum may represent the initial occupation of a people from the Great Basin/Lake Mojave/Silver Lake region with the continuing occupation representing a melding of SD and LJ cultural patterns. The Harris site Locus II as well as sites on the San Dieguito Plateau, may represent the continuation of a lithic tradition from ca. 10,000 to 3,500 years ago of producing finely worked bifaces, scrapers, and crescents from primarily fine-grained metavolcanic materials.

Middle Archaic Phase I (9000–7500 B.P.)

This phase represents the post-initial Early Archaic occupation and the more commonly found shell scatters with occupation sites primarily near the coast and lagoons. This is a formative time for lagoons and as such, lagoons are in excellent condition, with sea level rising during this period and tides able to flush lagoons, therein keeping a healthy habitat for a diverse, large in size, and abundant shellfish population.

Common at lagoon and coastal sites are simple shell scatters, as well as sites with fire hearths, shellfish, fish and mammal bone, milling tools, cobble tools (e.g., choppers, hammerstones, battered stones), flake tools, bone tools, *Olivella* sp. spire-removed beads, and burials, with little evidence of the SDCP (e.g., finely made bifaces, scrapers, or crescents of fine-grained metavolcanic material). However the SDCP is more common within the San Dieguito Plateau, an area adjacent and east of north SDC lagoons (see Figure 11). Sites on the San Dieguito Plateau date from 9000 to 3500 and contain both SDCP and LJCP.

Middle Archaic Phase II (7500–3500 B.P.)

The Middle Archaic Phase II is a continuation of the Middle Archaic Phase I, but reflects changing coastal and lagoon conditions as well as increased aridity beginning around 7000 B.P. (Spaulding 1990). Sand transport had a major impact on coastal regions and lagoons, with Masters reporting a change in rocky coast to sandy beach habitats in the La Jolla region after 5000 B.P. (Masters 2006) and the creation of San Diego Bay due to sand transport and wave shadow effect around Point Loma, leaving the mouth of the bay protected from closure by the shadow effect of Point Loma (Masters 1988:4–18). The creation of San Diego Bay ca. 7000–5000 B.P. provided both a new and significant resource for shellfish and fish.

Sutton (2009) reports the Northern Uto-Aztecan (NUA) had moved into the western Mojave Desert, the southern Sierra Nevada, and perhaps the southern San Joaquin Valley ca. 5000–3500 B.P. and then branched into Southern California by ca. 3500 B.P., which may account for the loss of Coso obsidian and other obsidian trade from the southern Sierra Nevada region into SDC.

By ca. 3500 B.P. with the stabilization of sea level, sand and cobble bars formed at the mouths of north SDC lagoons (Agua Hedionda, Batiquitos, San Elijo, and San Dieguito) causing these lagoons to fill with sediment. This lagoon sedimentation resulted in the reduction and/or loss of lagoon shellfish and fish in these once rich habitats, and therein depopulation of north SDC coastal lagoon areas until a reopening during the Late Period.

Terminology for this general time period includes the Encinitas Tradition, Millingstone Horizon, Topanga Complex, La Jolla, La Jolla Tradition/Complex, and Pauma Complex. Cultural material during the Middle Archaic Phase II includes Phase I materials (previously discussed) with the addition of a wider range of beads (stone, bone, and shell); a range of milling features (bedrock slicks and mortars); plummet stones; donut stones, discoidals, stone balls, cogged stones, pitted stones; and some bifaces including knives and Elko points (Figure 21).

Late Archaic (3500–1300 B.P.)

The Late Archaic begins with change for the north SDC lagoon occupants as sand and cobbles moved by ocean currents and wave action closed lagoon mouths. The closure of lagoon mouths was followed by lagoon siltation, loss of lagoon shellfish and fish resources, and depopulation of lagoon shorelines. For the San Elijo Lagoon, the lagoon was closed from ca. 3450–1050 B.P. (Byrd et al. 2004:346); and this was the general condition for Agua Hedionda, Batiquitos, and San Dieguito lagoons, thereby severely reducing north SDC lagoon food resources as documented by the general absence of archaeological sites adjacent to these lagoons ca. 3500–1500 B.P. However, Late Archaic occupation is documented at the Spindrift site; Peñasquitos and Tijuana lagoons, which continued to function as mudflats producing shellfish and fish; and at the San Diego Bay and river valley. During this time, populations may have been more focused on coastal resources from Peñasquitos to San Diego Bay to the Tijuana Estuary, as well as adjacent river valleys.

Along with the loss of lagoon resources in north SDC, a major drought from 2800–1850 B.P. was reported by Mensing (Mensing et al. 2013). Assuming drought conditions, Late Archaic sites may have moved to reliable water sources (e.g., springs and near river mouths), which may have been used repeatedly over the Late Holocene, with Late Archaic evidence of occupation in these river valleys buried by silt and sediment. Also, Late Archaic sites may reflect the initial formation of Late Period villages ca. 3000–2000 B.P., given basal radiocarbon dates for the villages of Ystagua, La Rinconada de Jamo, Sabre Springs, Cosoy, and Las Chollas.

Notable are the few sites and artifacts representing the Late Archaic. It is assumed that the atlatl was still in use, as were milling and cobble tools with occupation focused on coastal resources at Spindrift SDI-39, Peñasquitos Lagoon, Tijuana Lagoon, and San Diego Bay.

Late Period (1300 B.P. to Historic Contact)

The Late Period begins with the reopening of north SDC lagoons ca. 1500–1000 B.P. to ca. 500 B.P., as based on coring studies (Byrd et al. 2004; Gallegos 1985; Miller 1966) and the presence of radiocarbon-dated archaeological sites adjacent to these lagoons. These lagoons, although open to ocean flushing, probably functioned as

Figure 21. Features, Artifacts and Ecofacts from Dated ca. 7500–3500 B.P. (Middle Archaic) Sites.

mudflats and were not as productive in shellfish and fish, and not equal to the productive levels noted during the Early and Middle Holocene/Archaic. By 650–500 B.P., north SDC lagoon mouths were again blocked and therein closed to tidal flushing. During the Late Period, Peñasquitos and Tijuana lagoons continued as shellfish-producing mudflats; and San Diego Bay was healthy with major habitation sites found near each river mouth leading into San Diego Bay.

The Late Period includes major changes in land use, resource intensification, and technology reflected by the introduction of the bow and arrow; use of Obsidian Butte obsidian primarily for small arrow points; finely made arrow points from a variety of materials; beads of shell, bone, and stone; bone tools; shell fishhooks; increase in milling tools including manos, metates, stone bowls, bedrock mortars and slicks; ceramics for seed storage, water vessels, and smoking pipes; and a wide range of faunal remains including shell, fish bone, and small to large mammal bone.

Burials likely ended by ca. 1300 B.P. and cremation of the dead began. Resource intensification is noted by fire-affected rock features, most likely for pine nut and agave processing; and task-specific milling locations with primarily milling and maintenance tools (e.g., battered cobbles). Major inland sites were situated near water, grasslands, granitic rock, and oaks, with a focus on acorns and rabbits. Late Period coastal diet was more focused on coastal resources of shellfish and fish along with acorns and rabbits; and the inland diet was focused primarily on acorns and rabbits. Plant foods such as grass seeds were also an important part of the diet.

Ceramics may have been introduced ca. 1270–960 B.P. (J. Berryman 1981; Griset 1996; May 1976; Moriarty 1966). Yohe (1992, 1998), on the basis of his work at the Rose Springs site, suggests the introduction of the bow and arrow ca. 1500 B.P. For SDC, the introduction of the bow and arrow would postdate 1500 B.P., with Koerper et al. (1996) suggesting for Orange County a date ca. 1250 B.P. Koerper's use of ca. 1250 B.P. also appears reasonable for the introduction of the bow and arrow into SDC. SDC point types are primarily Cottonwood and Desert Side-notched.

Sometime after 1500 and perhaps more likely ca. 1250–1000 B.P., Northern Uto-Aztecan (NUA)/Luiseño settled in north and northeastern SDC, having moved south from areas presently identified as Los Angeles Basin and Orange County. The causal factors for NUA movement west and ultimately south into SDC is hypothesized as drought beginning in the Middle Holocene. The intrusion by both the Penutians and the NUA affected the Hokan in the northern, central, and southern portions of the state, with both the Penutians and NUA enlarging their territories; and Hokan lands becoming smaller and more fragmented throughout California. In southern California, Hokan is in the central and southern portions of SDC, extending east into Arizona, and south into Baja California (Golla 2007; Sutton 2009). Also, given that: (1) the Hokan phylum is the oldest of the western North American languages, estimated over 8,000 years (Golla 2007:78); and (2) the Hokan language is scattered as isolates across California, with the Kumeyaay in SDC one of the remnants (see Figure 10); it is possible that the Kumeyaay are related to the First People who settled in SDC. The best method to test this hypothesis is DNA.

Lake Cahuilla, a freshwater lake, was created by the flooding of the Colorado River into the Imperial Valley to the 12 m (40 ft.) shoreline at least four times between ca. 1250–250 B.P. (Laylander 1997; Waters 1983). A major freshwater lake resource 161 km long by 56 km wide (115 by 35 miles) when full to the 12 m shoreline would have attracted NUA/Takic from the north, Kumeyaay from SDC, and Yumans from the east to exploit shellfish, fish, birds, mammals, and plants. The last full stand of Lake Cahuilla is dated to ca. 250 B.P. (Laylander 1997). Also, the attraction of inland oaks and grasslands in SDC may have been the impetus for the Northern Uto-Aztecan/Takic (NUA) incursion from the north, into north SDC post 1500 B.P. as represented by the Luiseño.

Summary

Background, Setting, and Chronology

Chapter 1 provided a discussion on the earliest radiocarbon-dated sites in SDC and how the Kelp Highway is a viable model for the initial LJCP population of SDC to have settled in a coastal location and focused on ocean/coastal resources. Chapter 1 also discussed Early Holocene SDCP sites Windsong Shores SDI-10965, UCLJ-M-15, and the Harris site SDI-149, and why the Harris site Locus 1 E-Stratum should not be identified as a quarry or habitation site, but rather a lithic workshop with temporary campsites where Stage 3 tool production activities were conducted. Chapter 2 focused on the La Jolla Archaeological Area (e.g., Spindrift to the Chancellor's House); the Early Holocene setting; and a discussion of sites, cultural material, burials, and site status within the LJAA. Chapter 3 discussed the differences in how Rogers and Warren viewed the San Dieguito (SDCP) and how this affected the chronology of SDC. Warren kept to the tradition of Pleistocene-Holocene shoreline sites found near present-day inland dry lakes. While Rogers included the traditional materials found at Pleistocene-Holocene shoreline sites, he also included Elko points, which greatly extends the time range for San Dieguito (SDCP). For SDC, Warren identified five sites as San Dieguito (SDCP) (Warren et al. 1998), while Rogers identified 71 sites overall (19 within or adjacent to the San Dieguito Plateau), as having a San Dieguito component, as well as a region (San Dieguito Plateau) containing San Dieguito sites (SDCP). Chapter 4 provided a summary on Late Holocene and Late Period occupation, and Chapter 5 provided a chronology for SDC.

Native American occupation was affected by environmental change throughout the Holocene, which included sea level rise, sand transport, health of lagoons, and the creation of San Diego Bay and Lake Cahuilla. Fresh water, not always available in the desert, was always available in western SDC as a result of the interior mountain ranges and large catchments providing water through multiple river valleys to the coast throughout the Holocene.

Early Archaic (12,000–9000 B.P.) represents the initial occupation of SDC. This important period is singled out for the purpose of better understanding the initial population, date(s), areas populated, cultural material, activities conducted, burials, diet, and environmental setting. The end of the Pleistocene and beginning of the Holocene provided a rich coastal habitat that supported and facilitated population growth during the Early Holocene.

The Middle Archaic (Phase I 9000–7500 B.P. and Phase II 7500–3500 B.P.) is a continuation of the Early Archaic and is broken into two phases to reflect environmental change and adaptation to change, as well as artifact additions during these phases.

The Late Archaic (3500–1300 B.P.) is poorly represented in the archaeological record and likely reflects less of the archaeological record on the landscape due to drought, and siltation and closure of north SDC lagoons. Conversely, Peñasquitos and Tijuana lagoons continued to function as mudflats producing shellfish and fish for local occupants throughout the Holocene. And, San Diego Bay and river valley were also highly productive during the Middle Archaic Phase II, Late Archaic, and Late Period.

During the Late Period (ca. 1300 B.P. to historic contact), the environmental setting improves with the reopening of north SDC lagoons and full lake stands of Lake Cahuilla. During this time period, population growth was facilitated by innovation, technology, increased resource breadth, and resource intensification.

First People

The initial peopling and the following occupation, as well as people's adaptation to environmental change, is important to our understanding of the past 12,000 years of SDC history. In most—if not all—cases, the discussion has centered on collections of artifacts, whether they be identified as San Dieguito, San Dieguito Cultural Pattern (SDCP), Western Stemmed Point Tradition, La Jolla, or La Jollan Cultural Pattern (LJCP). However, this discussion always leads indirectly or directly to people. Who were the First People, where did they arrive from, where did they initially settle, and is there a relationship between First People and the Kumeyaay living here today? These questions have been addressed in this manuscript from the artifacts and ecofacts left across the landscape over the past 12,000 years. However this discussion will need DNA and numerous single-sample AMS radiocarbon dates to provide more definitive answers to these questions.

First People models include: Abandonment; Displacement, Acculturation, Transformation, and Non-transition, and these models assume San Dieguito (SDCP) as First People (Warren et al. 1998). Abandonment (e.g., a people came, a people left, a people came, etc.) is not supported, given the continuous radiocarbon dates for San Diego County. Displacement (e.g., the initial population was pushed out and replaced) is also not supported, given the absence of burials demonstrating evidence of warfare. Also, LJCP radiocarbon dates are equal to or earlier than SDCP dates. Acculturation and Transformation both identify SDCP as First People who became LJCP; and neither Acculturation nor Transformation is supported due to the presence of Early Holocene LJCP radiocarbon dates (e.g., Spindrift, Chancellor's House, Del Mar Man, and Remington Hills) and the continued SDCP presence of bifaces, scraping tools, and crescents on the San Dieguito Plateau dated to the Early and Middle Holocene. Non-transition (e.g., two modes of behavior within a single culture system) may best explain the types of artifacts and activities found on the San Dieguito Plateau.

Given the findings by Erlandson (Erlandson et al. 1996; Erlandson et al. 2007a,b; and Erlandson 2013) and others, a coastal route via the Kelp Highway may identify the avenue taken by SDC's First People, and provides the basis for the addition of models 6 and 7, with LJCP as the initial occupation (First People). Model 6 (Non-transition LJCP First People) identifies the LJCP as initially occupying San Diego County (SDC), with the LJCP adding SDCP tools for the purpose of better exploiting inland resources (e.g., collecting, hunting, and processing plant and animal resources).

Model 7 (Amalgamation), also identifies the LJCP as First People most likely in the La Jolla area (LJAA), but with an intrusion into north SDC by a people as represented by SDCP leaving the Great Basin drying lakes (e.g., Lake Mojave and Silver Lake) ca. 10,000–9,000 years ago and settling in north SDC as represented at Agua Hedionda SDI-10965 and UCLJ-M-15, and the Harris site SDI-149 Locus I E-Stratum.

For SDC, there are the "by land" and "by sea" options for First People. The "by land" option is represented by SDCP at Windsong Shores, UCLJ-M-15, and the Harris site Locus I E-Stratum. The "by sea" option is represented by Spindrift, Chancellor's House, Del Mar Man site, and Remington Hills. The "by land" option for First People does not account for LJCP radiocarbon dates as early or earlier than SDCP. Models 6 and 7 with LJCP representing First People, is supported by Late Pleistocene-Early Holocene radiocarbon dates, coastal site location(s), relatively large Early to Middle Holocene La Jolla population, rich environmental setting (e.g., La Jolla Bay, submarine canyons, lagoons, and springs), and provides the foundation for First People (LJCP) entering SDC ca. 12,000 to 10,000 years ago via the Kelp Highway.

Model 7, the "by sea" option is more complex but appears to answer the presence of both LJCP and SDCP in north SDC during the Early Holocene. This model identifies a people (LJCP) occupying and focusing on coastal resources, followed by an intrusion into north SDC by a people (SDCP) who left drying Great Basin lakes (e.g., Lake Mojave and Silver Lake) ca. 10,000–9000 B.P. as represented at Windsong Shores, UCLJ-M-15, and the Harris site. Also, the amalgamation provides an answer for LJCP and SDCP (e.g., milling tools, cobble tools, bifaces, scrapers, crescents, *Olivella* sp. spire-removed beads, hearths, burials, and faunal remains of shell, fish bone, and small to large mammal bone) found at sites on the San Dieguito Plateau. The San Dieguito Plateau appears to represent multiple modes of behavior (LJCP and SDCP) to best hunt, collect, and process a wide range of coastal and foothill resources, along with the tradition of finely working stone tools beginning ca. 10,000/9000 B.P. to 4000/3500 B.P. Assuming amalgamation of LJCP and SDCP as one people would also explain the presence of burials within the LJCP and the absence of burials within the SDCP. It is further hypothesized that the San Dieguito, La Jolla, Pauma Complex, and Late Period Diegueño/Yuman/Kumeyaay are historically related cultural units that are the result of genetically related populations; however, DNA will be necessary to prove or disprove this hypothesis.

Going Forward

Discoveries will continue to be made that contribute to the archaeological record; however, those areas (coastal, lagoon, and foothills) that may be critical to understanding the past may have been bulldozed or built over (e.g., LJAA and the San Dieguito Plateau). The archaeological history for these areas is now in reports, which may or may not be in state information centers. And artifacts from these important sites may or may not be accessible. If CRM work was conducted and reports and artifacts were not submitted/curated for these studies, then archaeologists, agency reviewers, Native Americans and developers may have actively or passively contributed to the loss of this 12,000-year history. Data collection has increased greatly over the past 50 years and curation of this information is critical for the understanding and documentation of this 12,000-year history. Cultural Resource Management reports are important and curation of each report provides important information, as does artifact curation. CRM has produced numerous special studies, such as radiocarbon dating, residue analysis, and obsidian hydration and sourcing that need to be compiled for on-going and future research.

Archaeologists need to use AMS for single item dating and not bulk sample dating; to bracket upper and lower site boundaries; to identify and focus on single deposit sites given the problems of bioturbation; to date the introduction of diagnostic artifacts such as the atlatl and arrow points, ceramics, mortars, stone bowls, and fishhooks; and to document the timing of the Luiseño into SDC. Re-dating of specific sites (especially Early Holocene sites) will be necessary as bulk samples were used and these are not equal to AMS single sample corrected dates.

The ability to use GPS, GIS, and modeling site/cultural material patterning by radiocarbon dates and environmental setting (e.g., sea level rise and change in setting, climate zone, soils, water, vegetation) through time should be built in the university system and/or CRM, and used as a research tool, teaching tool, and public information tool. Environmental data (i.e., soil, sedimentation rates, charcoal, shell, seeds and pollen) from archaeological sites as well as lagoon coring studies with associated radiocarbon dating would help to define the past 12,000 year environmental setting for SDC archaeological sites. And, the understanding of past environmental settings and change may assist in determining future environmental change.

As reported by SDC underwater archaeologist Roy Pettus (1982:73-75), offshore cultural resources are present and, "An extremely small amount of the total offshore area of San Diego County has been surveyed... The number of prehistoric sites and variety of artifacts which have been recorded... and the width of San Diego County's continental shelf indicate that the potential is high for undiscovered cultural resources." At a minimum, underwater survey and mapping to identify submerged cultural resources should be conducted for that portion of LJAA located west of the Spindrift site SDI-39/W-1 and W-2 including the relic Pleistocene/Holocene shoreline adjacent to La Jolla and Scripps submarine canyons. Survey work should include both a scuba transect survey, ship based sidescan sonar, marine magnetometer, and other evaluations/tests to identify anomalies and to test these anomalies using coring to determine the presence or absence of evidence of the earliest settlements in SDC. In addition, this work would assist in a management plan to study and preserve submerged cultural resources within the LJAA (see Figure 8).

DNA should be employed before we lose this information to reburial of past people's history. DNA from an individual tooth is being used in other parts of California, and the rational is that people lose teeth naturally over the course of their life. DNA results have connected present-day people to past people, thereby providing a more complete understanding overall and a powerful statement of adaptation and resilience over hundreds if not thousands of years.

Politics may and probably will change, and future generations will ask to see their history and not fully understand why bulldozers and others have buried their history. As Emma Lou Davis generally stated: It is a shared history—it is all of our story.

Epilogue

What do we take away from the story of a people who have lived here for over 10,000 years and live here today in the fabric of today's society as lawyers, teachers, firemen, mechanics, and musicians? A people who have survived through innovation, adaptation, and resilience. This more than 10,000-year-old story is one of survival through traditions, language, community, and reliance on low technology (low tech) for much of this time period. High tech is the story for only the past 100+ years. How do these technologies work and how will they work for us going forward?

Stuart (2000:XIV-XV) states, "[A] powerful society [high tech] . . . captures more energy and expends . . . it more rapidly than an efficient one [low tech]. Such societies tend to be structurally more complex, more wasteful of energy, more competitive, and faster paced than an efficient one. Think of modern urban America as powerful. . . . In contrast, an efficient society metabolizes its energy more slowly, and so it is structurally less complex, less wasteful, less competitive, and slower paced. Think of . . . contemporary Pueblo farmers in the American Southwest [or as SDCP/LJCP/Kumeyaay/Luiseño]. In competitive terms, the powerful society [high tech] has an enormous short-term advantage over the efficient one [low tech] if enough energy is naturally available to 'feed' it, or if its technology and trade can bring in energy rapidly enough to sustain it. But when energy (food, fuel, and resources) becomes scarce, or when trade and technology fail, an efficient society [low tech] is advantageous because its simpler, less wasteful structure is much more easily sustained in times of scarcity."

Low tech wins out against high tech during uncertain or unstable environmental, financial, or political conditions, and dependence on local resources may be the only option. Native Peoples who occupied SDC for over 10,000 years using low tech and efficient use of local resources could have continued their way of life indefinitely, therein providing stability in both certain and uncertain environmental times.

Today we are in high tech times, using energy, foods, and water from outside our local region and are dependent due to population size on these resources. Changes in rainfall are inevitable, as well as seismic activity and sea level rise, which will affect roads, energy transmission lines, food delivery systems, and gas, water, and sewer lines. Drought was identified as the cause of abandonment of the Anasazi Pueblos ca. 650–750 years ago, but recent research now adds politics and religion as additional causal factors. Politics and/or religion can play a hand in surviving environmental change, but only if used in a positive manner and in concert with science. Stuart concludes: "The Chacoans did not fail because they ran short of turquoise and macaws, which they prized. They failed because they ran out of essentials, so that their growth could not be sustained. At the end, they did not have enough water, corn, meat, or fuel. If modern societies fail, ours included, it will not be because they taxed widgets another 3 percent to create infrastructure or they could import fewer Mercedes. . . . It will be either because, besotted by the idea of growth, they ran out of irreplaceable resources—fossil fuel, water, farmland—or because they so flamboyantly increased the disparity in wealth that the moderating middle class vanished." (Stuart 2000: 200).

When you see a people using low tech—collecting and grinding seeds—are you really looking at the past or are you looking at the future: the people who will be left should high tech fail. Today's high tech is both common and expected to include high population density and long life with fewer health problems than those of past peoples. Population limits will be the most difficult for society as a whole, and for politicians and the general public whose jobs depend on increasing population and infrastructure needs, therein increasing high tech and everyone's vulnerability to unstable/uncertain conditions.

High tech is more fragile than low tech, and affects more people than ever before; but, high tech will not be able to fully protect the population from major environmental catastrophes of extreme rainfall changes, heat and drought, sea level rise, and seismic activity. However, high tech could assist low tech in providing solar energy for houses, machinery, and cars. Enhancement of low tech local native food plants and animals and enhancement of lagoons for the production of shellfish and fish for local use, could thereby provide a sense of independence, sustainability, and a sense of community. Learning to live in a hybrid high tech and low tech environment may provide the best of both worlds; and therein learning to live with native plants, animals, birds, and insects that have evolved to best live in the local but changing environment.

References

Agenbroad, Larry D., John R. Johnson, Don Morris, and Thomas W. Stafford Jr.
2005 Mammoths and Humans as Late Pleistocene Contemporaries on Santa Rosa Island. In: Garcelon, D. K., Schwemm, C. A. (Eds.), *Proceedings of the Sixth California Islands Symposium*, Institute for Wildlife Studies, Arcata, CA.

Bada, Jeffrey L., and Patricia M. Masters
1978 The Antiquity of Human beings in the Americas: Evidence Derived from Amino Acid Racemization Dating of Paleoindian Skeletons. *Society for California Archaeology Occasional Papers in Method and Theory in California Archaeology* 2:17–24.

Bada, Jeffrey L., R. A. Schroeder, and G. F. Carter
1974 New Evidence for the Antiquity of Man in North America Deduced from Aspartic Acid Racemization. *Science* 184:791–793.

Bamforth, D. B.
1991 Technological organization and hunter/gatherer mobility: A California example. *American Antiquity* 56:216–234.

Bastian, Anne
1977 The Aboriginal Use of Agave in Davis Valley. Master's thesis Department of Anthropology, University of California, Riverside.

Baumhoff
1955 Site record forms SDI-1 and SDI-2. Report on file, South Coastal Information Center, San Diego State University.

Beck, Charlotte, and George T. Jones
1997 The Terminal Pleistocene/Early Holocene Archaeology of the Great Basin. *Journal of World Prehistory* 11:161–236.
2013 Complexities of the Colonization Process: A View from the North American West. In: *Paleoamerican Odyssey*, Edited by K. Graf, C. Ketron, and M. Waters. Center for the Study of the First Americans, Dept. of Anthropology, Texas A&M University.

Becker, Mark S., and Dave Iversen
2004 Prehistoric Coastal Adaptations in Southern California: a Perspective from the Lithic Artifacts. In Results of NSF-Funded Archaeological and Paleoenvironmental Investigations at San Elijo Lagoon, San Diego County, California, by Byrd, Pope and Reedy. Report on file, South Coastal Information Center, San Diego State University.

Berryman, Judy
1981 Archaeological Mitigation Report for Santee Green SDI-5669. Report on file, South Coastal Information Center, San Diego State University.
1985 Redefining Type Sites—The Presence of Milling Implements at W-240: A San Dieguito "Type Site." Report on file, South Coastal Information Center, San Diego State University.

Berryman, Stan
1979 Results of the Archaeological Test on the Southern Portion of W-240, Scraper Hill. Report on file, South Coastal Information Center, San Diego State University.
1985 Final Archaeological Report on the Excavation on the Southern Portions of Site W-240, Scraper Hill. Report on file, South Coastal Information Center, San Diego State University.

Berryman, Judy, and Stan Berryman
1988 Archaeological Salvage Report for W-240: The Scraper Hill Site Escondido, California. Report on file, South Coastal Information Center, San Diego State University.

Bolton, H. E.
1926 *Historical memoirs of New California by Fray Francisco Palou, O.F.M.* New York: Russell & Russell.

Breschini, G., T. Haversat, and J. Erlandson
1996 *California radiocarbon dates.* 8th edition. Salinas: Coyote Press.

Brodie, Natalie, Jacqueline Hall, Michael Sampson, Michael Buxton, Christopher Morgan, Jason Miller, Mark Roeder, Jeffrey Homburg, Jason Windingstad, and Aharon Sasson
2014 Late Holocene Life Along Chollas Creek: Results of Data Recovery at CA-SDI-17203. Report on file, South Coastal Information Center, San Diego State University.

Broughton, J. M.
1997 Widening Diet Breadth, Declining Foraging Efficiency, and Prehistoric Harvest Pressure: Ichthyofaunal Evidence from the Emeryville Shellmound, California. *American Antiquity* 71:845–862.

Bucy, D. R.
1971 A technological analysis of a basalt quarry in western Idaho. Unpublished Ph.D. dissertation, Department of Anthropology, Idaho State University.

Bull, Charles S.
1976 Archaeological Investigations at Santa Fe Knolls. Report on file, South Coastal Information Center, San Diego State University.
1987 A New Proposal: Some Suggestions for San Diego Prehistory. In: San Dieguito-La Jolla Chronology and Controversy, edited by D. Gallegos. *San Diego County Archaeological Society Research Paper,* No. 1.

Byrd, Brian F., and L. Mark Raab
2007 Prehistory of the Southern Bight: Models for a New Millennium. In: *California Prehistory, Colonization, Culture, and Complexity*, edited by Jones and Klar, 223–224. AltaMira Press.

Byrd, Brian F., Kevin O. Pope, and Seetha N. Reedy
2004 In Results of NSF-Funded Archaeological and Paleoenvironmental Investigations at San Elijo Lagoon, San Diego County, California. Report on file, South Coastal Information Center, San Diego State University.

Carrico, Richard L.
1986 *Strangers in a Stolen Land.* American Indians in San Diego 1850–1880. San Diego State University, Publications in American Indian Studies, No. 2.

Carrico, Richard L., and Paul Ezell
1978 Archaeological Mapping and Testing of Harris Site and Adjacent Cultural Resources, Rancho Santa Fe Area, San Diego County, California. Report on file, South Coastal Information Center, San Diego State University.

Carrico, Richard L., and Dennis R. Gallegos
1989 Data Recovery Program for a Portion of Pump Station 64 Force Main Improvement within the southwestern portion of SDI-4609, the Village of Ystagua, Sorrento Valley. Report on file, South Coastal Information Center, San Diego State University.

Carrico, Richard L., Theodore G. Cooley, and Joyce M. Clevenger
1991 Archaeological Excavations at the Harris Site Complex, San Diego County, California. Report on file, South Coastal Information Center, San Diego State University.

Carter, George F.
1980 *Earlier Than You Think: A Personal View of Man in America*. College Station: Texas A&M University Press.

Chace, Paul G.
1980 An Archaeological Assessment of the Sorenson Property. Report on file, South Coastal Information Center, San Diego State University.

Cheever, Dayle, and Dennis R. Gallegos
1988 Data Recovery for Table Mountain Agave Roasting Pit, San Diego County, California. Report on file, South Coastal Information Center, San Diego State University.

Christenson, Lynne E.
1990 The Late Prehistoric Yuman People of San Diego County, California: Their Settlement and Subsistence System. Ph.D. dissertation, Department of Anthropology, Arizona State University, Tempe. University Microfilms, Ann Arbor.

Cochran, Glen E.
1965 Shoshonean Migration into Southern California: A Hypothesis and its Treatment. Senior thesis, Department of Anthropology, University of California, Riverside.

Cook, John R.
1985 An Investigation of the San Dieguito Quarries and Workshops near Rancho Santa Fe, California. Report on file, South Coastal Information Center, San Diego State University.

Couro, Ted, and Margaret Langdon
1975 *Let's Talk 'lipay Aa: An Introduction to the Mesa Grande Diegueño Language*. Banning: Malki Museum Press.

Cox, Virginia T.
1963 UCLJ-M-7: A La Jollan Site dated at 7530 ±120 years before present. Report on file, South Coastal Information Center, San Diego State University.

Crabtree, Robert H., Claude N. Warren, and D. L. True
1963 Archaeological Investigations at Batiquitos Lagoon, San Diego County, California. University of California, Los Angeles, Archaeological Survey Annual Report. 1962–1963:319–349.

Cressman, Luther S.
1960 Cultural Sequences at the Dallas, Oregon: a Contribution to Pacific Northwest Prehistory. *Transactions of the American Philosophical Society*, Vol. 50 (10).

Dalhberg, Patricia, Don Schmidt, and Richard Carrico
2007 National Register of Historic Places (NRHP) form for the William Black House (Chancellor's House), and archaeological site SDM-W-12 Locus A (SDI-4669) submitted in 2007 and accepted for placement on the NRHP in 2008 (#08000343).

Daugherty, R. D.
1956 Archaeology of the Lind Coulee site, Washington. *Proceedings of the American Philosophical Society* 100 (3):223–78.

Davis, E. L, C. W. Brott, and D. L. Weide
1969 The Western Lithic Co-tradition. *San Diego Museum Papers 6*. San Diego Museum of Man, San Diego.

Davis, Owen K.
2014 Pollen Analysis, Appendix C. In People in a Changing Land. The Archaeology and History of the Ballona in Los Angeles, California. Vol 1: Paleoenvironment and Culture History, Edited by Homburg, Douglass, and Reddy. Series Eds. D. Grenda, R. Ciolek-Torello, and J. Altschul.

Eighmey, James D., and Dayle M. Cheever
1993 The Villas at Stallions Crossing: Cultural Resource Testing at SDI-687, Archaic Occupations within the San Dieguito Valley. Report on file, South Coastal Information Center, San Diego State University.

Emory, K. C.
1960 *The Sea Off Southern California, a Modern Habitat of Petroleum*. New York: Wiley.

Engelhardt, Zephyrin, O.F.M.
1920 *San Diego Mission*. San Francisco: The James H. Barry Company.

Engstrand, I. W., ed., trans.
1975 Pedro Fages and Miguel Costanso: Two early letters from San Diego in 1769. *The Journal of San Diego History* 21(2):1–11.

Erlandson, Jon M.
2013 After Clovis-First Collapsed: Reimagining the Peopling of the Americas. In: *Paleoamerican Odyssey*, edited by K. Graf, C. Ketron, and M. Waters. Center for the Study of the First Americans, Dept of Anthropology, Texas A&M University.

Erlandson, J. M., T. C. Rick, T. L. Jones, and J. F. Porcasi
2007a One If by Land, Two If by Sea: Who Were the First Californians? In: *California Prehistory, Colonization, Culture, and Complexity*, edited by Jones and Klar, 53–62. AltaMira Press.

Erlandson, J. M., M. H. Graham, B. J. Bourque, D. Corbett, J. A. Estes, and R. S. Steneck
2007b The Kelp Highway Hypothesis: Marine Ecology, the Coastal Migration Theory, and the Peopling of the Americas. *Journal of Island and Coastal Archaeology* 2:161–74.

Erlandson, Jon M., Douglas J. Kennett, B. Lynn Ingram, Daniel A. Guthrie, Don P. Morris, Mark A. Tveskov, G. James West, and Phillip L. Walker
1996 An Archaeological and Paleontological Chronology for Daisy Cave (CA-SMI-261), San Miguel Island, California. *Radiocarbon*, Vol. 38, No. 2.

Ezell, Paul
1987 The Harris Site—An Atypical San Dieguito Site or Am I Beating a Dead Horse. In: San Dieguito-La Jolla: Chronology and Controversy, edited by D. Gallegos. *San Diego County Archaeological Society Research Paper*, No. 1.

Fenenga, Gerrit L., and Jerry N. Hopkins, eds.
2010 A Riddle Wrapped in a Mystery inside an Enigma: Three Studies of Chipped Stone Crescents from California. The Tulare Lake Archaeological Research Group. *Contributions to Tulare Lake Archaeology V*.

Fitzgerald, Richard T., Terry L. Jones, and Adella Schroth
2005 Ancient long-distance trade in Western North America: new AMS radiocarbon dates from Southern California. *Journal of Archaeological Science* 32:423–434.

Flenniken, J. Jeffrey, James D. Eighmey, and Meg McDonald
1998 Comparative Technological Lithic Analysis of Selected Temporally Diagnostic San Diego Sites. In Prehistoric and Historic Archaeology of Metropolitan San Diego: A Historic Properties Background Study. Report prepared for Metropolitan Wastewater by ASM. Report on file, South Coastal Information Center, San Diego State University.

Flenniken, J. Jeffrey, Jeffrey A. Markos, and Terry L. Ozbun
1993 Battered Implements: Mano and Metate Resharpening Tools from CA-SDI-10148. In: *Lithic Analysts Research Report* No. 33. Pullman, Washington.

Gallegos, Dennis R.
1985 Batiquitos Lagoon Revisited. *Casual Papers* 2(1):1–13.
1986 Early and Late Period Occupation at Rogers Ridge (SDI-4845, W-182), Carlsbad, California. Report on file SCIC, SDSU, San Diego, California.
1987 A Review and Synthesis of Environmental and Cultural Material for the Batiquitos Lagoon Region. In San Dieguito-La Jolla Chronology and Controversy, edited by D. Gallegos, 23–34. *San Diego County Archaeological Society Research Paper*, No. 1.
1991 Antiquity and Adaptation at Agua Hedionda, Carlsbad, California. In: *Hunter-Gatherers of Early Holocene Coastal California*, edited by J. M. Erlandson and R. H. Colten, 19–41. Cotsen Institute of Archaeology, University of California, Los Angeles.
2007 Cultural Resources Monitoring Report for the Carlsbad Municipal Golf Course, City of Carlsbad, California. Report on file, South Coastal Information Center, San Diego State University.
2012 Cultural Resource Monitoring for the Escondido Union High School District, Del Lago Academy, Escondido, California. Report on file, South Coastal Information Center, San Diego State University.

Gallegos, Dennis R., and Richard L. Carrico
1984 Windsong Shores Data Recovery Program for Site W-131, Carlsbad, California. Report on file, South Coastal Information Center, San Diego State University.
1985 The La Costa Site SDI-4405 (W-945): 7000 Years Before Present, Carlsbad, California. Report on file, South Coastal Information Center, San Diego State University.

Gallegos, Dennis R., Nina Harris, and Adella Schroth
1999 The 4,000 Year Old Lego Crescentic-Hearth Site (CA-SDI-12814) Carlsbad, California. Report on file, South Coastal Information Center, San Diego State University.

Gallegos, Dennis R., Carolyn E. Kyle, Adella Schroth, and Patricia Mitchell
1998 Management Plan for Otay Mesa Prehistoric Resources, San Diego, California. Reprint by Coyote Press. Report on file, South Coastal Information Center, San Diego State University.

Gamble, Lynn H., and Glenn S. Russell
2002 A View from the Mainland: Late Holocene Cultural Developments Among the Ventureno Chumash and the Tongva. In: *Catalysts to Complexity: Late Holocene Societies of the California Coast*, edited by J. M. Erlandson and T. L. Jones, 101–126. Cotsen Institute of Archaeology, University of California, Los Angeles.

Gifford, Edward W.
1916 Composition of California Shellmounds. *University of California Publications in American Archaeology and Ethnology* 12 (1): 1-29.

Golla, Victor
2007 Linguistic Prehistory. In: *California Prehistory, Colonization, Culture, and Complexity,* edited by Jones and Klar, 71–82. AltaMira Press.

Grenda, Donn R.
1997 Continuity and Change: 8500 Years of Lacustrine Adaptation on the Shores of Lake Elsinore. Prepared for LA Army Corps of Engineers by Statistical Research Inc., Tucson, Arizona. Technical Series 59.

Griset, Suzanne
1996 Southern California Brown Ware. Ph.D. dissertation, Department of Anthropology, University of California, Davis.

Gross, G. Timothy
2000 Archaeological Investigations on the Air Field Site, CA-SDI-13327 (SDM-W-180) Carlsbad, California. Report on file, South Coastal Information Center, San Diego State University.

Hanna, David C. Jr.
1980 A Cultural Resource Inventory of the University of California at San Diego. Report on file, South Coastal Information Center, San Diego State University.
1982 Malcolm J. Rogers: The Biography of a Paradigm. Master's thesis, Dept. Anthropology, San Diego State University, San Diego, CA.
1991 The Phase II Archaeological Test of Malcolm J. Rogers' Site SDM-W-181 at La Costa Town Center in the City of Carlsbad, California. Report on file, South Coastal Information Center, San Diego State University.

Hastings, Philip A, Matthew T. Craig, Brad E. Erisman, John R. Hyde, and Harold J. Walker
2014 Fishes of Marine Protected Areas Near La Jolla, California. *Southern California Academy of Sciences*, 200–231.

Haynes, C. Vance Jr., Donald G. Grey, Paul E. Damon, and Richmond Bennett
1967 Arizona Radiocarbon Dates VII, *Radiocarbon*, San Dieguito Series. Vol. 9, 9–10.

Hector, Susan M.
2007 Archaeological Investigations at University House Meeting Center and Chancellor Residence, CA-SDI-4669 (SDM-W-12), University of California at San Diego, La Jolla, California, 18–20. Report on file, South Coastal Information Center, San Diego State University.

Hedges, Ken
1970 An Analysis of Diegueño Pictographs. Unpublished master's thesis. Department of Anthropology, San Diego State University.
1973 Rock Art in Southern California. *Pacific Coast Archaeological Society Quarterly* 9(4):5–28.
1979 The Rancho Bernardo Style in Southern California. In: *American Indian Rock Art*, edited by F. Bock, K. Hedges, G. Lee, and H. Michaelis, Vol. 5. American Rock Art Research Association, El Toro.

Hedges, Ken, and Diane Hamann
1987 Pictograph Analysis, Appendix J. In: Archaeological Investigation at Westwood Valley, San Diego, California by R. Carrico and C. Kyle. Report on file, South Coastal Information Center, San Diego State University.

Hubbs, Carl L., George S. Bien, and Hans E. Suess
1960 La Jolla Natural Radiocarbon Measurements, *American Journal of Science Radiocarbon Supplement,* Vol. 2, 212, 220–221.
1962 La Jolla Natural Radiocarbon Measurements II. *Radiocarbon*, Supplement, v.4, 204–238.
1963 La Jolla Natural Radiocarbon Measurements III. *Radiocarbon*, Vol. 5, 260.
1965 La Jolla Natural Radiocarbon Measurements IV, *Radiocarbon*, Vol. 7, 104–109.

Ike, Darcy
1978 Letter to Patricia Collum and Appendices I-IV, UCSD, regarding the archaeological aspects of the UCSD "Knoll" property (W-5). Letter report dated April 4, 1978, prepared by Flower, Ike & Roth Archaeological Consultants and submitted to UCSD.

Ike, Darcy, J. Bada, P. Masters, G. Kennedy, and J. Vogel
1979 Aspartic Acid Racemization and Radiocarbon Dating of An Early Milling Stone Horizon Burial in California. *American Antiquity*, Vol. 44, No. 3.

Inman, Doug
1983 Application of coastal dynamics to the reconstruction of paleocoastlines in the vicinity of La Jolla, California. In: *Quaternary Coastlines and Marine Archaeology*, edited by Masters, P. M., Flemming, N. C. Academic Press, London, 1–49.

Jantz, Richard L., and Douglas W. Owsley
2000 Circumpacific Populations and the Peopling of the New World: Evidence from Cranial Morphometrics. Paper presented at Clovis and Beyond Conference, Santa Fe, New Mexico.

Jenkins, D. L., L. G. Davis, T. W. Stafford Jr., P. F. Campos, T. J. Connolly, L. S. Cummings, M. Hofreiter, B. Hockett, K. McDonough, I. Luthe, P. W. O'Grady, K. J. Reinhard, M. E. Swisher, F. White, B. Yates, R. M. Yohe II, C. Yost, and E. Willerslev
2013 Geochronology, Archaeological Context, and DNA at the Paisley Caves. In: *Paleoamerican Odyssey*, edited by K. Graf, C. Ketron and M. Waters.

Jertbert, Patricia
1986 The Eccentric Crescent: Summary Analysis. *Pacific Coast Archaeological Society Quarterly*, Vol. 22, No. 4, Oct. 1986.

Jones, George T., and Charlotte Beck
2012 The Emergence of the Desert Archaic in the Great Basin. In: *From the Pleistocene to the Holocene, Human Organization and Cultural Transformations in Prehistoric North America*, edited by C. B. Bousman and J. Vierra, 118. Texas A&M University Press.

Kaldenberg, Russell L.
1976 Paleo-Technological Change at Rancho Park North, San Diego, California. Master's thesis, San Diego State University, San Diego, California.
1982 Rancho Park North, A San Dieguito-La Jolla Shellfish Processing Site in Coastal Southern California. *Occasional Paper*, No. 6, IVC Museum Society, El Centro, California.

Kaldenberg, R. L. and P. H. Ezell
1974 Results of the Archaeological Mitigation of Great Western Sites A and C, Located on the Proposed Rancho Park North Development. Report on file, South Coastal Information Center, San Diego State University.

Kennett, Douglas J., Brendan J. Culleton, James P. Kennett, Jon M. Erlandson, and Kevin G. Cannariato
2007 Middle Holocene Climate Change and Human Population Dispersal in Western North America. *In: Climate Change and Cultural Dynamics: A Global Perspective on Mid-Holocene Transitions*, edited by D. G. Anderson, K. A. Maasch, and D. H. Sandweiss, 531–557. New York: Elsevier Press.

Knell, Edward J.
2010 Organization of Lithic Technology at the C. W. Harris Site, California: Type Site for the Early Holocene San Dieguito Complex. Paper presented at 2010 SAA Meeting, St. Louis.

Koerper, Henry C.
1981 Prehistoric Subsistence and Settlement in the Newport Bay Area and Environs, Orange County, California. Unpublished Ph.D. dissertation, Department of Anthropology, University of California, Riverside.

Koerper, Henry C., Paul E. Langenwalter, and Adella Schroth
1986 The Agua Hedionda Project: Archaeological Investigations at CA-SDI-5353 and CA-SDI-9649. Report on file, South Coastal Information Center, San Diego State University.

Koerper, Henry C., A. B. Schroth, R. D. Mason, and M. L. Pererson
1996 Arrow Projectile Point Types as Temporal Types: Evidence from Orange County California. *Journal of California and Great Basin Anthropology* 18:258–283.

Krantz, Grover S.
1978 Reply. In: *Society for California Archaeology Occasional Papers in Method and Theory in California Archaeology* No. 2.

Kroeber, Alfred
1925 *Handbook of the Indians of California.* American Bureau of Ethnology Bulletin 78, Washington, D.C.

Kyle, Carolyn E., Adella B. Schroth, and Dennis R. Gallegos
1997 Route 905 Cultural Resources Test Report for Sites CA-SD-6941, Loci G and Y; CA-SDI-11423, and CA-SDI-11424. Report on file, South Coastal Information Center, San Diego State University.
1998 Remington Hills Archaeological Data Recovery Program for Prehistoric Site (CA-SDI-11079, Otay Mesa, San Diego, California. Report on file, South Coastal Information Center, San Diego State University.

Laylander, Don
1997 The Last Days of Lake Cahuilla: The Elmore Site. *Pacific Coast Archaeological Society Quarterly* 33(1–2):1–138.
1989 Phase II Archaeological Investigations at Site CA-SDI-5383, Peñasquitos Area, San Diego, California. Report on file, South Coastal Information Center, San Diego State University.
2012 Research Issues in San Diego Prehistory. Submerged Sites, edited by D. Laylander, updated June 2005.

Lee, Melicent
1949 *Salt Water Boy.* Caldwell, Ohio: Caxton Printers.

Leftwich, James A.
1984 *La Jolla Life.* La Jolla, California: La Jolla Press.

Linick, T. W.
1977 La Jolla Natural Radiocarbon Measurements VII. *Radiocarbon,* Vol. 19, No. 1, 32–33.

Malies, Deedra, and Orton Knutson
1976 A Report of an Archaeological Survey done by Deedra Malies and Orton Knutson, student paper on file at Palomar College.

Masters, Patricia M.
1990s Shell analysis for W-11075 (W-3683). Ms on file with the author.
1988 Section 4, Paleo-Environmental Reconstruction of San Diego Bay, 10,000 years B.P. to Present. In: Five Thousand Years of Maritime Subsistence at Ballast Point Prehistoric Site SDI-48 (W-164), San Diego, California. Edited by D. Gallegos and C. Kyle. Reprint by Coyote Press in 1998. Report on file, South Coastal Information Center, San Diego State University.

2006 Holocene sand beaches of Southern California: ENSO forcing and coastal processes on millennial scales. *Palaeogeography, Palaeoclimatology, Palaeoecology*, 232.

Masters, Patricia M., and Ivano W. Aiello
2007 Postglacial Evolution of Coastal Environments. In: *California Prehistory, Colonization, Culture, and Complexity*, edited by T. Jones and K. Klar, 53–62. AltaMira Press.

Masters, Patricia M., and Dennis R. Gallegos
1997 Environmental Change and Coastal Adaptations in San Diego County During the Middle Holocene in *Archaeology of the California Coast During the Middle Holocene*, edited by J. Erlandson and M.A. Glassow, 11-21. Cotsen Institute of Archaeology, University of California, Los Angeles.

Masters, Patricia M., and Joan S. Schneider
2000 Cobble Mortars/Bowls: Evidence of Prehistoric Fisheries in the Southern California Bight. *USDI, Minerals Management Service*, Pacific OCS Region Camarillo, CA.

May, Ron
1976 An Early Ceramic Date Threshold in Southern California. *The Masterkey* 50(3). Southwest Museum, Los Angeles.

Mayes, Arion T.
2010 These Bones Are Read: The Science and Politics of Ancient Native America. *The American Indian Quarterly*, Vol. 34, No. 2, 131–156. University of Nebraska Press.

McDonald, Meg, and James D. Eighmey
1998 Late Period Prehistory in San Diego. In: Prehistoric and Historic Archaeology of Metropolitan San Diego: A Historic Properties Background Study. Report prepared for Metropolitan Wastewater by ASM. Report on file, South Coastal Information Center, San Diego State University.

McDonald, Meg, C. Serr, and J. Schaefer
1993 Phase II archaeological evaluation of CA-SDI-12809, a late prehistoric habitation site in the Otay River Valley, San Diego County, California. Report on file, South Coast Archaeological Information Center, San Diego State University.

Mealey, M. Marla
2006 Data Recovery at Storm-Damaged Sites in Torrey Pines State Reserve. Report on file, South Coastal Information Center, San Diego State University.

Mensing, Scott A., Saxon E. Sharpe, Irene Tunno, Don W. Sada, Jim M. Thomas, Scott Starratt, and Jeremy Smith
2013 The Late Holocene Dry Period: multiproxy evidence for an extended drought between 2800 and 1850 cal yr B.P. across the central Great Basin, USA. *Quaternary Science Reviews* 78, 266–282.

Miller, Jacqueline Neva
1966 The Present and Past Molluscan Faunas and Environments of Four Southern California Coastal Lagoons. Master's thesis, Department of Biology, University of California, San Diego.

Moriarty, James R. III
1966 Cultural Phase Divisions Suggested by Typological Change Coordinated with Stratigraphically Controlled Radiocarbon Dating at San Diego. *The Anthropological Journal of Canada* 4(4):20–30.
1967 Transitional Pre-Desert Phase in San Diego County, California. *Science* 155:553–556.

Moriarty, James R. III, and James Edward Moriarty IV
1982 An Anomalous Burial from the Spindrift Site in La Jolla, California. Ms. on file at the South Coastal Information Center, San Diego State University.

Moriarty, James R. III, George Shumway, and C. N. Warren
1959 Scripps Estates Site I (525): A Preliminary Report on an Early Site on the San Diego Coast. UCLA, *Archaeological Survey Annual Report Vol. 1.*

Morin, M.
1974 Site form for W-556. On file at the San Diego Museum of Man.

Morrato, Michael J.
1984 *California Archaeology.* New York: Academic Press.

Noah, Anna C., and Dennis R. Gallegos
2008 Class III Archaeological Inventory for the SDG&E Sunrise Powerlink Project, San Diego and Imperial Counties, California. Report on file, South Coastal Information Center, San Diego State University.

Norwood, Richard H., and Carol J. Walker
1980 The Cultural Resources of San Dieguito Estates. Prepared by Recon for Pardee Construction Co. Report on file, South Coastal Information Center, San Diego State University.

Palou, Fr. F.
1926 Historical memoirs of new California mission records, edited by R. F. Heizer, 160–161. *Reports of the University of California Archaeological Survey* 74.

Pettus, Roy
1982 Submerged Cultural Resources in San Diego County. *Casual Papers* 1(1): 72-87.

Pigniolo, Andrew R.
2004 Points, Patterns and People: Distribution of the Desert Side-Notched Point in San Diego County. *Proceedings of the Society for California Archaeology*, Volume 14, 27–39.
2013 Malcolm Rogers: Geoarchaeologist. *Pacific Coast Archaeological Society Quarterly* 48 (3-4):75–87.

Pigniolo, Andrew R., and Natalie Brodie
2009 Preliminary Draft Cultural Resource Monitoring and Data Recovery for the Princess Street/Spindrift Drive Underground Utility District: The Spindrift Site (CA-SDI-39/17372, SDM-W-1). Report on file, South Coastal Information Center, San Diego State University.

Pigniolo, Andrew R., and Tanya Wahoff
1998 Cultural Resource Evaluation and Data Recovery Program, Coast Apartments Renovation Project Site CA-SDI-525/SDM-W-9E/UCLJ-M-1. Prepared for University of California, San Diego. Report on file, South Coastal Information Center, San Diego State University.

Raven-Jennings, Shelly, and Brian F. Smith
1999 Final Report for Site SDI-8330/W-240 "Scraper Hill," Escondido, California. Report on file, South Coastal Information Center, San Diego State University.

Reddy, Seetha N.
1999 Plant Usage and Prehistoric Diet: Paleoethnobotanical Investigations on Camp Pendleton, Southern California. *Pacific Coast Archaeological Society Quarterly* 35(4):25–44.

Robbins-Wade, M.
1990 Prehistoric settlement pattern of Otay Mesa, San Diego County, California. Master's thesis, Department of Anthropology, San Diego State University.

Rogers, Malcolm J.
1920s Site record forms and field notes for sites: SDM-W-1/CA-SDI-39, W-2, W-5/SDI-4670, W-9/SDI-525, W-12/SDI-4669, W-34/SDI-10940, W-86/SDI-603, W-131/SDI-10965, W-151, W-179/SDI-4395, W-180/SDI-13327, W-181, 182/SDI-4845, and W-240/SDI-8330. Unpublished site records and notes on file at the San Diego Museum of Man and South Coastal Information Center, San Diego State University.
1926a Fossil Human Remains from the Vicinity of San Diego California. Field Notes on W-2 ca. 1926. Unpublished site records and notes on file at the San Diego Museum of Man.
1926 A Preliminary Survey of the La Jolla Finds. Manuscript on file at the San Diego Museum of Man.
1929 The Stone Art of the San Dieguito Plateau. *American Anthropologist* 31:454–467.
1929a Rogers notes on site W-151, dated Oct 7, 1929. On file at the San Diego Museum of Man.
1936 Yuman Pottery Making. *San Diego Museum Papers*, No. 2
1939 Early Lithic Industries of the Lower Basin of the Colorado River and Adjacent Desert Areas. *San Diego Museum Papers*, No. 3.
1943 Cemetery Notes on Burials from Site W-9. On file at the San Diego Museum of Man.
1945 An Outline of Yuman Prehistory. *Southwestern Journal of Anthropology*, Vol. 1, No. 2.
1966 *Ancient Hunters of the Far West*. Ed. Richard R. Pourade. San Diego: Union-Tribune.

Rosenthal, Jeffrey S., and Richard T. Fitzgerald
2012 The Paleo-Archaic Transition in Western California. In: *From the Pleistocene to the Holocene, Human Organization and Cultural Transformations in Prehistoric North America*, Eds. C. Britt Bousman and Bradley J. Vierra. Texas A&M University Press.

Rosenthal, J. S., W. R. Hildebrandt, and J. H. King
2001 Donax Don't Tell: Reassessing Late Holocene Land Use in Northern San Diego County. *Journal of California and Great Basin Anthropology* 23:179–214.

Roth, Linda, and Judy Berryman
1993 Survey, Significance Testing, and Proposed Mitigation on a Portion of SDM-W-1 (SDI-39) and Historic Evaluation of Parcel #346-461-6, City of San Diego, CA DEP No. 92-0719. Report on file, South Coastal Information Center, San Diego State University.
1996 Mitigation Report for a Portion of SDMM-W-12 (SDI-4669). TMI Environmental Services, Reno, Nevada. Report on file, South Coastal Information Center, San Diego State University.

San Diego Union
1950 *San Diego Union*, 11/21/1950.

Schmitt, Axel K., Arturo Martin, Daniel F. Stockli, Kenneth A. Farley, and Oscar M. Lovera
2012 (U-TH)/He zircon and archaeological ages for a late prehistoric eruption in the Salton Trough (California, USA). Publisher: Geological Society of America, URL: http://geology.gsapubs.org.

Schroth, Adella B.
1994 The Pinto Point Controversy in the Western United States. Ph.D dissertation. Department of Anthropology, University of California, Riverside.
1998 Lithic Analyis. In: Remington Hills Archaeological Data Recovery Program for Prehistoric Site (CA-SDI-11079, Otay Mesa, San Diego, California. Authors Kyle, Schroth, and Gallegos (ed.). Report on file, South Coastal Information Center, San Diego State University.

Schroth, Adella B., and J. Jeffrey Flenniken
1997 Section 8, CA-SDI-11424 Lithic Assemblage and Section 9 Intersite Lithic Studies. In: Route 905 Cultural Resources Test Report for Sites CA-SD-6941, Loci G and Y; CA-SDI-11423, and CA-SDI-11424. Authors Kyle, Schroth, and Gallegos (ed.). Report on file, South Coastal Information Center, San Diego State University.

Seibert D.
1978 A Preliminary Site Report on W-240, Escondido, California. Student paper on Palomar College excavation on file at Palomar Junior College, Anthropology Department.

Shipek, F.
1976 Site form W-1149, on file at the San Diego Museum of Man.
1989 An example of intensive plant husbandry: The Kumeyaay of Southern California. In: *Foraging and farming: The evolution of plant exploitation*, edited by D. R. Harris and G. C. Hilman, 99–110. London: Unwin Hyman.
1993 Kumeyaay Plant Husbandry: Fire, Water and Erosion Control Techniques. In: *Before the Wilderness: Environmental Management by Native Californians*. Menlo Park, California: Ballena Press.

Shumway, George, Carl L. Hubbs, and James Moriarty
1961 Scripps Estate Site, San Diego, California, A La Jollan Site Dated 5460–7370 Years Before Present. *Annals of the New Your Academy of Sciences* 93(3): 37–172.

SIO
1978 Scripps Institutution of Oceanography: Probing the Oceans 1936 to 1976. San Diego, Calif.: Tofua Press.

Smith, Brian F.
1986 A Brief Summary of Excavations, Evaluation of Uniqueness, and Impact Analysis for the Charles H. Brown, Sr. Site (W-1137). Report on file, South Coastal Information Center, San Diego State University.

Smith, David D., and Associates
1973 Archaeological Salvage of the Fox Point Site. Report on file, South Coastal Information Center, San Diego State University.

Spaulding, W. G.
1990 Vegetational and Climatic Development of the Mojave Desert: the Last Glacial Maximum to the Present. In: *Packrat Middens: the Last 40,000 Years of Biotic Change*, edited by L. L. Betancourt, T. R. Van Devender, and P. S. Martin. Tucson: University of Arizona Press.

Stafford, Thomas W. Jr., and Rose A. Tyson
1989 Accelerator Radiocarbon Dates on Charcoal, Shell and Human Bone from the Del Mar Site, California. *American Antiquity*, 54(2), 389–395.

Stafford, T. W. Jr., A. J. T. Jull, K. Brendel, R. C. Duhamel, and D. Donahue
1987 Study of Bone Radiocarbon Dating Accuracy at the University of Arizona NSF Accelerator Facility for Radioisotope Analysis. *Radiocarbon* 29, No. 1, 24–44.

Stuart, David E.
2000   *Anasazi America*. Albuquerque: University of New Mexico Press.

Sussman, Carol
1990   Artefact Assemblage, Typology, for SDI-11075 (W-3683). Supplement to Sussman and Masters 1990 report. Report on file with author.

Sussman, Carol, and Patricia M. Masters
1990   Survey of prehistoric resources at W-3683 [CA-SDI-11075] and in the vicinity of the Proposed IGPP Expansion. Report on file with authors.

Sutton, Mark
2009   People and Language: Defining the Takic Expansion into Southern California. *Pacific Coast Archaeological Society Quarterly*, Vol. 41, Nos. 2 and 3.

Taylor, R. E., L. A. Payne, C. A. Prior, P. J. Slota, R. Gillespie, J. A. J. Gowlett, R. H. Hedges, A. J. T. Tull, T. H. Zabel, D. J. Donahue, and R. Berger
1985   Major Revisions in the Pleistocene Age Assignment for North American Human Skeletons by C-14 Accelerator Mass Spectrometry; None Older than 11,000 C-14 years B.P., *American Antiquity* 50:136–140.

True, D. L.
1958   An Early Complex in San Diego County, California. *American Antiquity*, Vol. 23, No.3, 255–263.
1966   Archaeological differentiation of Shoshonean and Yuman speaking groups in southern California. Ph.D. dissertation. Los Angeles: Department of Anthropology, University of California, Los Angeles.

True, D. L., and Paul D. Bouey
1990   Gladishill: A Probable San Dieguito Camp Near Valley Center, California. *New World Archaeology, The Institute of Archaeology, UCLA*, Vol. VII, No. 4.

Tuthill, Carr, and A. A. Allanson
1954   Ocean Bottom Artifacts. *The Master Key*, Southwest Museum, LA, Vol. 28, 222–232.

Vaughan, Sheila J.
1982   A Replicative Systems Analysis of the San Dieguito Component at the C. W. Harris Site. Master's thesis Department of Anthropology, University of Nevada, Las Vegas.

Warren, Claude N.
1967   The San Dieguito Complex: A Review and Hypothesis. *American Antiquity* 32(2).
1968   Cultural Tradition and Ecological Adaptation on the Southern California Coast. In: Archaic Prehistory in the Western United States, C. Irwin, Williams, ed. *Eastern New Mexico University Contributions in Anthropology* 1(3). Portales, New Mexico.

Warren, Claude N., ed.
1966   The San Dieguito Type Site: M. J. Rogers' 1938 Excavation on the San Dieguito River. *San Diego Museum Papers* No. 5, Oct. 1966, San Diego, CA.

Warren, Claude N., and H. Thomas Ore
1978   Approach and process of dating Lake Mojave artifacts. *The Journal of California Anthropology* 5(2):179–187.

Warren, Claude N., and M. G. Pavesic
1963   Shell midden analysis of site SDI-603 and ecological implications for cultural development of Batiquitos Lagoon, San Diego County, California. *University of California Archaeological Survey Annual Report* 5:411–438.

Warren, Claude N., and D. L. True
1961   The San Dieguito Complex and its Place in California Prehistory. *University of California, Los Angeles, Archaeological Survey Annual Report* 1960–1961.

Warren, Claude N., Gretchen Siegler, and Frank Dittmer
1998   Paleoindian and Early Archaic Periods. In: Prehistoric and Historic Archaeology of Metropolitan San Diego: A Historic Properties Background Study. Report prepared for Metropolitan Wastewater by ASM. Report on file, South Coastal Information Center, San Diego State University.

Warren Claude N., D. L. True, and A. A. Eudey
1961   Early gathering complexes of western San Diego County. *University of California, Los Angeles, Archaeological Survey Annual Report* 3:1–106.

Waters, Michael R.
1972   Archaeological Excavation of the Center Hill Site SDM-W-179, San Diego County, California. Report on file with the author.
1983   Late Holocene Lacustrine Chronology and Archaeology of Ancient Lake Cahuilla, California. *Quaternary Research* 19:73–387.

Waters, M. R., and T. W. Stafford Jr.
2013   The First Americans: A Review of the Evidence for the Late-Pleistocene Peopling of the Americas. In: *Paleoamerican Odyssey*, Eds. K. Graf, C. Ketron, and M. Waters.

Wells, S. G., R.Y Anderson, L. D McFadden, W. J Brown, Y. Enzel, and J. L. Miossec
1989   Late Quaternary paleohydrology of the eastern Mojave River drainage basin, southern California Quantitative assessment of the late Quaternary hydrologic cycle in a large arid watershed. *New Mexico Water Resources Research Institute*, Technical Report 242–250.

West, James G., and Jon. M. Erlandson
1994   A Late Pleistocene pollen record from San Miguel Island, California: Preliminary results. *American Quaternary Association Program and Abstracts*. 13th biennial meeting, Minneapolis: 256.

West, James G., and Kelly R. McGuire
2004   9500 Years of Burning Recorded in a High Desert Marsh. *Proceedings of the Spring-fed Wetlands: Important Scientific and Cultural Resources of the Intermountain Region*, 2000. www.wetlands.dri.edu.

West, James G., and W. Woolfenden, J. A. Wanket, and R. S. Anderson
2007   Late Pleistocene and Holocene Environments. In: *California Prehistory, Colonization, Culture, and Complexity*, edited by T. Jones and K. Klar. AltaMira Press.

Willig, Judity A., and C. Melvin Aikens
1988   The Clovis-Archaic Interface in Far Western North America. In: *Early Human Occupation in the Far Western North America: The Clovis-Archaic Interface*, edited by J. A. Willig, C. M. Aikens, and J. L. Fagan. Nevada State Museum Anthropological Papers 21, Carson City.

Wilson, Diane Drake
2001   Report on Kumeyaay Cultural Affiliation. Submitted by the UCLA NAGPRA Coordinating Committee, October 2001. Report submitted with NRHP nomination for the Chancellor's House prepared by Dalhberg, Schmidt and Carrico in 2007.

Winterrowd, C. L., and D. S. Cardenas
1987   An Archaeological Indexing of a Portion of the Village of La Rinconada de Jamo SDI-5017 (SDM-W-150). Report on file, South Coastal Information Center, San Diego State University.

Yohe, Robert M. II
1992   A Reevaluation of Western Great Basin Cultural Chronology and Evidence for the Timing of the Introduction of the Bow and Arrow to Eastern California Based on New Excavations at the Rose Spring Site (CA-INY-372). Ph.D. dissertation, Department of Anthropology, University of California, Riverside.
1998   The Introduction of the Bow and Arrow and Lithic Resource Use at Rose Spring (CA-INY-372). *Journal of California and Great Basin Anthropology* 20(1):26–52.

Index

Abandonment, Model 1, 3, 48, 52, 53, 56, 57, 66, 87, 93
accelerator mass spectrometry (AMS), 13, 111
Acculturation, Model 3, 3, 66, 93
acorn, 70, 76
adze, 60
Agua Hedionda Lagoon, 11, 14, 21, 57
Agua Hedionda site UCLJ-M-15, xv, 3, 6–9 11, 13, 21, 23, 67, 85, 88, 92, 93
Amalgamation, Model 7, 66, 67, 85, 93
amulet, 58, 60
Anza-Borrego Desert State Park, 71
Archaic, xv, xvi, 1, 40, 53, 55, 57, 65, 83, 85, 87, 88, 89, 91, 92, 102, 105, 109, 111, 112
Argopecten, 6, 14, 27, 37, 52, 53, 54, 57, 58, 60
Arlington Springs, 3
arrow point, 21, 37, 80
arrow shaft straightner, 43
artifact, 33, 35, 37, 45, 48, 52, 55, 57, 58, 60, 65, 71, 76, 81, 82, 85, 87, 92, 94, 118
Artifact Scatter, 71
Astraea, 32, 34, 37, 38
auditory exostosis, 40, 86

Baja California, 91
basket, 40, 86
Batiquitos Lagoon, xi, 4, 50, 52, 54, 56, 57, 69, 71, 101, 103, 112, 118
bead(s), 3, 6, 11, 12, 21, 33, 36, 38, 39, 43, 48, 52, 54, 60, 65, 67, 86–89, 91, 93
Bedrock Milling, 71, 76
Beringia, 1
biface, 11, 18, 19, 20, 21, 38, 52, 53, 58, 60, 63, 65, 80, 81
bird(s), 3, 14, 37, 52, 56, 60, 69, 70, 91, 98
bone tools, 36, 38, 43, 48, 65, 87, 88, 91
bowls, 32, 38, 77, 80, 91, 94, 107
burial(s), 1, 6, 13, 23, 26, 32–40, 42, 43, 48, 53, 54, 56, 57, 62, 65–67, 86–88, 91–94, 105, 108, 109

Cactus Street site SDI-11424, 60
Cahuilla, xv, 70, 76, 80, 82, 91, 92
California State Artifact, 60
California State University Northridge (CSUN), 26
Camp Callan, 35, 36
canoes, 33, 77
Casa Diablo obsidian, 70
Center Hill Site SDI-4395/W-179, 49–52, 112
Ceramic Scatter, 71, 76
Chancellor's House, SDI-4669, xiii, xv, 3, 6–10, 21, 23, 26, 27, 34, 38, 39, 40, 42, 43, 85–87, 92, 93, 101, 104, 109, 113
Channel Islands, 32, 67, 70, 87
chaparral, 4, 54
charmstone, 32
Chendytes lawi, 14
chert, 11, 14, 20, 36, 53, 77, 81
chopper, 36, 58
Coast Apartments, 35, 37, 108
coastal sage scrub, 4, 54
Coastal Zone, 71, 87
cobble-based tool, 66
cogged stones, 89
Colorado Buff, 33
core, 1, 19, 53, 54, 58, 60, 63, 69, 80, 81
Coso obsidian, 54, 70, 71, 89
Cosoy, 77, 89
Cottonwood triangular point, 80, 82, 91
cremation, 70, 77, 79, 82, 83, 91
crescent, 36, 53, 58, 60, 62, 105
crescents, xv, 1, 3, 11, 14, 15, 16, 21, 23, 43, 45, 46, 47, 48, 53, 54, 55, 56, 60, 62, 65, 66, 67, 85, 86, 87, 88, 93, 102
CRM, xi, xiii, xv, 33, 94
CSUN, 26, 38, 39
Cultural Resource Management, xv, 94
Cupeño, 70

Daisy Cave SMI-261, 3, 4, 102
Del Mar Man SDI-10940, xv, 6–10, 13, 21, 23, 83, 85, 93
Desert Side-notched (DSN), 80, 82, 91, 108
desert zone, 76
Diegueño, 32, 33, 39, 54, 71, 79, 94, 101, 104
discoidal, 43
Displacement, Model 2, 3, 66, 93

Donax, 34, 37, 76, 109
donut stone, 36, 38, 43, 55, 89
Early Archaic, xv, xvi, 83, 85, 87, 88, 92, 112
ecofact, xv, 52, 63, 65, 93
Elko, 58, 60, 62, 65, 88, 89, 92
Encinitas Tradition, 1, 54, 89

factory, 16, 18, 19, 20, 21
felsite, 11, 13, 20, 45, 48, 57, 85
fire-affected rock, 34, 53, 91
First People, xiii, xv, xvi, 3, 21, 23, 42, 43, 53, 66, 67, 82, 85, 86, 91–93
fish bone, 37, 54, 66, 67, 86, 91, 93
fish hook, 38
Fish Springs obsidian, 87
flake tools, 11, 35, 36, 38, 43, 53, 54, 56, 60, 67, 88
flintnappers, 81

Gabrielino, 70, 79
Gladishill, 63, 65, 88, 111
gorges, 37, 38, 77
Great Basin, xv, 1, 2, 3, 14, 21, 23, 42, 62, 65, 67, 85, 87, 88, 93, 99, 105, 106, 107, 109, 113
Great Western site. See Rancho Park North.

habitation, 11, 18–21, 37, 45, 54, 57, 63, 65, 69, 71, 76, 80, 81, 85, 87, 88, 91, 92, 107
Haliotis, 11, 27, 37
hammerstones, 1, 13, 14, 21, 35, 36, 38, 43, 48, 52, 53, 54, 55, 56, 60, 65, 88
Harris, C.W., site, xi, xiii, xv, xvi, 3, 6, 16, 17, 18, 19, 20, 21, 43, 45, 48, 53, 57–60, 62, 63, 65, 67, 80, 81, 83, 85, 88, 92, 93, 100, 101, 102, 105, 111
Hokan phylum, 40, 71, 85, 91

Imperial Valley, xi, 33, 70, 71, 82, 91, 118
Institute of Geophysics and Planetary Physics (IGPP), 35
Interior zone, 69, 71, 76
Ipai, 1, 71, 80
Isolate Find, 71

Kelly, Allan O., SDI 9649, 60
Kelp Highway, xv, 3, 6, 11, 85, 86, 92, 93, 102
knives, 13, 14, 16, 20, 39, 45, 52, 54, 55, 58, 60, 62, 66, 82, 85, 89
Kumeyaay, xi, xv, 1, 33, 39, 40, 42, 48, 57, 67, 70–72, 77, 79, 80, 82, 91, 93, 94, 97, 110, 113

La Costa Site SDI-4405, 47, 51, 60, 61, 103
La Jolla, xiii, xv, 1, 3, 5, 6, 13, 14, 23, 25–35, 37, 38, 39, 40, 42, 43, 45, 48, 52–58, 60, 67, 69, 81, 82, 85–87, 89, 92, 93, 94, 100, 102, 103, 104–106, 108, 109
La Jolla Archaeological Area (LJAA), 3, 23, 26–29, 39, 42, 43, 66, 67, 69, 82, 85, 86, 92–94
La Jolla Bay, 3, 6, 23, 26, 27, 86, 87, 93
La Jolla Beach and Tennis Club, 27, 32
La Jolla Caves, 6, 26, 27
La Jolla Cultural Pattern (LJCP), 1, 3, 13, 39, 42, 45, 48, 52, 53, 56, 57, 65–67, 69, 81, 85, 87, 88, 92–94, 97
La Jolla Shores W-2, xiii, 25–31, 33, 34, 43, 109
La Jolla Submarine Canyon, 26, 27, 32, 33, 35, 86
La Jollan (LJ), 6, 11, 13, 35, 38, 39, 53, 60, 66, 88, 92, 101, 110
La Punta, 21, 77
La Rinconada de Jamo, 77, 89, 113
Laevicardium elatum, 58
Lake Cahuilla, 70, 76, 79, 80, 91, 92, 106, 112
Lake Elsinore, 55, 104
Lake Mohave, 1, 14, 16
Lake Mojave, 1, 3, 14, 67, 85, 88, 93, 111
Lake Mojave Culture, 1
Las Chollas, 77, 89
Last Glacial Maximum (LGM), 1, 25, 110
Late Archaic, xv, xvi, 83, 89, 92
Late Holocene, xv, 4, 21, 57, 65, 67, 69, 70, 71, 73, 76, 80, 81, 82, 83, 89, 92, 100, 103, 107, 109, 112, 118
Late Period, xv, xvi, 1, 21, 33, –35, 39, 43, 52, 54, 67, 69–71, 76, –83, 89, 91, 92, 94, 103, 107

Late Pleistocene, 1, 2, 3, 4, 6, 25, 82, 93, 99, 112
Legoland site SDI-12814, 62
Lind Coulee, 1, 14, 101
Lithic Scatter, 71
Little Ice Age, 4, 69
Los Angeles Basin, 69–71, 91
Lower Cliff site W-2240, 34, 35
Luiseño, xi, xv, 1, 70–72, 76, 77, 79, 80, 82, 91, 94, 97

manos, 1, 6, 33, 35, 36, 38, 52, 53, 55, 57, 60, 63, 77, 91
Maritime Zone, 71
Medieval Climatic Anomaly (MCA), 4, 69
metates, 1, 6, 14, 32–36, 38, 39, 52, 53, 56, 57, 60, 77, 87, 91
midden(s), xiii, 1, 3, 6, 13, 14, 25–27, 33–38, 43, 45, 48, 52, 54–58, 71, 86, 87, 110, 112
Middle Archaic, xv, xvi, 55, 83, 87, 88–90, 92
Middle Midden SDI-4670/W-5, xiii, 27–29, 34, 38, 43, 87
Millingstone Horizon, 1, 89
millingstones, 16
Model 1. See Abandonment, Model 1
Model 2. See Displacement, Model 2
Model 3. See Acculturation, Model 3
Model 4. See Transformation, Model 4
Model 5. See Non-transition, Model 5 (SDCP First People)
Model 6. See Non-transition, Model 6 (LJCP First People)
Model 7. See Amalgamation, Model 7
Mojave Desert, 70, 71, 89, 110
Mono Craters obsidian, 70, 87
mortars, 32, 35, 36, 77, 89, 91, 94, 107
Most Likely Descendant (MLD), 42
Mt. Hicks obsidian, 70
Mytilus, 27, 34–38, 52, 54, 57, 87

nets, 37, 77, 86
Newport Bay, 55, 106
Non-transition, Model 5 (SDCP First People), 3, 48, 52, 54–56, 60, 66, 87, 93
Non-transition, Model 6 (LJCP First People), 3, 67, 87, 93

North Hill W-181, 45–51, 53, 54, 60, 104, 109
Northern Uto-Aztecan (NUA), 69, 70, 71, 89, 91
NRHP, 42, 101, 113
oak, 4, 11, 70
Obsidian Butte, 33, 77, 80–82, 91
Olivella, 3, 6, 11, 12, 33, 36, 37, 38, 43, 48, 52, 54, 60, 67, 86, 87, 88, 93
Orange County, 69, 70, 80, 91, 106
Ostrea, 37, 52, 54, 57
Otai, 77
Otay Management Plan Area (OMPA), 21, 23, 60, 62
Otay Mesa, 11, 21, 60, 86, 103, 106, 109, 110, 118

Paisley Caves, 1
Penutian, 70

Rancho Cielo, 18–21, 45, 48, 85
Rancho Park North SDI-4392/W-49, 46, 48, 50–52, 55, 60, 105
reamer, 38, 52
Remington Hills SDI-11079, xv, 3, 6–11, 12, 21, 23, 60, 71, 83, 85, 86, 93, 106, 110
resource intensification, xv, xvi, 76, 82, 91, 92
Revelle Hall, 36
Roasting Pit, 71, 76, 101
Rock Art, 79, 104
Rock Features, 39, 71, 76, 91
Rock Shelter, 71
Rogers Ridge SDI-4845/W182, 45, 47, 49–51, 53, 54, 60, 103
Rose Springs site, 91

Sabre Springs, 77, 89
Salton Brown, 33
San Diego Bay, 4, 57, 69, 71, 83, 89, 91, 92, 106
San Diego County (SDC), xiii, xv, xvi, 1, 3, 4, 6, 11, 14, 18, 21, 23, 25, 26, 43, 45, 48, 56, 62, 63, 65–67, 69–71, 76, 77, 79–83, 85–89, 91–94, 97, 118
San Diego State University (SDSU), 35, 52, 103
San Dieguito (SD), 14, 34, 35, 38, 39, 45, 48, 52–54, 57, 58, 60, 62, 63, 65, 66, 81, 85, 88

San Dieguito Cultural Pattern (SDCP), 1, 3, 13, 39, 42, 48, 52, 53, 56–58, 60, 62, 63, 65–67, 85, 87, 88, 92,–94, 97
San Dieguito Lagoon, 6, 13
San Dieguito Plateau (SDP), 45, 48
San Elijo Lagoon, 4, 69, 89, 99, 100
San Felipe obsidian, 80
San Miguel Island, 4, 102, 112
Santiago Peak Volcanics, 20, 45
scraper, xv, 6, 11, 13, 14, 16, 20, 21, 32, 33, 35, 36, 38, 43, 45, 48, 52–55, 57, 58, 60, 62, 63, 65, 67, 82, 85, 87, 88, 93
Scraper Hill SDI-8330/W-240, xiii, 46–48, 54–56, 60, 99, 100, 108
Scraper-Maker, xiii, 1, 45, 53, 60
Scraper-Maker Hill SDI-13327/W-180, 46, 47, 49–51, 53, 60
scraping tools, 1, 11, 35, 56, 60, 65, 66, 88, 93
Scripps Estates SDI-525, -11019/W-9, xi, xiii, 23, 26–29, 31, 34–37, 40, 43, 57, 87, 108
Scripps Institution of Oceanography (SIO), 27, 34, 36, 87
Scripps Submarine Canyon, 26, 86
sea level, xv, 3, 4, 11, 13, 21, 25, 26, 27, 32, 33, 35, 37, 43, 56, 67, 69, 83, 86–89, 92, 94, 97, 98

shell, 1, 6, 13, 14, 21, 26, 27, 33–38, 48, 52–55, 57, 58, 60, 65, 67, 77, 86–89, 91, 93, 94
Shell-Midden [people], xiii, 1, 3, 56
shellfish, xv, 1, 3, 4, 6, 13, 14, 21, 23, 25, 27, 33, 34, 35, 37, 42, 48, 52–57, 60, 62, 66, 69, 70, 76, 83, 85–89, 91, 92, 98, 105
Sierra Nevada (Sierras), 14, 67, 70, 71, 89
Silver Lake, 1, 3, 14, 16, 23, 67, 85, 88, 93
Spindrift SDI-39/W-1, xiii, xv, 6–10, 21, 23, 25, 27–34, 39, 42, 43, 57, 69, 85–87, 89, 92–94, 108
stone balls, 14, 36, 38, 43, 89
Sugarloaf obsidian, 11, 70

Takic language, 70
temporary camp, 16, 21, 54, 63, 71, 76, 92
teshoa, 1, 52, 56, 81
Tijuana Lagoon, 3, 11, 21, 69, 77, 86, 89
Tipai, 1, 71, 80
Tivela Proxy, 35
Tivela stultorum (pismo clam), 27, 36, 38, 40
Tizon Brown Ware, 33
Topanga Complex, 89
Torrey pines, 25, 34, 35, 76, 107

trail, 71
Transformation, Model 4, 3, 13, 48, 52, 66, 93
transitional, 69, 71, 76, 85

University of California San Diego (UCSD), 3, 6, 13, 26, 34, 37, 86, 87, 105
Upper Cliff site SDI-11075, 27, 34, 87

village, 21, 33, 45, 77–81, 100

Western Lithic Co-Tradition, 1, 14, 102
Western Pluvial Lakes Tradition (WPLT), 1, 14, 65
Western Stemmed Point Tradition (WSPT), 1, 14, 92
Windsong Shores SDI-10965, xv, 3, 6–10, 14, 15, 21, 23, 43, 46–50, 55, 57, 60, 63, 67, 70, 85, 88, 92, 93, 103, 109
workshop, 18–21, 63, 65, 85, 92

Younger Dryas, 25
Ystagua, 77, 80, 81, 89, 100
Yuman, 1, 6, 33, 35, 42, 48, 53, 54, 57, 67, 70, 71, 79, 82, 94, 101, 109, 111

About the Author

The author began his career in archaeology in 1969 working for State Parks, then the Bureau of Land Management Desert Planning Staff (1975–78), followed by work in the private sector with site density and significance modeling for Wirth's Sun Desert Powerline Project; WESTEC for desert and SDC archaeological studies (1978–1990); SRI-Principal Investigator (2009–2012); and Gallegos & Associates from 1990 to present. These studies included surveys, excavations, artifact analysis, report preparation, and editing for projects throughout San Diego County and the Southern California desert. Publications for Mr. Gallegos and Mr. Gallegos with others include: Cultural Resource Inventory of the Central Mojave and Colorado Desert Regions; Class II Cultural Resource Inventory, East Mesa and West Mesa Region, Imperial Valley; Batiquitos Lagoon Revisited; Early Man and a Cultural Chronology for Batiquitos Lagoon; a Review and Synthesis of Environmental and Cultural Material for the Batiquitos Lagoon Region; Relocation of the Ballast Point Tryworks Oven Foundation; Patterns and Implications of Coastal Settlement in San Diego County: 9000 to 1300 Years Ago; a Review and Synthesis of the Archaeological Record for the Lower San Diego River Valley; Environmental Change and Coastal Adaptations in San Diego County; Five Thousand Years of Maritime Subsistence at Ballast Point Prehistoric site SDI-48 (W-164); Management Plan for Otay Mesa Prehistoric Resources; Archaeology in America, San Diego Area, Coastal Southern California, Ancient Coastal sites; and Southern California in Transition: Late Holocene Occupation of Southern San Diego County, California.